A LEARNING GRAMMAR OF ENGLISH

Norman Coe

Nelson

THOMAS NELSON & SONS LIMITED
Nelson House Mayfield Road
Walton-on-Thames Surrey KT12 5PL

PO Box 18123 Nairobi Kenya

Watson Estate Block A 13 Floor
Watson Road Causeway Bay Hong Kong

116-D JTC Factory Building
Lorong 3 Geylang Square Singapore 14

THOMAS NELSON AUSTRALIA PTY LIMITED
19-39 Jeffcott Street West Melbourne Victoria 3003

NELSON CANADA LIMITED
81 Curlew Drive Don Mills Ontario M3A 2RI

THOMAS NELSON (NIGERIA) LIMITED
8 Ilupeju Bypass PMB 21303 Ikeja Lagos

British Library CIP Data
Coe, Norman
    A learner's grammar of English.
    1. English language – Text-books for foreigners
    I. Title
    428'.2'   PE1128

ISBN 0 17 555281 9
NCN 8666/73

First published 1980
© Norman Coe 1980

Illustrations by Robert Nicholls.

Phototypeset by Tradespools Ltd, Frome, Somerset.

Printed in Hong Kong

Acknowledgements

I have spent many months writing and rewriting this book, and during that time I have had the help of various colleagues. I would especially like to thank Ann Brumfit, Hilary Rees-Parnall, Lucy Saunders and Gerry Sweeney, who looked through complete early drafts and made very many useful comments and criticisms. I would also like to thank Shaaban Afifi, Kazamiera Asarabowska, Bill Bain, Emanuela Bertolini, Gean Cases, Ilene Chester, Neus Domingo, Alexandra Florea, W S Fowler, Maria Rosa Furriol, Carl James, György Kemény, Mariadorra Mazza, Carroll Mortera, Rhian Owen, Robin Rycroft, Dolores Soler and Margareta Volarić for reading parts of an early draft and for their advice.

I also, of course, owe a great debt to the masters in this art – I am only their disciple – who have written grammar books before me. I would particularly like to mention Randolph Quirk, Sidney Greenbaum, Geoffrey Leech, Jan Svartvik, R A Close and A S Hornby, whose books have been of enormous value to me.

Last, but by no means least, my warmest thanks go to my wife, Rosa – who married me in the middle of this – for, among many other attributes, her long-tried patience.

Norman Coe
Barcelona 1979

Acknowledgements

Contents

Part 2 Adjectives, adverbials and prepositional phrases

Adjectives

Adverbials

Prepositional phrases

Part 3 Verb phrase

Introduction   89

Be, have

Modals, etc.

Part 4 Sentence processes

Part 5 Types of complement

Part 6 Co-ordination and subordination

Appendixes

Index of grammatical terms functions etc.

Index of words

Tables

Conventions

35	Number of a section
5	Number of an example sentence
35.5	Example 5 in section **35**
5a, 5b, 5c	Alternative structures with the same or similar meaning
A, B, C, D, etc.	Different speakers
(that)	Part of a sentence that is optional in the context, e.g. **I said (that) I was there.** This sentence can be with or without **that,** with the same meaning.
/	Separates two possible answers in the context, e.g. C: Are you English? D: **Yes, I am. / No, I'm not.** Here, **Yes, I am** and **No, I'm not** are both possible answers to the question.
relative clause, noun, etc.	Grammatical words are in italic, e.g. Sometimes *past verb* forms do not refer to past time.
x for to do x	Incorrect form; this is always contrasted with the correct form e.g. I've cut my hand. (*Not* x the hand x)
« »	Compare
«	See, refer to in an earlier section.
»	See, refer to in a following section.
[1] [2] etc.	These footnotes appear at the end of each section.

General introduction

This grammar is a reference book for foreign learners of English, and I hope that it will also be useful to their teachers. Reference is easy because there are three possible ways to do it. Suppose you want to find, for example, **the**; you can

either a) look in the Contents, p v, for the sentence(s) with **the** in **bold** type

or b) look in the Index of grammatical terms, functions etc., p 223, for *definite article*

or c) look in the Index of words, p 227, for **the**.

In addition, sections have references to related sections and examples.

The book has six Parts and an Appendix. Each Part deals with a particular area of English grammar. However, it is impossible to divide English perfectly into six pieces; consequently, although most information about, for example, *verbs* is in Part 3: *Verb phrase*, there is also certain information in other Parts and the Indexes will always guide the reader.

Each of the six Parts begins with an Introduction, with general explanations and guidance for the whole Part. After the Introduction, there are many short sections and each section deals with a specific point.

The explanations are as simple as possible, but it is always necessary to use special words to talk about different features of grammar, for example *count noun* and *mass noun*, or *present simple* and *past simple*. In this book, these words are written in italics. This is to remind the reader that they are grammatical names; they are not descriptions of structures or meanings. For example, although things that we can count are usually *count nouns*, this is not always true: we count money every day, but the word **money** is not a *count noun* (» **3**). Similarly, the *past simple* is not very simple, and it does not always refer to past time, (» **241**). For explanations of grammatical names, look at the Index of grammatical terms, functions etc. for the most important references, which are underlined.

The grammar concentrates on British English. Most of the examples are suitable for speaking and writing and also for both formal and informal situations. However, sometimes it is necessary to mention points that are not suitable for all circumstances; these examples are described as either 'formal style' or 'informal style', and in both cases these examples are contrasted with standard examples.

PART 1

Noun phrase

Introduction

A *noun phrase* is a word or group of words that can be *subject* or *object* in a sentence, and can also join with a *preposition* to make a *prepositional phrase* (» **99–106**). If a *noun phrase* has only one word, then it is either a *noun* (1; » **1–12**) or a *pronoun* (2; » **42–54**), e.g.

   1   dogs; cheese; happiness; Mary
   2   she; him; that; somebody; myself

If a *noun phrase* has two or more words, then one word is the *head word*, printed in **bold** type in examples 3–10, and the other words *modify* the meaning of the *head word*. The *head word* is either a *noun* (3–6) or a *pronoun* (7–10). A *noun* can be *premodified*[1] by an *adjective* (3; » **68**), or *postmodified*[1] by a *prepositional phrase* (4; » **55**) or by a *clause*[2] (5; » **56–67**), or it can have both types of modification (6), e.g.

   3   the **cheese**; big **dogs**; some new **bread**; the pretty little **girl**
   4   the **girl** in the corner; the **bread** that we bought
   5   **dogs** that bite; **girls** that I have met
   6   the pretty little **girl** in the corner; big **dogs** that bite

Indefinite pronouns (» **50–52**) can be *postmodified* by an *adjective* (7; » **52**), or by a *prepositional phrase* (8; » **55**), or by a *clause*[2] (9; » **56, 59–67**), or by more than one of these (10), e.g.

   7   **somebody** strong; **something** new
   8   **something** in the air; **anybody** in the audience
   9   **no one** to talk to; **something** that has just arrived
  10   **anybody** brave in the audience; **something** pretty that isn't expensive

---

[1] *Premodify* means 'go before (a word) and modify its meaning', e.g. **big** *premodifies* **dogs** in 3. *Postmodify* means 'go after (a word) and modify its meaning', e.g. **in the corner** *postmodifies* **girl** in 4.

[2] *Clauses* that can *postmodify* a *noun* or *pronoun* are of three types:

    an **-ing** *clause*, e.g. **standing on the chair** (» **56**)
    a *relative clause* (» **58–64**)
    a **to** *clause*, e.g. **to talk to, to cut these with** (» **65–67**)

Nouns

There are three kinds of *nouns*: *count nouns* (» **1**), *mass nouns* (» **2–4**) and *proper nouns* (» **5–7**). The differences between them are grammatical:

a) only *count nouns* have both *singuar* and *plural* forms (but » *proper nouns*, **7**)

b) only certain *determiners* go with *singular count nouns* (» Table 1, Column B)

c) only certain *determiners* go with *plural count nouns* (» Table 1, Column D)

d) only certain *determiners* go with *mass nouns* (» Table 1, Column F)

e) *proper nouns* normally have no *determiner* (but » **6, 7**).

Determiners

Determiners are a small group of special *adjectives*; there can never be more than one *determiner* in a *noun phrase*, and it is normally the first word, (but all (» **33**), both (» **35**) and half (» **254**) can go before a *determiner*), e.g.

11   **this** big red car; **her** big red car; **every** big red car

Table 1 shows the possible combinations of *determiners* and related words with *count nouns* and *mass nouns*, and also with *pronoun* **one**(**s**) (» **49**). It also shows which *pronouns* can refer to the *noun phrase* in question.

Table 1 *Determiners* and related words

A	B singular count noun	C one	D plural count noun	E ones	F mass noun	G pronoun
a, an (13)	cup	[1]	—	—	—	one[2]
all (33)	—	—	cups	[1]	milk	all[2]
any (20, 21)	cup	one[3]	cups	[1]	milk	any[2]
both (35)	—	—	cups	[1]	—	both[2]
each (36)	cup	one	—	—	—	each[2]
either (38)	cup	one	—	—	—	either[2]
enough (32)	—	—	cups	[1]	milk	enough[2]
every (37)	cup	one[3]	—	—	—	—
(a) few[4] (25, 26)	—	—	cups	[1]	—	(a) few[2]
(a) little[5] (25, 26)	—	—	—	—	milk	(a) little[2]
a lot of (24)	—	—	cups	[1]	milk	a lot[2]
many (23)	—	—	cups	[1]	—	many[2]
more, most (27)	—	—	cups	[1]	milk	more[2], most[2]
much (23)	—	—	—	—	milk	much[2]
my[6] (44)	cup	[1]	cups	[1]	milk	mine[7]
neither (38)	cup	one	—	—	—	neither[2]
no (22)	cup	one[3]	cups	[1]	milk	none[2]
some (20, 21)	cup	[3]	cups	[1]	milk	some[2]
such a (40)	cup	[1]	—	—	—	—
such (40)	—	—	cups	[1]	milk	—
that, this (19)	cup	one	—	—	milk	that, this
the (14)	cup	[8]	cups	[8]	milk	it, they, them
these, those (19)	—	—	cups	[1]	—	these, those
what a (41)	cup	[1]	—	—	—	—
what (41)	—	—	cups	[1]	milk	—
what (159)	cup	—	cups	—	milk	what
which (161)	cup	one	cups	ones	milk	which[2]
a whole (34)	cup	one	—	—	—	—
the whole (34)	cup	—	—	—	» 34	the whole[2]
whose (162)	cup	—	cups	—	milk	whose
'zero' (17, 18)	—	—	cups	—	milk	they, them, it

Notes to Table 1

Cup(s) is an example that represents all *count nouns*; **milk** is an example that represents all *mass nouns*.

Determiners are in bold type, e.g. **a, an**.

Where no word is given (—), the corresponding form does not exist.

Example A: **a, an**
Column B shows that we can use **a** or **an** with a *singular count noun*, e.g. **a cup, an egg**, etc; Column C shows that we cannot say x a one x

but we can say **a big one, an old one,** etc. Column D shows that we cannot use **a** or **an** with a *plural count noun*, so e.g. *Not* x̶ ̶a̶ ̶c̶u̶p̶s̶ ̶x̶. Column E shows that we cannot use **a** or **an** with **ones,** so *Not* x̶ ̶a̶ ̶o̶n̶e̶s̶ ̶x̶. Column F shows that we cannot use **a** or **an** with a *mass noun,* so e.g. *Not* x̶ ̶a̶ ̶m̶i̶l̶k̶ ̶x̶. Column G shows that we use *pronoun* **one** to refer to a *noun phrase* with *determiner* **a** or **an,** e.g. **I didn't buy a cup, but Helen bought one,** i.e. **one** means 'a cup', and *pronoun* **one** can be *postmodified* by an **of** *phrase,* e.g. **one of the cups,** etc.

Example B: **all**
Table 1 shows that we can say **all cups, all ideas,** etc. (Column D). We can say **all big ones, all old ones,** etc. (Column E). We can say **all milk, all beauty,** etc. (Column F). And the appropriate *pronoun* is **all,** which can be *postmodified* by an **of** *phrase,* e.g. **all of the cups,** etc.

———

[1] *Phrases* with **one** or **ones** are only possible with an *adjective,* e.g. **a big one,** but *Not* x̶ ̶a̶ ̶o̶n̶e̶ ̶x̶, etc.

[2] These *pronouns* can be *postmodified* by an **of** *phrase,* e.g. **one of the cups,** etc.

[3] **Any one** and **every one** can be used for people or things; **anyone, everyone, no one** and **someone** are only used for people.

[4] or **fewer** or **fewest.**

[5] or **less** or **least** (but » **29**).

[6] or another *possessive adjective* (» **44**).

[7] or another *possessive pronoun* (» **46**).

[8] **The** cannot go with **one** or **ones** alone, but we can say e.g. **the big one, the happy ones,** etc., and also **the one in the corner, the ones that came,** etc.

1 Their **son** washed the **dishes**.

Son and **dishes** are *count nouns*; they have *singular* and *plural* forms, e.g. **son, sons; dish, dishes**[1], etc. They go with certain *determiners* (« Table 1, p 3) and they can be *premodified* by *adjectives* (1, 4). When a *singular noun* is *subject*, it normally has a *singular verb* (1, 2); when a *plural noun* is *subject*, it normally has a *plural verb* (3, 4; but » also **8**), e.g.

1 My sister has bought some new cassettes.
2 His idea was not original.
3 His ideas were not original.
4 Do those old ladies live in that house?

However, we usually treat quantities of money (5), distance (6) and time (7) as *singular*, e.g.

5 A: Is £25 a lot of money for you?
   B: Yes, it is.
6 12 miles is a long way. (« » **185**)
7 Two hours isn't enough. (» **97**.10)

---

[1] For the spelling of regular *plural nouns* » **256**; for *nouns* with irregular *plural* forms » **257**.

2 **Food** is more important than **art**.

Here, **food** and **art** are *mass nouns*, i.e. these words do not refer to individual foods and arts, but to food and art in general, so it would not make sense for **food** and **art** to be *plural*. When words are used as *mass nouns*, they do not have *plural* forms. *Mass nouns* go with certain *determiners* (« Table 1, p 3) and they can be *premodified* by *adjectives* (2, 4). When a *mass noun* is *subject*, it has a *singular verb* (1–4), e.g.

1 Does this coffee come from Brazil?
2 Foreign travel is the best education.
3 Cheese tastes best without bread.
4 Commercial television depends on advertising.

However, many words that are normally *mass nouns* can also be used as *count nouns*. In this use they have *plural* forms and they go with the *determiners* for *count nouns* (« Table 1, p 3), e.g.

5 Would you like a coffee? (i.e. a cup of coffee; « » 1)
6 One of the best English cheeses comes from Cheddar. (i.e. kinds of cheese; « » 3)
7 My mother bought a colour television. (i.e. a television set; « » 4)

3 There isn't much **furniture** in the flat.

Furniture is a *mass noun*. Certain words are *mass nouns* in English, but the corresponding words in other languages are *count nouns*. The most common ones are: **advice, bread, cutlery, evidence, furniture, grass, hair[1], information, knowledge, lightning, luggage, money, news, progress, research, rubbish, spaghetti, thunder, weather, work**, e.g.

1   Let me give you some advice. (*Not* ~~x an advice x~~)
2   Is there any interesting news? (*Not* ~~x Are there x~~)
3   We didn't do any research on rabbits. (*Not* ~~x researches x~~)
4   Is her hair turning grey? (*Not* ~~x Are her hairs x~~)

If it is important to refer to a unit, then we say e.g. **a piece of advice, a piece of news**, etc., but it is normally not important and we simply use **some** (1) or **any** (2, 3) for an indefinite quantity. There are special words for some units of *mass nouns*, e.g. **coin** for a piece of money, **loaf** for a unit of bread, etc.

---

[1] **Hair** can also refer to a single hair and then it is a *count noun*, e.g.

5   My father has several grey hairs. (« » 4)

4 **Smoking** cigarettes is bad for you.

Here, **smoking** is a *mass noun*. The **-ing** *form* of all *main verbs* can be used as a *mass noun*; in this use the **-ing** *form* is often called a *gerund*. This use of the **-ing** *form* has no progressive meaning, and so we can make *gerunds* from *verbs* that do not normally have *progressive* forms (6, 7; » **142**). These **-ing** *forms* are like other *mass nouns* because they can have *determiners* (1, 2) and *adjectives* (2) but they are also like *verbs* because they can have *objects* (3, 5–7) and *adverbials* (4). *Noun phrases* with an **-ing** *form* are used like other *noun phrases*, i.e. as *subject* (1, 2, 6), as *object* of certain *verbs* (4, 7; » **199, 200**), *complement* of **be** (3), and after *prepositions* (5; » **79, 99**), e.g.

1   Their painting is better than their drawing.[1] (i.e. their skill at painting is better than their skill at drawing)
2   Her excellent sewing has won many prizes.
3   Their hobby is building model boats.
4   Jack doesn't like working late at night.
5   Are you interested in visiting the town museum?
6   Understanding a language is not the most difficult aspect.
7   Would you mind seeing the film again?

Note: When a sentence refers to a particular planned event, we cannot use an -ing *clause* as the *complement* of **be**; we use a **to** *clause*, e.g.

    8   Was their plan to steal the money? (*Not* x̶ ̶s̶t̶e̶a̶l̶i̶n̶g̶ ̶x̶)

    9   Our idea is to leave after lunch. (*Not* x̶ ̶l̶e̶a̶v̶i̶n̶g̶ ̶x̶)

---

[1] Certain -**ing** *forms* can also be *count nouns*. In 1, **painting** and **drawing** refer to skills, and they are *mass nouns*. However, the same sentence could also refer to things, i.e. a painted picture and a drawn picture. In this case they are *count nouns* and we could use *plural* forms, e.g.

    10   Their paintings are better than their drawings.

For the spelling of -**ing** forms » **256.4.**

5 **Mary** has never met **Mr Jones**.

Mary and **Mr Jones** are *proper nouns*. These *nouns*, including titles, e.g. **Mr, Mrs,** etc., have a capital first letter. They do not normally have *determiners* or *adjectives*, but » **6**[1]. We use *proper nouns* for people, e.g.

    1   Helen was talking to Dr Brown.

    2   Did Miss Johnson write a letter to President Carter?

    3   Inspector Smith didn't interview Mr and Mrs Smith. (« » **6**.5)

We often use **mother, mum, mummy, father, dad, daddy** and other words for close relatives as *proper nouns*, i.e. they have a capital first letter and no *determiner*, e.g.

    4   Hello, Mum. Where's Dad?

But when these words are used as *count nouns*, they have no capital letter and they have normal *determiners*, e.g.

    5   She asked her mum where her dad was.

6 On **Saturday** we went to **Brighton**.

Saturday and **Brighton** are *proper nouns*. They begin with a capital letter and do not normally have *adjectives* or *determiners* (but « » **7**). We use *proper nouns*, normally without **the**[1], for:

a) days, months and names of holidays, e.g.

    1   I'm going to see him on Tuesday. (« » **3**)

    2   This year Easter is in April. (« » **4**)

Seasons can go with or without a capital letter and with or without **the**, e.g. **in (the) Summer, in (the) summer.**

b) towns, e.g. **London, Sheffield, Paris**
counties, provinces, etc., e.g. **Yorkshire, California, Bavaria**
countries, e.g. **England, Bulgaria, Japan**
continents, e.g. **Europe, Africa, Asia**
a single mountain, e.g. **Mount Everest, Mount Palomar**
a single lake, e.g. **Lake Windermere, Lake Geneva**
In names, **mount** and **lake** have a capital first letter.

c) roads, e.g. **Oxford Street, Chesterfield Road, Fifth Avenue**
parks, e.g. **Regents Park, Hyde Park, Green Park**
buildings, e.g. **Buckingham Palace, York Minster,
Westminster Abbey**
But we talk about **the High Street** of a town or village, and there are a few names of roads that have **the**, e.g. **The Mall, The Strand.** When we specify a building with an **of** *phrase* we also use **the**, e.g. **the Palace of Westminster, the University of Sussex, the Museum of Modern Art.**

———

[1] All *proper nouns* must have a *determiner*, usually **the**, when they are *postmodified* by a *prepositional phrase* (3) or by a *restrictive relative clause* (4, 5):

3   The Tuesday after next is a holiday. (« » 1)
4   Do you remember the Easter (that) we spent in Austria?
     (« » 2)
5   Inspector Smith didn't interview the Mr and Mrs Roberts
     (that) I know. (« » 5.3)

7 Did **the Mackeys** stay at **the Grand?**

The Mackeys and **the Grand** are *proper nouns*. We normally use **the** with *proper nouns* for:

a) *plural* surnames when we refer to a married couple or to a whole family, e.g.
the Rycrofts (i.e. Mr and Mrs Rycroft, and perhaps including their children)

b) other *plural proper nouns*, i.e.
groups of mountains, hills, e.g. **the Pyrenees, the Alps,
the Pennines**
groups of islands, e.g. **the Hebrides, the Canaries,
the West Indies**
certain countries, e.g. **the Netherlands, the United States,
the Philippines**

The following places also have **the: the West End, the East End, the City** (three areas of London); **the Ruhr, the Saar, the Ukraine, the**

Crimea, the East, the Far East, the Middle East, the West, the Mid-west, the Soviet Union, the Hague.

c) rivers, e.g. **the (River) Thames, the (River) Rhine**
   seas, e.g. **the Black Sea, the Mediterranean (Sea), the Dead Sea**
   canals, e.g. **the Suez Canal, the Panama Canal**
   oceans, e.g. **the Pacific (Ocean), the Atlantic (Ocean)**

In names, **river, sea** and **ocean** have a capital letter, but these words are often omitted.

d) pubs, e.g. **the Red Lion, the King and Queen**
   hotels, e.g. **the Devonshire (Hotel), the Cumberland (Hotel)**
   cinemas, theatres, e.g. **the ABC (Cinema), the Globe (Theatre)**
   museums, galleries, e.g. **the British Museum, the Tate (Gallery)**

In names, **hotel, cinema, theatre, museum** and **gallery** have a capital letter, but these words are often omitted.

e) newspapers, e.g. **the Daily Mirror, The Guardian**

When **the** is part of the name, it also has a capital letter, but **the** is normally not used with magazines and journals, e.g. **Cosmopolitan, Private Eye, New Society.**

f) ships, trains, e.g. **the Queen Elizabeth, the Flying Scotsman**

8 The Canaries is the place that my family like best.

The Canaries is *plural* in form; **family** is *singular*. If we consider these *nouns*, called *collective nouns*, as units, then we use a *singular verb, pronoun*, etc. (1); if we consider them as several individuals, then we use a *plural verb, pronoun*, etc. (2), but often there is little difference in meaning (3a, b):

1 A crowd is more than the sum of its individuals.
2 The crowd are now singing one of their favourite songs.
3a Ford is going to replace its present models.
3b Ford are going to replace their present models.

Collective nouns can be *count nouns* (1, 2) or *proper nouns* (3). There are not many *count nouns* that are *collective nouns*; the most common ones are: **cast, committee, couple, crew, crowd, family, gang, government, group, jury, majority, minority, pair, staff, team.**

There are many *proper nouns* that are *collective nouns*, including the names of most large organisations and companies, e.g. **the Cabinet, Congress, Parliament, Labour** (i.e. the Labour Party); **the BBC[1], the GLC[1], the Foreign Ministry,** and other public authorities; **Ford,**

ICI[1], **the British Steel Corporation,** and other companies; **Arsenal, England,** and other sports teams; **the United Nations; the United States, the Philippines,** and other countries with *plural* names.

There are also a number of *nouns* which are *singular* in form but which normally take a *plural verb*, *pronoun*, etc. The most common ones are: **the aristocracy, the clergy, the intelligentsia, the nobility, the police, the press, the proletariat, the public,** e.g.

4   The police were wearing their summer uniforms.

---

[1] **BBC** means British Broadcasting Corporation; **GLC** means Greater London Council; **ICI** means Imperial Chemical Industries.

Also » **257**.

9   A boathouse.
A houseboat.

a boathouse

a houseboat

Noun phrases with *nouns* before the *head noun* are a complex and changing area of contemporary English. Here we give some guidance to their structure and meaning, but rules that cover all types are impossible. The main points are:

a) the *head noun* is always the last one, so:

> **A boathouse** is a building for storing boats. **A houseboat** is a kind of boat.
> **A food factory** is a kind of factory. **Factory food** is a kind of food.
> **A shop workers' pay dispute** is a kind of dispute.

b) every *noun* modifies the one immediately after it (» **69**), e.g.

> **A shop workers' pay dispute** is a kind of dispute.
> What kind of dispute? A dispute over pay.
> What kind of pay? Pay for workers.
> What kind of workers? Workers in shops.

In other words, it is a dispute over the pay for workers in shops.

There are several types of *noun phrase* with one *premodifying noun*:

a) The *premodifying noun* is the material or a main ingredient, e.g. **silver spoons** (i.e. spoons made of silver), **gold ring, fish soup, apple pie**[1], **orange marmalade**[1], **clay pipe, wax doll**.

b) The *premodifying noun* refers to the purpose of the *head noun*, which is a container, e.g. **soup tin** (i.e. a tin for soup), **coffee pot, wine glass, egg-cup, match-box**[1], **bookcase**[1], **teapot**. These phrases refer to the containers only, not the contents (« » **30**). There are similar phrases where the *head noun* is not a container, e.g. **tennis shoes** (i.e. shoes for tennis), **eye shadow**[1], **cat food**[1], **lamp-post, shoe-leather**[1], **toothbrush**[1], **saucepan, wallpaper**[1]. There is a tendency to join the two words in writing, but there is no rule for those which are two words, those which have a hyphen (-), and those which are written as one word. Learners should consult a good dictionary.

a soup tin

a tin of soup (» **30**)

c) The *premodifying noun* is an -*ing form* and refers to the purpose of the *head noun*, e.g. **driving school** (i.e. school for driving), **cooking apples, climbing boots, drawing pins, scrubbing brush, rocking-chair, ironing-board, walking-stick**. There is a tendency to join the two words with a hyphen (-), but there is no rule for those that have a hyphen and those that do not. Learners should consult a good dictionary.

Also » **69**.

d) The *premodifying noun* is a thing; the *head noun* is a part of it, e.g. **chair leg** (i.e. leg of a chair), **garage door, table top, kitchen sink, garden fence, bedroom window, picture frame**, etc. These phrases, when the meaning is 'part of' are more common than e.g. **the leg of the chair** (» **102**). There are similar phrases that refer to the *head noun* in a certain place, e.g. **village church, country house, park bench, corner shop**, etc.

e) The *head noun* is a story, etc., about the *premodifying noun*, e.g. **love story, detective story**[1], **cowboy film**[1], **war poem**.

With more than one *premodifying noun*, the meaning becomes even more complicated. Here are some examples of *noun phrases* with two, three and four *premodifying nouns*: **fish canning machinery** (i.e. machinery for the canning of fish), **Finance Committee Chairman** (i.e. chairman of the committee on finance), **Government Crisis**

Talks[2] (i.e. talks on the crisis by the government), **Leeds University Chess Champion** (i.e. the champion at chess for the University of Leeds), **Yorkshire County Cricket Club** (i.e. the club for cricket for the county of Yorkshire), **Long-distance Lorry Drivers' Pay Rise**[2] (i.e. rise in the pay for the drivers of lorries that go long distances).

---

[1] The *premodifying noun* is *singular* even when it has a plural meaning, e.g. **orange marmalade** is made from oranges, **a match-box** is for matches, **eye shadow** is for eyes, and **a cowboy film** is about cowboys, etc. However, *nouns* that have only a *plural* form, or a *plural* form with a special meaning, have the *plural* form in this use too, e.g. **news bulletin, clothes brush, glasses case**, etc. Notice also: **a ten-penny stamp, a three-year-old child, three five-pound notes**, etc., where the *premodifying noun* is also *singular*.

[2] Newspaper headlines are often *noun phrases* like these.

10 Mary's coat was in my brother's bedroom.

Mary's and **brother's** are the *possessive* form of *nouns*. For the spelling, follow this procedure: Step 1, add an apostrophe (') to the *noun*; Step 2, if the last letter is not **s**, add an **s**[1], e.g.

Noun	girl	girls	Mary	Mr Smith	Mrs Jones	woman	women
Step 1	girl'	girls'	Mary'	Mr Smith'	Mrs Jones'	woman'	women'
Step 2	girl's	girls'	Mary's	Mr Smith's	Mrs Jones'	woman's	women's

The *possessive* form shows a meaning relation with the other *noun*, but there are several possible meanings, including possession[2], e.g.

Mike's records	i.e. records owned by Mike
Mike's mother	i.e. a family relation
Mike's boss	i.e. a work relation
Mike's hair	i.e. part of a whole
Mike's favourite actor	i.e. the actor he likes best

The *possessive* form can *premodify* a *noun* (1, 2) or can go alone, without a *noun*, if we can understand the *noun* from the context (3):

1　Mary's brother is called Peter.
2　The girls' bicycles are over there.
3　Mrs Johnson's hair is fair, but her daughter's is quite dark. (i.e. her daughter's hair)

The *possessive* form has the same *determiners* as the corresponding *noun*, so **Mary's brother** in 1 because Peter is the brother of Mary (*Not* ~~x the Mary x~~), but **the girls' bicycles** in 2 because the bicycles belong to the girls.

With such close units as **mother-in-law, someone else**, etc., the apostrophe and **s** go at the end of the *noun phrase*, e.g. **my mother-in-law's car, someone else's coat**, etc.

The *possessive* form of periods of time is used in such expressions as: **today's newspaper, this week's programmes, an hour's work, three days' journey, a month's salary.**

---

[1] *Nouns* ending in **s** pronounced /z/ have in fact two possibilities, e.g. **Mrs Jones' son**, or **Mrs Jones's son**. *Nouns* ending in **s** pronounced /s/ must add **s**, e.g. **the boss's car, Lewis's manager**.

[2] These different meanings can also be expressed by an **of** *phrase*; for a comparison of the use of *possessives* with **of** *phrases* » **102**.

11 I think there's a **dentist's** next to the **butcher's**.

I think there's a dentist's next to the butcher's.

We use **dentist's** to mean 'dentist's surgery' and **butcher's** to mean 'butcher's shop'. We cannot use these short forms for the places of all trades and professions, but the most common ones are: **baker's, barber's, butcher's, chemist's, chiropodist's, dentist's, doctor's, florist's, greengrocer's, grocer's, hairdresser's, newsagent's, tobacconist's**, e.g.

    1   You really should go to the hairdresser's, Jim.
    2   Can you buy stamps at a tobacconist's in England?

12 I met a **friend of Susan's** at the party.

A friend of Susan's is a *double possessive*, i.e. it has both **of** and a *possessive* form (**Susan's**). In these phrases the *possessive* must refer to a definite person; it can be a *possessive pronoun*, but not a *personal pronoun* (1, 2):

1 He's had some books of mine for months. (*Not* x of me x)
2 Are the Greens relatives of yours? (*Not* x of you x)
3 A friend of Peter's was on the train. (*Not* x of Peter x)

A friend of Peter's implies that Peter has more than one friend; **Peter's friend** would refer to Peter's only friend or to a friend previously mentioned.

13 Kate ate a banana and **an** apple.

A and **an** are the *indefinite articles*; they belong to the class of *determiners*. We use **a(n)** with *singular count nouns*, **a** before a consonant sound and **an** before a vowel sound, e.g. **a girl, a large animal, a thought, a university, an engineer, an honest man, an apple, an early train.**

The basic use of **a(n)** is for a person or thing that we cannot, or do not want to, identify specifically (1, 2), or when we mention an unidentified person or thing for the first time (3, 4), or when we classify a person or thing (5, 6):

1 The police are looking for a man in a red car.
2 I'd like a record of Beethoven's Fifth Symphony.
3 An old man was talking to a little boy. The man seemed very friendly but the boy looked frightened.
4 They have a flat here and a house in Brighton, but the house is very old. (« » **14**.1)
5 Mrs Briggs is a dentist. (« » **17**.3)
6 Is that an African elephant? (« » **17**.4)

We do not normally use *singular count nouns* alone, without a *determiner*, so e.g.

7 My sister is a nurse. (*Not* x is nurse x)
8 Do they have a car? (*Not* x have car x)

We do not use **a(n)** with words used as *mass nouns* (« **2**), so:

9 Iron is heavier than water.
10 They like strong coffee.

But when the same words are used as *count nouns*, **a(n)** is possible:

11 We had to buy a new iron. (« » 9)
12 Would you like a coffee? (« » 10)

We do not normally use **a(n)** with *proper nouns* (« **5**), but we use **a(n)** with someone's name when we only know the name but do not know who the person is, e.g.

13   A Mrs Richards telephoned while you were out. (i.e. someone called Mrs Richards, but I don't know who she is)

Note: We use **one**, not **a(n)** when there is a contrast with other numbers (14) or with **another** (15) or **others** (16):

14   There were two tigers but only one lion. (*Not* x a lion x)
15   They wandered from one place to another. (*Not* x a place x)
16   One teacher stayed but all the others went home. (*Not* x a teacher x)

14 **The** ink was in **the** cupboard.

The is the *definite article*; it belongs to the class of *determiners*. We use **the** with *count nouns*, e.g. **the girl, the large animals**, and with *mass nouns*, e.g. **the water, the terrible weather**.

The basic use of **the** is to identify specific people and things. There are three ways to specify the people or things:

a) First, when we mention someone or something that has already been mentioned, e.g.

1   They have a flat here and a house in Brighton, but the house is very old. (« » **13**.4)
2   Yesterday we had both cheese and ham, but the cheese has gone bad. (« » **18**.2)

b) Second, the *noun phrase* can be made specific with a *postmodifying phrase*; this can be a *prepositional phrase* (3–5; » **55**), an **-ing** *clause* (6; » **56**), or a *restrictive relative clause* (7; » **58–62**):

3   Do you know the girl in the corner?
4   I admire the patience of research workers. (« » **18**.3)
5   They are experts on the folk music of India[1]. (« » **18**.4)
6   The big dogs sitting over there are Alsatians. (« » **17**.2)
7   The wood (that) we bought was expensive. (« » **18**.1)

The big dogs sitting over there are Alsatians

c) Third, when the situation itself limits the possibilities to one, i.e. one possibility, though not necessarily one object (9, 10), e.g.

8   Let's go to the park this afternoon.
9   Don't the stars look bright tonight?
10   The children have gone to a party.

In cases like these we understand which park, which stars, which children, etc., from the situation.

The is also used with certain words to refer to an institution in general. These include: **the church, the cinema, the opera, the press, the radio, the telephone, the theatre**, e.g.

11   A: Do you often go to the theatre? (i.e. go to see plays)
     B: No, but we often go the cinema. (i.e. go to see films)

Names of meals do not normally have **the**, e.g.

12   We have lunch at half past one.

However, we use **the** to refer to a specific meal, e.g.

13   I enjoyed our visit very much except for the lunch.

The alone cannot be *postmodified*, but **the one**(s) can, e.g.

14   A: Give me a sharp knife, please.
     B: Do you want the one in the box or the one (that) I bought yesterday. (Also » **19**.14, 15)

----

[1] **The folk music of India** and **Indian folk music** mean the same thing; the first is not more definite than the second. The same is true of similar expressions, e.g. **the literature of Greece** and **Greek literature**. In each case the first alternative needs **the** because of the **of** *phrase*.

For another use of **the** » **249**.

15 **The young** have little sympathy for **the old**.

We can use **the** with certain *adjectives* to refer to a whole class of people; the *adjectives* describe a human condition. Those that are regularly used in this structure are: **young, old, rich, poor, blind, deaf,** but you will sometimes meet others, e.g. **lame, good, bad, living, dead.** When these phrases are *subject*, they have a *plural verb*:

1   Nowadays the blind are well cared for. (i.e. blind people)

These phrases cannot be used for an individual, so:

2   The blind man was well cared for. (*Not* x The blind was x)

16 My mother's **English** but my father's a **Swede**.

English is an *adjective*; **Swede** is a *noun*. These nationality words have a capital first letter. There are different groups:

country	adjective	singular noun	plural noun

a) the *adjective* is different from the *noun*; the *singular noun* ends in **man**, the *plural noun* in **men**:

England	English	Englishman	Englishmen
France	French	Frenchman	Frenchmen
Holland	Dutch	Dutchman	Dutchmen
Ireland	Irish	Irishman	Irishmen
Scotland	Scottish	Scotsman	Scotsmen
	(or **Scots**)	(or **Scot**)	(or **Scots**)
Wales	Welsh	Welshman	Welshmen

b) the *adjective* is different from the *noun*; the *singular noun* adds **s** to form the *plural*:

Arabia	Arabian[1]	Arab	Arabs
Denmark	Danish	Dane	Danes
Finland	Finnish	Finn	Finns
Iceland	Icelandic	Icelander	Icelanders
Poland	Polish	Pole	Poles
Spain	Spanish	Spaniard	Spaniards
Sweden	Swedish	Swede	Swedes
Turkey	Turkish	Turk	Turks

c) the *adjective* is the same as the *singular noun*; the *singular noun* adds **s** to form the *plural*:

Africa	African	African	Africans
Cyprus	Cypriot	Cypriot	Cypriots
Czechoslovakia	Czech	Czech	Czechs
Egypt	Egyptian	Egyptian	Egyptians
Germany	German	German	Germans
Greece	Greek	Greek	Greeks
India	Indian	Indian	Indians
Iran	Iranian	Iranian	Iranians
Iraq	Iraqi	Iraqi	Iraqis
Israel	Israeli	Israeli	Israelis
Italy	Italian	Italian	Italians
Kuwait	Kuwaiti	Kuwaiti	Kuwaitis
Mexico	Mexican	Mexican	Mexicans
Nigeria	Nigerian	Nigerian	Nigerians
Pakistan	Pakistani	Pakistani	Pakistanis

Phillipines	Filipino	Filipino/a	Filipinos/as
Thailand	Thai	Thai	Thais
U.S.A. (or America)	American	American	Americans
U.S.S.R. (or Russia)	Russian	Russian	Russians

and many other nationality words ending in **an** including: **Argentina, Argentinian; Asia, Asian; Belgium, Belgian; Brazil, Brazilian; Europe, European; Hungary, Hungarian; Indonesia, Indonesian; Kenya, Kenyan; Malaysia, Malaysian; Norway, Norwegian.**

d) the *adjective* is the same as both the *singular* and the *plural nouns*:

China	**Chinese**	**Chinese**	**Chinese**

and also: **Japan, Japanese; Portugal, Portuguese; Switzerland, Swiss; Vietnam, Vietnamese.**

We normally use *adjectives* to talk about a person's nationality, eg.

1a   Juan is Spanish; Britta is Swedish. (*Not* x a Spanish x; *Not* x a Swedish x)

We sometimes use a *noun* to talk about a man's nationality, but for women we use the *adjective* alone (1a) or **a(n)** + the *adjective* + **woman** or **girl**:

1b   Juan is a Spaniard; Britta is a Swedish girl. (*Not* x Britta is a Swede x)

2   Ove is a Swede; Maria is a Spanish girl. (*Not* x Maria is a Spaniard x)

We can refer to individuals with the *noun*. A *singular noun* usually refers to a man (3); for women we tend to use **a(n)** + the *adjective* + **woman** or **girl** (4):

3   I met an American. (i.e. a man)

4   I met an American woman.

When the *noun* is *plural*, it refers to men or to men and women (5); for women alone we tend to use the *adjective* + **women** or **girls** (6):

5   The school is full of Spaniards. (*Not* x Spanish x; i.e. men, or men and women)

6   The school if full of Spanish girls.

For generalisations about people, the words in group (**a**) have two alternatives: the *plural noun* alone (7a) or **the** + the *adjective* (7b); the words in groups (**b**) and (**c**) have two alternatives: the *plural noun*, with or without **the** (8); the words in group (**d**) have only one possibility: **the** + the nationality word (9):

7a   Frenchmen drink a lot of wine. (*Not* x The Frenchmen x)

7b   The French drink a lot of wine.

8   (The) Swedes are generally tall.
9   The Swiss like to be neutral.

For languages we normally use the *adjective* alone, e.g.

10   Ken speaks Spanish and French.

_____

[1] **Arabic** for the language.

17 **Onions** are good for you.

We use *plural count nouns*, e.g. **onions**, without a *determiner*[1] when we talk in general about a class of people or things (1, 2) and for classifying people or things (3, 4):

1   Lawyers earn more than teachers.
2   Do you like big dogs? (« » **14**.6)
3   Both Mr and Mrs Briggs are dentists. (« » **13**.5)
4   Are those African elephants? (« » **13**.6)

When we want to identify specific people or things, we use **the** (« **14**); for an indefinite quantity we use **some** or **any** (» **20, 21**)

When we refer to groups of people by race, etc., or to species of animals, there are alternative structures with **the** or a(n) and a *singular noun*, with similar meaning, e.g.

5a American Indians have tremendous stamina.
5b The American Indian has tremendous stamina.
5c An American Indian has tremendous stamina.

_____

[1] This is sometimes called the *zero determiner*.

18 She likes **art** and **classical music**.

Words used as *mass nouns* go without a *determiner*[1] when we talk about something in general, e.g.

1   Wood is expensive in England. (« » **14**.7)
2   Cheese goes bad quickly in summer. (« » **14**.2)
3   Scientific research requires patience. (« » **14**.4)
4   They are experts on Indian folk music. (« » **14**.5)

However, when we want to identify specific examples of things, we use **the** (« **14**); when we talk about an indefinite quantity, we use **some** and **any** (» **20, 21**)

_____

[1] This is sometimes called the *zero determiner*.

19 **This** picture is interesting. **That's** interesting as well.

This and **that** are *demonstratives*; they are either *determiners* (1–6) or *pronouns* (7, 8). The forms are:

singular	**this**	**that**
plural	**these**	**those**

We use **this** and **that** with *singular count nouns* (1, 2) and with *mass nouns* (5, 6); we use **these** and **those** with *plural count nouns* (3, 4). We usually use **this** and **these** for people and things that are near the speaker, and **that** and **those** for people and things further away from the speaker.

1 Look at this stamp!
2 Does that shop sell foreign newspapers?
3 These apples aren't English.
4 You must clean those shoes.
5 This soup is very tasty.
6 That traffic yesterday was terrible.

Look at this stamp!

You must clean those shoes.

We can use *demonstratives* as *pronouns*, i.e. without a *noun*, when we can understand the *noun* from the context, e.g.

> 7 Look at this! (« » 1)
> 8 These aren't English. (« » 3)

If a *singular count noun* is explicit in the context, e.g. **book** in 9, then we can use **this one** or **that one** to refer to it, e.g.

> 9 A: Would you like this book or that one? (i.e. that book)
> B: I'd like that one, please.

If a *noun* has not been mentioned, then we must use **this** or **that** alone without **one** (7). In the *plural* we use **these** and **those** without **ones**, e.g.

> 10 C: Which of these flowers do you like best?
> D: These are prettier than those.

We often use these words to identify people, e.g.

> 11 Kate, let me introduce you. This is my mother, and these are my sisters, Helen and Sarah.

In reply to a question with **this** or **that** asking us to identify someone, we can answer with **it**, e.g.

> 12 E: Who's that?
> F: It's my brother.

However, we use other *personal pronouns*, not **it**, to refer to someone that is already identified (» **42**).

On the telephone the caller uses **this** to identify himself or herself and **that** to ask for the identity of the listener, e.g.

> 13 Hello! This is Ann. Is that Mr Bright?

This one, that one, these and **those** can be *postmodified* by a *prepositional phrase* (14; » **55**) or a *restrictive relative clause* (15; » **58–62**):

> 14 Bring me that one in the corner.
> 15 Not many people came, but those who did were quite satisfied.

20 I bought **some** postcards but I didn't get **any** stamps.

Some and **any** are *determiners* (1–4) and *pronouns* (6–9); they go with *plural count nouns*[1, 2] (1, 2) and *mass nouns* (3, 4). In *statements* with a *negative* word we use **any**[2]; the meaning of **any** together with a *negative* word is 'no' or 'none'. We use **some** in *positive statements* to talk about an indefinite quantity. (For **some** and **any** in *questions* » **21, 253**)

1   They had some very interesting books.
2   I didn't buy any apples. (i.e. I bought no apples)
3   She gave me some fresh cream to take home.
4   He never spends any money on the house. (i.e. he spends no money)

Any alone is not *negative*, so *Not* x I bought any apples x (« » 2), *Not* x he spends any money x (« » 4).

Sentences without **some** or **any** that refer to an indefinite quantity, e.g. **There's butter in the cupboard** or **I haven't got cigarettes** are infrequent and often sound strange, so students should avoid them. However, we must omit **some** and **any** when we classify something (« **17**), e.g.

5   Those aren't Indian elephants; they're African elephants. (« » **17**.4)

We can use **some** and **any** as *pronouns*, i.e. without a *noun*, when we can understand the *noun* from the context, e.g.

6   A: Have we got any jam?
      B: Yes, I bought some today.
7   I looked at several books, but there weren't any that I found useful.

Pronouns **some** and **any** can also have an **of** *phrase*, e.g.

8   There were a lot of children. Some of them were carrying flowers.
9   We very rarely see any of our relatives.

Some is indefinite, so it is not used to specify a small quantity, e.g. as an answer to the *questions* **How much** and **How many**. For this we use **a little** and **a few** (» **25**), e.g.

10   C: How many were there?
       D: Just a few. (*Not* x just some x)

We can use both **some** and **a few** with periods of past time, e.g. **some weeks ago**, or **a few weeks ago**, with similar meaning. But for future time, only **a few** is possible, e.g. **in a few days**, *Not* x in some days x.

---

[1] We also use **some** when the particular person, thing, etc., is unknown, or when we do not want to be specific. In this use **some** can go with a *singular count noun*, e.g.

11   E: Where did this magazine come from?
      F: Oh, some friend of Ken's brought it. (i.e. a friend of Ken's, but I don't know who)
12   G: Where did you buy this camera?
      H: I bought it at some shop in Oxford Street. (i.e. a shop in Oxford Street, but I don't remember which)

² We can also use **any** and its combined forms, i.e. **anything, anybody,** etc., in *positive statements* to mean 'it doesn't matter which'. In this use **any** can go with a *singular count noun* (13):

    13   I: Which newspaper shall I buy?
            J: Any newspaper will do. (i.e. it doesn't matter which)
    14   Anybody can answer the next question. (i.e. it doesn't matter who answers)
    15   K: Where do you want me to put the basket?
            L: Put it anywhere for the moment. (i.e. it doesn't matter where)

Notice also the difference between these pairs of sentences:

    16   Mick is cleverer than anybody. (i.e. Nobody is cleverer than Mick)
    17   Bill is cleverer than some people. (i.e. Bill is not cleverer than everybody)
    18   This is too much for anybody. (i.e. This is too much for everybody, it doesn't matter who)
    19   This is too much for some people. (i.e. but not for everybody)

21 Do they need **any** extra workers?
Would you like **some** tea?

We use **some** and **any** in *questions*, but they have different expectations. The more normal situation is when we have no particular expectation or when we expect a negative answer; here we use **any**, e.g.

    1   Have you got any brothers or sisters?
    2   Did Helen take any money with her?

But when we expect or hope that the answer will be positive, we use **some**, e.g.

    3   Would you like some cake?¹
    4   Could you bring some of your records to the party?

Reported questions (» **178**) follow the expectation of the corresponding question:

    5   They asked if Helen had taken any money with her. (« » 2)
    6   My wife asked them if they would like some cake. (« » 3)

---

¹ This is a sincere offer. On the other hand, **Do you want any cake?** sounds reluctant.

22 They had **no** food and **no** tickets.

Here, **no** is a *determiner*; it goes with *count nouns*, usually *plural* (1, 2) but occasionally *singular* (3), and with *mass nouns* (4a, 5). **No** is *negative*; it expresses the absence of something:

1   The sign said, 'No dogs or other animals.'
2   There are no trees in their garden.
3   No parent should behave like that.
4a The school has no money for books.
5   No help was offered.

When **no** is not part of the *subject* (4a), sentences often sound strange; we often prefer to express the same meaning with **not** or **n't** and **any** (« » also 12), e.g.

4b The school hasn't any money for books.

A *clause* does not normally contain more than one *negative* word, so *Not* x The school hasn't no money x (« » 4a, b).

No is also the *negative* answer, e.g.

6   A: Can you come tomorrow?
    B: No, I can't.

Normally **no** has only these two uses[1], i.e. *determiner* and *negative* answer. We use **not** or **n't** to make *negative* sentences with *auxiliary verbs* (7), *adjectives* (8), *adverbs* (9), *pronouns* (10), *prepositional phrases* (11), and *determiners* (12):

7   They didn't ask for the money.
8   C: I think they said it was a black car.
    D: Not black, they said blue.
9   Mary can play the guitar, but not very well.
10 E: Who's done this?
    F: Not me.
11 I've seen the teapot somewhere, but not in the kitchen.
12 Not many people went to the concert.

Similarly with other *determiners*: **not a clever boy, not any trouble, not much milk, not enough patience, not the right book,** etc.

No is not a *pronoun*; the corresponding *pronoun* is **none** (13–16), which can be *postmodified* with an **of** *phrase* (14–16). When **none** is not the *subject* we often prefer **not** or **n't** with **any** instead (13, 14). When **none** is *subject* and corresponds to a *plural noun*, it can have either a *singular* or a *plural verb* (15):

13 G: How many fish did you catch?
    H: I didn't catch any. (or I caught none)
14 We didn't go in any of the caves. (or We went in none of the caves)

15　None of the boys is very athletic. (or boys are very)
16　None of the food has gone bad.

We usually avoid the phrases **no things** and **no people**; we express this meaning with **nothing** (» **50**) and **nobody** or **no one** (» **51**).

---

[1] However, we can use **no** with *comparatives*: **no bigger, no better, no less**, etc., e.g.

17　This programme is no better than the last one.

We also use **no** in the fixed expressions **no good, no use** and **no point**, which all mean 'hopeless, useless', e.g.

18　It's no good crying about it. (*Not* x There's no good x)
19　There's no use worrying about it. (or It's no use)
20　There's no point in asking again. (*Not* x It's no point x)

Notice the use of the **-ing** *form* with all these phrases.

23　Did you have **much** trouble?　There weren't **many** cars in town.

Much is a *determiner* (1, 2) and a *pronoun* (5); **many** is an *adjective*[1] (3, 4) and a *pronoun* (6). **Much** goes with *mass nouns* and **many** goes with *plural count nouns*, but mostly only in *questions* (1, 3, 5) and *negative statements* (2, 6). Both **much** and **many** mean 'a large quantity', and both can be *premodified* by **very** (1, 4):

1　Do you drink very much tea?
2　You haven't done much work today.
3　Are there many good cinemas in Sheffield?
4　I don't buy very many books.
5　A: Have you saved any money?
　　B: Not much. (i.e. not much money)
6　They expected a lot of people, but not many came. (i.e. not many people)

In *positive statements* **much** is rare but is sometimes used in formal style (7); **many** is not so unusual (8):

7　The government has done much for old age pensioners.
8　Many birds come here in the spring. (« » **24**.1)

However, **much** and **many** in *positive statements* often sound strange, and students should use **a lot (of)** instead (» **24**). Notice that **much** and **many** appear normally in *positive statements* if they are *premodified* by **too** (» **31**), **as** (» **70**) or **so** (» **75**).

Quite and **rather** cannot *premodify* **much** and **many**, so *Not* x̶ ̶q̶u̶i̶t̶e̶ m̶a̶n̶y̶ ̶x̶, *Not* x̶ ̶r̶a̶t̶h̶e̶r̶ ̶m̶u̶c̶h̶ ̶x̶, (but » **24**).

---

¹ **Many** is not a *determiner* because it can go with a *determiner*, especially **the**, e.g.

 9   We had to solve the many problems that arose.

For **how many, how much** » **165**.

24   She uses **a lot of** eggs in her cooking.

A lot of is a phrase that goes with *plural count nouns* (1, 4) and *mass nouns* (3, 5) in *positive statements* (1–3), *negative statements* (5) and *questions* (4). As *subject*, the *noun* after **of** determines the *verb*, i.e. a *count noun* has a *plural verb* (1) and a *mass noun* has a *singular verb* (2). **A lot** (**of**) means 'a large quantity' and has the alternative form **lots** (**of**). **A lot** (**of**) can be *premodified* by **rather** (3) or **quite** (6) but **lots** (**of**) cannot:

 1   A lot of birds come here in the spring. (« » **23**.8)
 2   Lots of food is wasted.
 3   They used rather a lot of paint.
 4   Do English people eat a lot of potatoes?
 5   They don't like a lot of noise in the house.

Without a *noun*, we use **a lot** (or **lots**):

 6   A: Did they use a lot of paint?
      B: Yes, they used quite a lot.
 7   Jenny knows a lot about the theatre.

You will also meet **a good deal** (**of**) and **a great deal** (**of**) with *mass nouns* and **a large number** (**of**) with *count nouns*, with similar meaning to **a lot** (**of**).

25   There were **a few** people in the park. Put **a little** water in the soup.

A few goes with *plural count nouns* (1, 2); **a little** goes with *mass nouns* (3). We can *premodify* **a few** and **a little** with **only** or **just** (4), and with **quite** (2). Both **a few** and **a little** mean 'a small quantity', but both phrases imply a positive or optimistic view of the quantity compared with what you expect (« » **few** and **little**, **26**); **a few** and **a little** tend to go with **some** *words* (2; » **253**):

1 It was raining but there were a few people in the park. (i.e. not many people, but more than you expect on a rainy day; «» **26**.1)

2 Quite a few students have made some useful suggestions. («» **26**.2)

3 A: Is there anything to eat? I'm starving.
   B: Well, there's a little cold meat, I think.

It was raining but there were a few people in the park.

We can use **a few** and **a little** alone, i.e. without a *noun*, when we can understand the *noun* from the context, e.g.

4 C: Would you like· some tea?
   D: Just a little, please.

Note: If the *noun* after **a little** can be both *count* and *mass*, then the phrase will have two possible meanings, e.g. **a little cheese** can mean either 'a small (whole) cheese' (*count*) or 'not much cheese' (*mass*).

26 **Few** companies have shown any interest. The council has given us **little** encouragement.

Few and **little** are *adjectives* (1–3) and *pronouns* (4). **Few** goes with *plural count nouns* (1, 2); **little** goes with *mass nouns* (3). We can *premodify* these words with **very** (4). Both **few** and **little** mean 'a small quantity'[1], but both words imply a negative or pessimistic view of the quantity compared with what you expect («» **a few** and **a little, 25**);

few and **little** go with **any** *words* (2; » **253**). The meaning of **few** and **little** is often expressed with **not many** (1, 2) and **not much** (3):

 1   It **was** a pleasant day but there weren't many people in the park. (or but there were few people; i.e. not many people but you expect more on a pleasant day; « » **25**.1)

 2   Not many students have made any useful suggestions. (or Few students; « » **25**.2)

 3   We haven't got much milk. (or We have little milk.)

It was a pleasant day but there were few people in the park.

We can use **few** and **little** alone, i.e. without a *noun*, when we can understand the *noun* from the context, e.g.

 4   A: How many people came?
     B: Very few.

---

[1] Notice that **few** and **little** do not imply smaller quantities than **a few** and **a little**; the quantity may be the same but the expectation different (« » **25**.1, 2 and **26**.1, 2).

27 She earns **more** money than I do.

More is an *adjective* (1–4) and a *pronoun* (5); it is the *comparative* of both **many** and **much** (« **23**). **More** goes with *plural count nouns* (1, 2) and with *mass nouns* (3, 4).

We use **more** to talk about a greater quantity; the comparison is expressed with **than**. **More** with *count nouns* can be *premodified*, with various meanings, by **even, far** (2), **plenty, several, many, a lot, lots, some, a few, any, no** and numbers, but not **very** alone (3)[1]:

    1   This year we took more photos than last year.
    2   They had far more paintings than I had expected.

More with *mass nouns* can be *premodified*, with various meanings, by **even** (5), **plenty, far, much** (4), **a great deal, a good deal, a lot** (3), **lots, a little, some, any** and **no,** but not **very**[1]:

    3   It was a lot more trouble than we thought. (*Not* x~~very more trouble~~ x)
    4   They spent much more money than I did[2].

We use *pronoun* **more,** i.e. without a *noun,* when we can understand the *noun* from the context, e.g.

    5   Last year we took a lot of photos, but this year we took even more. (i.e. more photos)

We use **one more** in a comparison with **than** (6) or if we want to emphasise the number (7):

    6   The Smiths made one more journey than we made.
    7   Give me one more card, please.

If we do not want to emphasise the number **one,** we use **another,** e.g.

    8   Give me another card, please.

With numbers there is an alternative structure, e.g.

    9a Their flat has two more bedrooms than ours.
    9b Their flat has two bedrooms more than ours.

We also use **more** to mean 'extra, in addition', without an explicit comparison, e.g.

    10   Would you like some more soup?
    11   I've spent all my money. Can I have some more?

The *superlative* form corresponding to **more** is **the most,** which can be an *adjective* (12) or a *pronoun* (13):

    12   Who ate the most food?
    13   We all ate a lot, but Paul ate the most.

We all ate a lot, but Paul ate the most.

[1] **Very much more** can *premodify mass nouns*, e.g. **very much more trouble**; **very many more** can *premodify plural count nouns*, e.g. **very many more paintings.**

[2] For *pronoun* forms after **than** » **71.**

Also » **72.**

28 This car uses **less** petrol than our old one.

Less is an *adjective* (1, 2) and a *pronoun* (3); it is the *comparative* of **little** (« **26**) and goes with *mass nouns*. We use **less** to talk about a smaller quantity; the comparison is expressed with **than**. **Less** can be *premodified*, with various meanings, by **even, much** (2), **far** (3), **a good deal, a great deal, a little, any** and **no,** but not **very:**

1 Less rain fell last month than in any month since June 1946.
2 There was much less opposition than we expected.

We use *pronoun* **less,** i.e. without a *noun,* when we can understand the *noun* from the context, e.g.

3 We thought there would be a lot of opposition, but there was far less than we expected. (« » 2)

The *superlative* form corresponding to **less** is **the least,** which can be an *adjective* (4) or a *pronoun* (5):

4 Of all the pupils Sarah causes the least trouble.
5 The least (that) you can do is to listen. (i.e. the minimum)

Also » **29.**

29 There are **fewer** students this term than last term.

Fewer is an *adjective* (1, 2) and a *pronoun* (3); it is the *comparative* of **few** (« **26**) and goes with *plural count nouns*. We use **fewer** to talk about a smaller number; the comparison is expressed with **than**. **Fewer** can be *premodified*, with various meanings, by **even** (3a) **far, a lot, a good deal, a great deal, no** and numbers, but not **very**. In informal style **less**[1] is often used instead of **fewer** with *count nouns*, and **less** can then be *premodified*, with various meanings, by **even** (3b), **far, a lot, a few, no** and numbers, but not **very:**

1 Children have fewer teeth than adults. (or have less teeth[1])
2 There were fewer people than at the last concert. (or were less people[1])

We use *pronouns* **fewer** and **less**, i.e. without a *noun*, when we can understand the *noun* from the context, e.g.

    3a She has few books in French and she has even fewer in Spanish.

    3b She hasn't got many books in French, and she's got even less in Spanish.[1]

We always use **less**, not **fewer**, with quantities of time, distance and money, e.g. **less than five hours, less than two miles, less than ten pounds,** etc.

The *superlative* form corresponding to **fewer** is **the fewest,** but we usually avoid this form and express the meaning with **fewer** (or **less**)[1] **than anyone,** etc., e.g.

    4 This town has fewer people out of work than any other town in the country. (or has less people[1])

---

[1] Some people consider the use of **less** with *plural nouns* incorrect.

30 We need three **pounds of** rice, two **tins of** soup and **a couple of** big tomatoes.

Pound, tin and **couple** are *count nouns*; they refer to units or quantities and are followed by **of** plus a *plural count noun* (1, 2) or a *mass noun* (3–5). *Determiners* etc. go with the unit word, e.g. **pound, tin couple,** not with the *noun* after of (5, 6). When it is *subject*, a *singular* unit usually goes with a *singular verb* (1, 2) and a *plural* unit goes with a *plural verb* (3, 4):

    1 A pair of old trousers was lying on a chair.
    2 A box of chocolates is a welcome gift.
    3 Two jars of jam have fallen off the table.
    4 Three pounds of beef are needed for this recipe.
    5 Have you ordered many pints of milk?
    6 Have you ordered much milk?

The unit word can be a measure (A), a container (B) or another quantity (C). Here are some typical examples; notice that every unit word can be *singular* or *plural* whether it is followed by a *count noun*, e.g. **apples, crisps, socks,** or a *mass noun*, e.g. **oil, jam, meat:**

A measures	B containers	C other quantities
a pound of apples two pounds of apples a litre of oil ten litres of oil	a packet of crisps ten packets of crisps one jar of jam many jars of jam	one pair of socks four pairs of socks a slice of meat three slices of meat

Unit words in Column A include: **gram, kilo, ounce, pound, ton; centimetre, kilometre, metre; foot, inch, mile, yard; litre, pint, gallon,** etc.

Unit words in Column B include : **bottle, box, can, cup, glass, jar, packet, pot, spoonful, tin,** etc. Phrases with these unit words mean the container and its contents, e.g. **a tin of soup** means 'a tin with soup in it', (« » **9b**).

Unit words in Column C include: **bar** (**of chocolate, soap**), **bit, couple, drop** (**of water, oil,** etc.), **loaf** (**of bread**), **pair** (**of socks, glasses, trousers, shoes,** etc.), **piece, slice,** etc.

31 I heard **too much** talk and saw **too little** action.

Too much and **too little** go with *mass nouns* (1, 2b); with *plural count nouns* we use **too many** and **too few** (3b, 4). For emphasis **far** can *premodify* all these phrases (5), and **much** can *premodify* **too much** (1) and **too little**. **Rather** can also *premodify* these phrases. We use **too much** and **too many** for a quantity that is excessive for a certain purpose; we use **too little** and **too few** for a quantity that is not sufficient for a certain purpose (» **77**). We express the relation to the purpose with a **for** *phrase* (1), a **to** *clause* (2), or with both (3). If the purpose can be understood from the context, it can be omitted (4). We often prefer **not enough** to express the meaning of **too little** and **too few** (2a, 4a).

    1   There's much too much food for me.
    2a There isn't enough snow to go skiing.
    2b There's too little snow to go skiing.
    3a We haven't got enough eggs for me to make six omelettes.
    3b We've got too few eggs for me to make six omelettes.
    4   Those children eat too many sweet things.

These phrases can be used as *pronouns*, i.e. without a *noun*, if we can understand the *noun* from the context, e.g.

    5   I wanted to know how many spectators there were, but there were far too many to count.

Note: **Too much cold air** means 'too much air that is cold', i.e. **too much** modifies **air**, not **cold**. If the air is too cold, then we say **air that is too cold**.

Also » **77**.

32 Are there **enough** screws to finish the job?

Here, **enough** is a *determiner*; it goes with *plural count nouns* (1, 2) and with *mass nouns* (3, 4). We use **enough** for a quantity that is sufficient for a certain purpose (» **78**). We express the relation to the purpose with a **for** *phrase* (1), a **to** *clause* (2), or both (3). If the purpose can be understood from the context, it can be omitted (4):

1   Have we got enough eggs for six omelettes?
2   We didn't buy enough apples to make a pie.
3   My aunt sent enough wool for me to make two jumpers.
4   Many people don't get enough fresh air.

We can use **enough** as a *pronoun*, i.e. without a *noun*, when we can understand the *noun* from the context, e.g.

5   We can borrow some chairs from the neighbours, but we still won't have enough.

Note: **Enough warm water** means 'enough water that is warm', i.e. **enough** modifies **water**, not **warm**. If the water is sufficiently warm, we say **water that is warm enough**.

Also » **78**.

33 **All** animals need water.

All goes first in a *noun phrase* (» **69**), before a *determiner*, which can be **the** (1), **this, that** (2), **these, those**, or a *possessive* (3, 4); with a *determiner* or a *possessive*, **of** can follow **all**, with the same meaning (1–4). **All** can also go without either a *determiner* or a *possessive* (5, 6). **All** goes with *count nouns*, usually *plural* (3, 4, 6) or with *mass nouns* (1, 2, 5).

All refers to every individual in a group of three or more, or to every part of something. In 5 and 6 the meaning includes everything; otherwise the meaning is restricted by the *determiner* or the *possessive* (1–4):

1   All (of) the drinking water comes from the stream.
2   Someone has to move all (of) that coal.
3   The dealer looked at all (of) my stamps.
4a   All (of) Sarah's friends came to see her.
5   All art is useless.
6   All motor vehicles must be insured.

With a *determiner* or *possessive*, when **all** is part of the *subject*, there is an alternative structure, with the same meaning, with **all** in *mid-position*, e.g.

> 4b Sarah's friends all came to see her.
> 7 Sarah's friends were all there.

We usually avoid **all** (**the**) **things** and **all** (**the**) **people** and also *pronoun* **all**; we express this meaning with **everything** (» **53**) and **everybody** or **everyone** (» **54**), e.g.

> 8 Everything was dirty. (*Not* x All was x)
> 9 We gave everybody a drink. (*Not* x We gave all x)

We usually avoid **all the** with *singular count nouns*; we express this meaning with **the whole** (» **34**), e.g.

> 10a It rained the whole day.
> 11 The whole house was filled with smoke.

However, with *singular* units of time, e.g. **day**, **week**, **year**, we can use **all** without **the**, e.g.

> 10b It rained all day.

With *pronouns*, **all** has different alternatives:

	subject	*object* or after a *preposition*
personal pronouns	all of it, it all[1] all of us (12a), we all[1] (12b) all of you, you all[1] all of them, they all[1]	all of it, it all all of us, us all all of you, you all all of them (13a), them all (13b)
demonstrative pronouns	all (of) this (14a), this all[1] (14b) all (of) that, that all[1] all (of) these, these all[1] all (of) those, those all[1]	all (of) this all (of) that all (of) these all (of) those (15)

All cannot go alone before a *personal pronoun* (12, 13):

> 12a All of us were tired and all of us felt hungry. (« » **35**.4a)
> 12b We were all tired and we all felt hungry. (*Not* x All we x)
>   (« » **35**.4b)
> 13a The manager spoke to all of them. (« » **35**.5a)
> 13b The manager spoke to them all. (*Not* x all them x)
>   (« » **35**.5b)
> 14a All (of) this seems childish.
> 14b This all seems childish.
> 15 We had to move all (of) those. (« » **35**.6)

---

[1] **All** after the *subject* goes in *mid-position* (12b, 14b).

34 The children prepared the **whole** meal.

Whole is an *adjective* that goes with a *singular count noun* or an abstract *mass noun*[1]. With a definite *determiner* there are two alternative structures:

the whole house	or	**the whole of the house**
that whole business	or	**the whole of that business**
her whole story	or	**the whole of her story**

However, with **a(n)** we use only the first structure, e.g. **a whole cake**. With *proper nouns* we use only the second structure, e.g. **the whole of Scotland**. Both structures have the same meaning: 'complete, but possibly in parts or pieces':

1 Did they tell you the whole truth?
2 The cakes are very big. Can you eat a whole one?
3 The whole of our house smelt for days.

We can also use **whole** after a *count noun* to mean 'complete and unbroken; in one piece', e.g.

4 Bill swallowed the biscuit whole. (i.e. without cutting or breaking it)

_____

[1] i.e. a *noun* that refers to an abstract concept, e.g. **truth, life, attention, concentration, business, effort,** etc.

35 **Both** windows were broken.

Both goes first in a *noun phrase* (» **69**), before a *determiner*, which can be **the** (1a), **these** or **those,** or a *possessive* (2a); with a *determiner* or a *possessive*, **of** can follow **both,** with the same meaning (1a, 2a). **Both** can also go without either a *determiner* or a *possessive* (1b). **Both** goes with *plural count nouns* and refers to the two members of a definite group of two:

1a The police surrounded both (of) the houses.
1b The police surrounded both houses.
2a Both (of) my sister's legs ached.

With a *determiner* or a *possessive*, when **both** is part of the *subject*, there is an alternative structure, with the same meaning, with **both** in *mid-position*, e.g.

2b My sister's legs both ached.
3 My sister's legs were both bleeding.

Both can go with the *pronouns* **we, us, you, they, them, these** and

those with the same structures as **all** with *pronouns* (« **33**), e.g.

4a Both of us were tired and both of us felt hungry.
(« » **33**.12a)
4b We were both tired and we both felt hungry.
(« » **33**.12b)
5a The manager spoke to both of them. (« » **33**.13a)
5b The manager spoke to them both. (« » **33**.13b)
6 We had to move both (of) those. (« » **33**.15)

For **both . . . and** » **227**.

36 **Each** member is allowed two tickets.

Each is a *determiner* (1–3) and a *pronoun* (4–8); we use **each** with a *singular count noun* (1, 2) or **one** (3). **Each** refers to the separate individuals in a group that contains two or more people or things:

1 Each patient receives individual attention.
2 Do they provide each child with his own materials?
3 They considered the suggestions carefully, for each one had something to offer.

We can use **each** alone, i.e. without a *noun*, when we can understand the *noun* from the context, e.g.

4 The three boys were questioned. Each told a different story. (i.e. each boy)

We can use *pronoun* **each** with an **of** *phrase*, e.g.

5a Each of the boys told a different story.

With a *plural subject* **each** can also go in *mid-position*, e.g.

5b The boys each told a different story.
6 We are each going to write a separate letter.

We also use **each** alone as the last word in the sentence, and we understand from the context whether it refers to the *subject* (7) or the *object* (8), e.g.

7 These oranges cost ten pence each. (i.e. each orange costs ten pence.)
8 Mrs Smith gave the girls one pound each. (i.e. one pound to each of the girls)

37 **Every** box is like this one.

Every is a *determiner*. We use **every** to talk about all the individuals in a group of three or more people or things; its meaning is plural but it goes with a *singular noun, verb,* etc., e.g.

1   Every job has its bad points. (i.e. All jobs have their bad points)
2   Were there mistakes on every page of the book?
3   They go fishing almost every weekend.

Every cannot go alone, i.e. without a *noun*; instead we use **every one** (two words), which can be for people or things:

4   Several girls came and my mother interviewed every one.
5   A: Have you looked in all the cupboards?
    B: Yes, I've looked in every one.

However, **everyone** (one word) can only refer to people (» **54**).

We use **every** with an *ordinal* number (» **254**), e.g. **every second, every third, every fourth,** etc. **Every second** has the alternative form **every other.**

1   Every second house has a chimney. (or Every other house)
2   Every third house has a flat roof.
3   Every fourth house has a garage.

38 I don't like **either** of them. I like **neither** of them.

Either and **neither** are *determiners* (1a, b) or *pronouns* (2–4). They go with a *singular noun* and as *subject* go with a *singular verb*[1] (3, 4). **Either** means 'one of two'; **neither** means 'not one or the other of two':

1a They did not accept either suggestion.
1b They accepted neither suggestion.
2   Have the police found either of the parents?
3   Neither of the twins is very clever.
4   Neither of us wants to go to the meeting.

---

[1] You will also meet **neither** with a *plural verb*, e.g. **are** in 3, **want** in 4, but some people consider this incorrect.

For another use of **either** » **226**; for another use of **neither** » **228**.

39 Can you play any **other** tunes?

Other and **another** are *adjectives* (1–4) and *pronouns* (5, 6); **others** is a *pronoun* (7). The forms are:

	indefinite		definite	
	adjective	pronoun	adjective	pronoun
singular count noun	another book another one	another	the other book the other one	the other
plural count noun	other books other ones	others	the other books the other ones	the others
mass noun	other work	other	the other work	the other

Another is always written as one word. Definite *noun phrases* can be made with different *determiners* and *possessives*, e.g. **every other book, those other books, Mary's other work, the other, your others**, etc. These words can refer to things that are different (1, 2, 4, 6), or to things that are similar but in addition to one previously mentioned (3, 5):

1 I don't like this music. Put another record on.
2 There weren't many children, but there were lots of other people.
3a I didn't make these shelves, but I made the other ones.
3b I didn't make these shelves, but I made the others.
4 She doesn't like melon. Is there any other fruit?
5 I like that record. Have you got another (one) by the same group?
6 I quite like this cheese, but I'd rather have the other.

Other cannot go with, or instead of, a *singular count noun*, so *Not* x put other record on x in 1, *Not* x have you got other (one) x in 5.

Other cannot be used in the sense of 'next' or 'last', so:

7 It isn't this street; it's the next one. (*Not* x the other x)
8 We didn't go last week but the week before. (*Not* x the other x)

40 He's **such** a fool (that) you can't talk to him.

Such is an *adjective*; **such** goes with a *singular count noun* with **a(n)** (1, 4), with *plural count nouns* (2) and with *mass nouns* (3, 5). We use

such to express the fact that someone or something has a quality that has certain consequences, which we express with a **that** *clause*, with optional **that**, e.g.

1 She's such a liar (that) you can't believe anything she says.
2 They were such big pears (that) we only got three in a kilo.
3 It was such delicious ice-cream (that) I asked for some more.

We also use **such** in sentences without a **that** *clause* as an exclamation, e.g.

4 Jill was such a helpful girl! (« » **41**.1, **75**.5, **76**.2)
5 They talk such rubbish!

We also use **such** to mean 'of this type, of that type', but we often express this meaning with **like this** or **like that**, e.g.

6 A: Tim never listens to what you say.
   B: Such people annoy me. (or People like that annoy me; i.e. people of that type annoy me)

We can also make explicit the relation between people of a certain type and a particular person with **such as**, e.g.

7a I'm surprised you employ such people as Tom. (i.e. people like Tom)
7b I'm surprised you employ people such as Tom.

We cannot use **such** with an *adjective* alone; instead we use **so** (» **75**). However, we can use **one(s)** instead of a *count noun*, e.g. **such a small one, such big ones**, if we can understand the *noun* from the context.

41 **What** lovely flowers those are!

Here, **what** is an *adjective*; **what** goes with *singular count nouns* with **a(n)** (1), with *plural count nouns* (2), and with *mass nouns* (3). **What** is used here for exclamations, and in this use does not have the *verb* form or word order of a *question*, e.g.

1 What a helpful girl Jill was! (*Not* x was Jill x; « » **40**.4, **75**.5, **76**.2)
2 What terrible risks they took! (*Not* x did they take x)
3 What nonsense!

We cannot use **what** with an *adjective* alone; instead we use **how** (» **76**). However, we can use **one(s)** instead of a *count noun* if we can understand the *noun* from the context, e.g. **What a small one!, What big ones!**

For other uses of **what** » **159, 181**.

42 **You** and I must talk about this problem.

You and I are *personal pronouns*. The *subject* forms are:

(referring to one)	I	you	he, she, it
(referring to two or more)	we	you	they

I refers to the person who is speaking or writing (1). **We** includes the person who is speaking or writing; **we** sometimes includes 'you' (2) and sometimes it does not (3). We use **you** to talk to one (4) or more than one person (5). **He** is for a male person (6) and sometimes for a male animal. **She** is for a female person (7) and sometimes for a female animal. **It** is for a thing (7, 8), animal, place (10) or idea, and sometimes for a human baby. We use **it** to refer to *mass nouns* (7), *singular count nouns* (8) and certain *proper nouns* (10). **They** is the *plural* of **he, she** (11) or **it** (12). **It** and **they** can only refer to definite *noun phrases* (8, 9, 12, 13).

1. I am English.
2. A: Can we go there this afternoon? (here, **we** means 'A and B')
   B: Yes, we can go in my car. (here, **we** means 'B and A')
3. C: Would you and Pat like to come to the party?
   D: Yes, thank you, we would. (here, **we** means 'D and Pat')
4. Andrew, can you help me, please? (here, **you** means 'Andrew')
5. Listen, children. You must be more careful. (here, **you** means 'children')
6. Mr Booth came once but he never came again.
7. Susan didn't like the food. She said it was cold.
8. E: Has that parcel come?
   F: Yes, it came this morning. (« » 9)
9. G: Has a parcel come?
   H: Yes, one came this morning, but I don't know if it's the one you mean. (*Not* x it came x; « » 8)
10. London is an interesting place, but it's too big.
11. I: Are your sisters in?
    J: No, they've gone to the cinema.
12. K: Have those parcels come?
    L: Yes, they came this morning. (« » 13)
13. M: Have any parcels come?
    N: Yes, some came this morning, but I don't know if they're the ones you mean. (*Not* x they came x; « » 12)

He, she, it, we and **they** are not used with a *noun phrase*, so:

14. Jim is my brother. (or He is; *Not* x Jim he is x)
15. The women stayed. (or They stayed; *Not* x The women they x)
16. Mary and I argued. (or We argued; *Not* x Mary and I we x)

43 Fred telephoned **me** yesterday.

Me is a *personal pronoun*. The *object* forms are:

(referring to one)	**me you**	**him, her, it**
(referring to two or more)	**us you**	**them**

The reference of these forms corresponds to the *subject* forms (« **42**). We use the *object* forms as *direct object* (1, 2, 4) as *indirect object* (6) and after a *preposition* (7). **It** and **them** can only refer to definite *noun phrases* (2–5):

1   Susan has just hit me.
2   You don't need to carry your case. I'll carry it.
3   A: Have you got a case?
    B: No, I haven't got one. (*Not* x it x)
4   Would you like one of these biscuits? I made them today.
5   C: Did you buy any biscuits?
    D: No, I didn't get any. (*Not* x them x)
6   Mary was pleased because my father gave her some flowers.
7   I know Gerry. I work with him.

We also use these forms, especially **me,** as *complement* of **be** (8) and alone as the answer to a question (9a):

8   Look at this photo. This is me and this is my boyfriend.
9a E: Who's going to do it?
    F: Not me.

In formal style, in answer to questions we use the *subject* form and the appropriate *auxiliary*, e.g.

9b E: Who's going to do it?
    F: I'm not.

We also prefer the *subject* form as the *complement* of **be** when the *pronoun* is modified by a *restrictive relative clause*, e.g.

10   Ask your mother. It was she who wrote the letter.

We cannot express possession with these forms, so *Not* x this book is to me x, *Not* x this book is of me x. Instead we use *possessive adjectives* (» **44**) or *possessive pronouns* (» **46**).

44 **Your** brother has borrowed **my** bike.

Your and **my** are *possessive adjectives*; they belong to the class of *determiners*. The forms are:

(referring to one)	**my**	**your**	**his, her, its**
(referring to two or more)	**our**	**your**	**their**[1]

All of these words can be used with *singular* or *plural noun phrases*, e.g. **my book, my books; her friend, her friends;** they can go with *singular count nouns* (1), *plural count nouns* (2) or *mass nouns* (3):

    1   They were working in their garden.
    2   Do your cousins live in Guildford?
    3   I admire her determination.

We can use a *possessive adjective* with another *adjective* and **one(s)** instead of a *count noun* if we can understand the *noun* from the context, e.g.

    4   These aren't my new boots; they're my old ones.

We cannot use *possessive adjectives* without a *noun* or **one(s)**; instead we use *possessive pronouns* (» **46**).

We normally use *possessive adjectives*, not **the,** to refer to parts of the body, e.g.

    5   I've cut my hand. (*Not* x the hand x)
    6   Can she touch her toes? (*Not* x the toes x)

But we say **She hit him on the head** because the *object* **him** already specifies the person concerned; the *passive* form of this is **He was hit on the head.**

We can use **own** after a *possessive adjective*, but not after **the,** for emphasis, e.g.

    7   They weren't working in their neighbours' garden; they were working in their own (garden).

---

[1] In informal style we use **their** to refer to **everybody** or **everyone** and sometimes also to **somebody, someone, anybody** and **anyone,** when either we do not know whether the people in question are male or female, or it is not important, e.g.

    8a I've told everybody to bring their notebooks.
    9   Somebody's put their wet clothes on top of mine.
    10a Has anyone forgotten to tell their parents?

However, some people consider this incorrect, and prefer not to use **their** here but instead to use **his or her** (10b) or simply **his** (8b) (including males and females), e.g.

    8b I've told everyone to bring his notebook.
    10b Has anyone forgotten to tell his or her parents?

But we always avoid several repetitions of **his or her** in the same passage.

For *personal pronoun* **one** » **45**.

45 What language do **they** speak in Yugoslavia ?

The *personal pronouns* that we use with a general meaning are **you** (1), **one** (2), **we** (4) and **they** (5–7); only **one** goes with a *singular verb*. The *possessive* corresponding to **one** is **one's**.

We use **you** to mean people in general, e.g.

> 1 A: How do you get to the station from here?
> B: You walk straight down this road.

One has a similar meaning to **you**, but it is formal style. **One** always includes the speaker, e.g.

> 2 When one gets older, one loses the will to work. (i.e. when people, including me, get older, they lose the will to work)

If the speaker excludes himself or herself, then **one** cannot be used:

> 3 People have lost the will to work. (i.e. people in general, but not including me)

We is used when the speaker identifies with the people in question; **they** is used when the speaker does not identify with the people.

For example, an Englishman would say:

> 4 In England we begin school when we are five.

On the other hand, someone who is not English would say:

> 5 In England they begin school when they are five.

They is often used to talk about impersonal authorities, e.g.

> 6 When are they going to do something for pensioners?
> 7 Have you heard? They're going to build a new town hall.

46 This record is **mine**.

Mine is a *possessive pronoun*. The forms are:

(referring to one)	**mine**	**yours**	**his, hers, its**
(referring to two or more)	**ours**	**yours**	**theirs**

All these words can stand for *singular* or *plural noun phrases*, e.g. **mine** for **my book** or **my books**; **ours** for **our dog** or **our dogs**.

We use a *possessive pronoun*, instead of a *possessive adjective* and a *noun*, when we can understand the *noun* from the context, e.g.

> 1 A: Is that Mrs Thomson's hat?
> B: No, hers is blue. (i.e. her hat)
> 2 Can we go in your car? There's something wrong with ours. (i.e. our car)

We cannot use these *pronouns* with *determiners*, so *Not* x the hers x in 1, *Not* x the ours x in 2. We cannot use *possessive pronouns* with *adjectives* or with *nouns*; instead we use *possessive adjectives* (« **44**).

47 I didn't recognise **myself** in the film.

Here, **myself** is a *reflexive pronoun.* The forms are:

(referring to one) **myself   yourself   himself, herself, itself**
referring to two   **ourselves yourselves themselves**
or more)

There is also the formal style **oneself** (4) corresponding to *pronoun* **one** (« **45**).

We use a *reflexive pronoun* when the *subject* is identical with the *direct object* (1, 4), the *indirect object* (2) or with the *noun* after a *preposition*[1] (3):

1   Did you hurt yourself while you were climbing?
2   We often buy ourselves flowers. (i.e. the flowers are for us; « » **48**.2)
3   They all had to paint a picture of themselves.
4   One can cut oneself on these things.

If we mention a part of the body with *verbs* like **hurt, cut,** etc., we do not use a *reflexive*, e.g.

5   Did you hurt your arm while you were climbing. (« » 1)

We can also use the *reflexive* forms as *emphatic pronouns;* these go at the end of the sentence (6) or, especially with a specific comparison, immediately after the *noun* or *pronoun* that they emphasise (7):

6   They painted the whole flat themselves. (i.e. this emphasises that nobody helped them)
7   David's friends didn't win anything, but he himself won the 100 metres.

---

[1] *Prepositions* of place, and also **with,** often do not have *reflexive pronouns*, e.g.

8   They kept their children near them.
9   She took my camera with her.

48 We often lend **each other** records.

Each other is a *noun phrase;* it has the alternative form **one another.** These phrases can be *direct object* (1), *indirect object* (2), and can follow a *preposition* (3). Both have *possessive* forms: **each other's** and **one another's** (4). We use these phrases to describe a two-way situation or action, e.g.

1   Mary and John help each other with their homework. (i.e. Mary helps John and John helps Mary)
2   Sally and I often buy each other flowers. (i.e. Sally buys flowers for me and I buy flowers for her; « » **47**.2)
3   They all took several photos of one another.
4   We often look after one another's children.

49 Do you mean the big house or the little **one**?

One is a *singular pronoun* (1); the *plural* form is **ones** (2) and the *singular possessive* form is **one's** (3). We use these words with *adjectives* to refer to a *count noun* when we can understand the *noun* from the context, e.g.

1 We haven't got any small cabbages. Would you like this big one instead. (*Not* x this big instead x)
2 The young children have gone home, but the older ones are still at school. (*Not* x the older are x)
3 A: Do you know that tall girl's parents?
    B: No, but I know the little one's mother.

For *determiners* that go with **one(s)** « Table 1, p18.

50 I think there's **something** behind the door.

Something, anything and **nothing** (» 253) are *indefinite pronouns.* We use these words to talk about an indefinite thing, i.e. when we cannot give the thing a name or description, e.g.

1 I think the dog can smell something.
2 Jim didn't bring anything when he came.
3 Nothing ever happens in this town.

Anything alone is not *negative*, so *Not* x Jim brought anything x in 2.
Also « **20²**

51 **Somebody** telephoned while you were out.

Somebody, anybody and **nobody** (» 253) are *indefinite pronouns*; they have the alternative forms **someone, anyone** and **no one** (normally written as two words.) We use these words to talk about an indefinite person, i.e. when we cannot give the person a name or description, e.g.

1 Molly was talking to somebody.
2 Is there anybody at the bus-stop?
3 Nobody lives in that house.

Anybody or **anyone** alone is not *negative*, e.g. *Not* x Anybody lives x in 3.
Also » **20²**.

52 I need **somebody** strong to help me.

Adjectives can *postmodify indefinite pronouns* **somebody, anybody, nobody, someone, anyone, no one, something, anything, nothing** and also *indefinite adverbs* **somewhere, anywhere, nowhere.** The *adjectives* themselves can be modified (2, 4), e.g.

    1   A: I'd like to speak to you.
         B: Is it something important?
    2   There was nobody very interesting at the dinner.
    3   Do you know anywhere nice round here?
    4   There isn't anybody stupid enough to volunteer.

Adjective **else** goes after these words to mean 'more' (5) or 'different' (6), e.g.

    5   I've had a sandwich, but I'd like something else.
    6   I can't tell her the news. Someone else must tell her.

Also » **55, 56, 59.**

53 **Everything** is made of atoms.

Everything is a *pronoun*; when it is *subject*, it goes with a *singular verb* (1). **Everything** refers to all the things in the world or in a particular place that we understand from the context, e.g.

    1   Everything has gone wrong.
    2   They lost everything in the fire.

We can specify a place or a group of things with a *prepositional phrase* (3) or a *restrictive relative clause* (4), e.g.

    3   They inspected everything in our suitcases.
    4   Tell me everything that happened.

You will sometimes meet **all** (**the**) **things,** with the same meaning as **everything,** but in many situations this sounds strange and learners should always use **everything** for this meaning.

54 **Everybody** needs to eat and sleep.

Everybody is a *pronoun*; it has the alternative form **everyone.** When **everybody** is *subject*, it goes with a *singular verb* (1, 3). **Everybody** refers to all the people in the world or in a particular place that we understand from the context, e.g.

    1   Everybody likes to be happy.
    2   Pollution affects everyone.

We can specify a particular place or group of people with a *prepositional phrase* (3) or a *restrictive relative clause* (4):

3 Everybody in this room is connected with education.
4 Everybody (that) I know wanted a change.

You will sometimes meet **all (the) people** with the same meaning as **everybody,** but in many situations this sounds strange and learners should use **everybody** for this meaning.

For **every one,** « 37.

55 Did you notice **the girls at the bus-stop** ?

Structure:

	A deter- miner	B (adjec- tive)	C noun or one(s)	D prepositional phrase	
1	The		car	in front of ours	was Peter's.
2 Can you see	those		cows	in that field?	
3 Whose are	the		ones	on the table?	
4	A	tall	man	with brown hair	stood up.

The *prepositional phrase* (D) describes the *noun* (C); when the *determiner* (A) is definite (1–3, 5, 6), the description is definite, i.e. it identifies a particular person or thing, or particular people or things, e.g.

5 A: Which woman are you talking about?
  B: The one beside that tree.

The description is usually of position (1–3, 5), but we also use **with** to describe people's features (4) and **in** to talk about their clothes:

6 I don't know the girl in the blue dress. (i.e. the girl wearing the blue dress)

Indefinite pronouns and *adverbs* (« **52**) can also be *postmodified* by *prepositional phrases*, e.g.

7 Someone on the bus told me about the fire.
8 Is their house anywhere near the station?

We can also use certain *adverbs* to *postmodify nouns* and describe their position, e.g. **that boy over there, the people behind, those plants outside.**

56 The people playing tennis were friends of mine.

Structure:

		A *deter-* *miner*	B *(adjec-* *tive)*	C *noun or* **one**(s)	D *-ing clause*	
1		The		dogs	eating those bones	look hungry.
2		A	young	girl	smoking a cigar	approached us.
3	Peter's	that		man	standing with Pat.	
4	Give me	those	small	ones	lying over there.	

The **-ing** *clause* (D) describes the *noun* (C); when the *determiner* (A) is definite (1, 3, 4), the description is definite, i.e. it identifies a particular person or thing, or particular people or things. The **-ing** *form* has a *progressive* sense here (» **138**), i.e. it describes an action in progress at the time, which can be past (5), present (6), or future (7):

> 5 There was a man smoking in the library. (i.e. who was smoking)
>
> 6 The lady talking to Tom works at the bank. (i.e. who is talking)
>
> 7 We have to get our instructions from a man wearing a black hat. (or in a black hat; i.e. who will be wearing; « » **55**.6)

Indefinite pronouns (« **52**) can also be *postmodified* by **-ing** *clauses*, e.g.

> 8 There was somebody smoking in the library.

When we talk about position, we can omit the **-ing** *form* if the *verb* is not important (« **55**), e.g.

without **-ing** *form*	with **-ing** *form*
the girls beside me	the girls sitting beside me
the lamp in the corner	the lamp standing in the corner
the baby on the carpet	the baby lying on the carpet

57 The girl mentioned in the report was innocent.

A *noun*, e.g. **girl**, is sometimes *postmodified* by a *past participle* phrase, e.g. **mentioned in the report**; this is equivalent to the *noun* with a *restrictive relative clause* (» **58–61**) in the *passive*:

    1   The girl (who was) mentioned in the report was innocent.

If the *past participle* phrase has commas, then it is equivalent to a *non-restrictive relative clause* (» **58, 63**), e.g.

    2   The Festival Hall, (which was) completed in 1951, has excellent acoustics.

This type of *noun phrase* sometimes sounds strange, and learners should normally use the corresponding *relative clauses* to express this meaning.

It is, however, perfectly normal after certain *verbs*, including **find, hear, keep, leave, like, make, prefer, see** and **want**, e.g.

    3   Jack found the money hidden in a drawer.
    4   Do they always keep the dog tied to the gate?
    5   I don't particularly like potatoes baked in their jackets.
    6   The boss wants the job finished by tomorrow.

For **have** and **get** in a similar structure » **175**.

58 The circle that has an L inside is on the left.

The square, which has a T inside, is at the top.

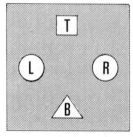

In the diagram there are four shapes. There is only one square and one triangle, so we can understand completely **the square** and **the triangle** in these sentences:

    1   The square is at the top.
    2   The triangle is at the bottom.

However, there are two circles, so we cannot understand completely **the circle** in the sentences:

    3   The circle is on the left.
    4   The circle is on the right.

If we read these sentences, we ask: 'Which circle?' In other words, we must identify a particular circle in order to know which one we are talking about, so:

    5   The circle that has an L inside is on the left.
    6   The circle that has an R inside is on the right.

Clauses like these that identify a person or thing, or people or things, are called *restrictive relative clauses* (» **59–62**). They are essential to the meaning of the sentence, so they are not separated with commas (,).

As we said earlier, we do not need to identify **the square** and **the triangle**, but we can still give extra information about them, e.g.:

    7   The square, which has a T inside, is at the top.
    8   The triangle, which has a B inside, is at the bottom.

Clauses that give extra information but which do not identify are called *non-restrictive relative clauses* (» **63**). They are not essential to the meaning of the sentence, so they are separated with commas.

59 I like **the girl that sang**.

The girl is a *noun phrase* that is *postmodified* by **that sang**, which is a *restrictive relative clause* (« **58**). The *relative pronoun* is **that**; it has the following forms:

	subject of the *relative clause*	*object* of the *relative clause*
for people	**that** (3a), **who** (3b)	**that** (5a), 'zero' (5b) **who** (5c), **whom** (5d)
for things, ideas	**that** (4a), **which** (4b)	**that** (6a), 'zero' (6b) **which** (6c)

Subject and *object* here refer to the *relative clause* alone; all *relative clauses* can *postmodify* the *subject* (**5**), *object* (**6**) or *complement* (**4**) of the whole sentence.

Whom is formal style.

'Zero' means that we can omit the *relative pronoun* when it is *object* of the *clause*. The different forms do not change the meaning of the sentence, so we can always use **that** for *restrictive relative clauses* (but » **60, 63**).

A *restrictive relative clause* restricts the meaning of the *noun* to a particular person or thing, or particular people or things, i.e. it gives essential information and tells us which – or what kind of – person, thing, etc., is the topic of the sentence (« **58**). Consider these conversations:

1 A: I was talking to an old lady.
   B: Which one?
   A: The old lady that sells flowers. (» 3)
2 C: *Family Connection* is a film.
   D: What kind of film?
   C: A film that deals with social problems. (» 4)

Obviously we can combine the information into one sentence, e.g.

3a I was talking to the old lady that sells flowers.
3b I was talking to the old lady who sells flowers.

4a *Family Connection* is a film that deals with social problems.
4b *Family Connection* is a film which deals with social problems.

5a Has the boy that the police arrested confessed?
5b Has the boy the police arrested confessed?
5c Has the boy who the police arrested confessed?
5d Has the boy whom the police arrested confessed?

6a The article mentions several books that I have read.
6b The article mentions several books I have read.
6c The article mentions several books which I have read.

I was talking to the old lady who sells flowers.

The *relative pronoun,* even when it is omitted (5b, 6b), replaces the *personal pronoun* that is necessary if there are two short sentences, e.g.

7 I was talking to an old lady. She sells flowers. (*Not* x an old lady that she sells x; « » 3a)
8 The article mentions several books. I have read them. (*Not* x The article mentions several books (that) I have read them x; « » 6a, b)

Indefinite pronouns and *adverbs* (« **52**) can also be *postmodified* by *restrictive relative clauses,* e.g.

9   Something (that) she said made me suspicious.
10 Is there anything (that) I can do?

60 My parents know **the people (that) I work for**

(That) I work for is a *restrictive relative clause* (« **58**) with a *preposition* (**for**). **For** is at the end of the *clause*, but in meaning it goes with the *relative pronoun* **that**. In formal style there is sometimes an alternative structure with the *preposition* first in the *clause*, before the *pronoun*:

  1   My parents know the people for whom I work.

With a *preposition* the *relative pronoun* has the following forms:

	preposition at end of *clause*	*preposition* first, before *pronoun*
for people	**that, who, whom,** 'zero' (2a)	**whom** (2b)
for things, ideas	**that, which** 'zero' (3a)	**which** (3b)

Whom is formal style. 'Zero' means that we can omit the *relative pronoun* when the *preposition* is at the end.

In general, both simple *prepositions*, e.g. **for, in**, and also compound ones, e.g. **in front of**, can go in both positions, e.g.

  2a The lady (that) I was sitting behind was wearing an enormous hat. (or The lady who(m) I was sitting behind)
  2b The lady behind whom I was sitting was wearing an enormous hat.
  3a Show me the boxes (that) the dolls are packed in. (or the boxes which the dolls are packed in)
  3b Show me the boxes in which the dolls are packed.

However, with *main verb* **be** the *preposition* only goes at the end (4); we also prefer the *prepositions* of *prepositional verbs* (» **191**) at the end (5):

  4   The man (that) I was in front of kept coughing.
  5   I didn't like the music (that) they were listening to.

61 I met **the girl whose picture was in the paper.**

Whose picture was in the paper is a *restrictive relative clause* (« **58**); **whose** is the *possessive* form of **who**, but can be used for both people (1) and things, ideas, etc., (2). **Whose** can combine such sentences as **I know a boy** and **His father died last week**:

  1   I know a boy whose father died last week.

Similarly, from **She agreed to certain changes** and **Their conse-quences were not clear at the time**:

> 2a She agreed to certain changes whose consequences were not clear at the time.

For things and ideas there is an alternative structure in formal style with **of which**:

> 2b She agreed to certain changes the consequences of which were not clear at the time.

62 Do you know **the factory where Mr Bingham works**?

Where Mr Bingham works is a *restrictive relative clause* (« **58**); **where** is a *relative adverb*. If the preceding *noun* refers to a place, we can use **where** instead of a *preposition* and a *relative pronoun* (1). If the preceding *noun* refers to a time, we can use **when** (2); if the preceding *noun* is **reason**, we sometimes use **why** (3):

> 1a That's the shop where she bought the gloves.
> 2a Wasn't 1966 the year when it rained so much?
> 3a Do you know the reason why she resigned? (i.e. the reason for which she resigned; *Not* x reason for why x; *Not* x reason because x)

Some people prefer to avoid **where, when** and, especially, **why** as *relative adverbs*, and instead use a *preposition* and a *relative pronoun* (1b, 2b); with **why** we can simply omit **the reason** (3b):

> 1b That's the shop in which she bought the gloves.
> 2b Wasn't 1966 the year in which it rained so much?
> 3b Do you know why she resigned?

63 **York, which is in the north**, has a magnificent cathedral.

Which is in the north is a *non-restrictive relative clause* (« **58**); **which** is the *relative pronoun*, and can have the following forms:

	subject of relative clause	*object* of relative clause	after a *preposition*
for people for things, ideas	**who** (1) **which** (4)	**who**(m), (2) **which** (5)	**whom**(3) **which** (6)

Subject and *object* here refer to the *relative clause* alone; this *clause* can go with the *subject* (2, 4, 6), *object* (3, 5), *complement* (1), etc., of the whole sentence.

In writing[1], we use *non-restrictive relative clauses* to give extra information about a person or thing, e.g.

1 The most important members of the committee are her parents, who are both lawyers.
2 The prime minister, who(m) many people recognised, stood talking to the police.
3 The director interviewed all the salesmen, to whom a report had already been sent.
4 Bakewell, which is an old town, is still important today.
5 Nobody supported the young man's plan, which most people considered far too radical.
6 The central streets, through which little heavy traffic passes, will be closed to motor vehicles.

The *relative pronoun* can be preceded by **all of, both of, most of, many of, some of, one** etc. **of, none of**, e.g.

7 The microphones, all of which had been carefully checked, were then set up on the stage.
8 The police interviewed several young men, three of whom had previous convictions.

---

[1] In speech, *non-restrictive relative clauses* are rare; instead we prefer *co-ordinated simple clauses* (» **226**), e.g.

9 York is in the north and it has a magnificent cathedral. (« » section heading)

64 Ann came early, which surprised everybody.

Which surprised everybody is a *sentence relative clause*; it refers to the whole of the previous *clause*, i.e. **Ann came early**. In this use **which** is the only *relative pronoun*; it is normally *subject* of the *clause*, and it is preceded by a comma (,) e.g.

1a The cases had names on, which made distribution easy.
2 Nobody asked our opinion, which annoyed me intensely.

The same meaning can be expressed in two short sentences, e.g.

1b The cases had names on. This made distribution easy.

65 I need **some scissors to cut this paper (with)**.

Structure:

A *noun phrase*	B **to** *infinitive*	C *(noun phrase)*	D *preposition*
a pen something a good surface	to write to put to roll out	these flowers the dough	with in on

The *noun phrase* (A) is an instrument or object for a particular purpose (» **252**); *preposition* **with** is optional when there is a *noun phrase* after the *verb* (2):

1　Is there a bowl to wash in? (i.e. a bowl in which we[1] can wash; « » 4)
2　I haven't got any glue to stick this (with). (i.e. glue with which I[1] can stick this)
3　Here's a mat to stand the hot dishes on. (i.e. a mat on which you[1] can stand the hot dishes)

---

[1] or somebody else; in all these sentences we understand the unmentioned *subject* of the **to** *infinitive* (B) from the context. If this *subject* is not clear, we can make it explicit with a **for** *phrase*, e.g.

4　Is there a bowl for the children to wash in? (« » 1)

Also » **252**.

66 Mrs Lee is **the best person to ask**.

Structure:

A **the**	B *(superlative adjective)*	C *noun*	D **to** *clause*
the the the	best most interesting	time woman place	to get there to talk to to stay

When there is no *superlative*, e.g. **the place to stay**, 'best' is understood, i.e. this means 'the best place to stay', e.g.

1   The time to go is during the festival. (i.e. the best time (that) you[1] can go)
2   The easiest way to get there is by taxi. (i.e. the easiest way (that) they[1] can get there)

---

[1] or somebody else; we understand the unmentioned *subject* of the **to** *clause* (D) from the situation. If the *subject* is not clear, we can make it explicit with a **for** *phrase*, e.g.

3   The easiest way for your parents to get there is by taxi. (« » 2)

67 The Johnsons were **the first guests to arrive**.

Structure:

A the	B adjective	C noun	D to clause
the	first	person	to finish the exam
the	only	car	to break down
the	next	train	to arrive at Platform 3

The *adjectives* (B) can be the *ordinal numbers* (» **254**) and also **next**, **last** and **only**. These *adjectives* (except **only**) can go alone, i.e. without a *noun* if we can understand the *noun* from the context, e.g.

1   There was a majority of men students at the meeting, but the first (student) to speak was a girl.

But **only** must have a *noun* or *pronoun* **one**, e.g. **the only student to speak,** or **the only one to speak,** *Not* x the only to speak x.

This structure corresponds in meaning to a *restrictive relative clause* (« **58–62**) and the *noun* (C) corresponds to the *subject* of the *clause*, e.g.

2   The first news to reach us was not very encouraging. (i.e. the first news that reached us)
3   Eva was the only person to be promoted. (i.e. the only person that was promoted)

PART 2

Adjectives, adverbials and prepositional phrases

Introduction

Adjectives (**68–82**)

Adjectives, which are in **bold** type in 1–8, can go alone (1; » **68**), can *premodify* a *noun* (2; » **68**), and can *postmodify* a *pronoun* (3; « **52**), e.g.

    1   **green; tall; French; interesting**
    2   **green** apples; a **French** town
    3   something **interesting**; somebody **intelligent**

Certain *adjectives* can be *premodified* by certain *adverbs* (4; » **74–77**), and can be *postmodified* by **enough** (5; » **78**) or by a *prepositional phrase* (6; » **79**) or a *clause* (7; » **80–82**), e.g.

    4a   completely **dry**; very **nice**; too **large**
    5   **big** enough; **clever** enough
    6   **lucky** at cards; **used** to getting up
    7   **sure** to break something; **free** to choose

Most short *adjectives* have *comparative* and *superlative* forms (8; » **71, 72**), e.g.

    8   **small, smaller, smallest**.

Adverbials (**83–98**)

Adverbials have various forms (» **83**): they can be single words, i.e. *adverbs* (9), or *prepositional phrases* (10), or *clauses* (11), e.g.

    9   **quickly; always; very; too**
    10   **into that room; along the corridor; on Friday**
    11   **so that it fell; to fetch some food**

Certain *adverbs* can be *premodified* by other *adverbs* (12a), and certain short *adverbs* can have *comparative* and *superlative* forms (13; » **71**), e.g.

    12a   too **quickly**; so **often**; very **clearly**
    13   **fast, faster, fastest**

Certain *adverbs*, e.g. **completely, very, too, so,** can modify *adjectives* (4b) or other *adverbs* (12b). Otherwise the main use of *adverbials*, in

bold type in 14–16, is to *modify* a *verb*, e.g.

4b **completely** dry; **very** nice; **too** large
12b **too** quickly; **so** often; **very** clearly
14 They spoke **slowly**.
15 He walked **along the corridor**.
16 She went **to fetch some food**.

Prepositional phrases (**99–106**)

A *prepositional phrase* consists of a *preposition* (» **99**), which is in **bold** type in 17, and a *noun phrase*, e.g.

17 **on** the table; **in front of** me; **because of** the fire

Prepositional phrases, which are in bold type in 18–21, have various uses. Their main uses are as *adverbials* that *modify verbs* (18), but they can also *postmodify nouns* (19; « **55**), *pronouns* (20; « **52**) and *adjectives* (21; » **79**), e.g.

18 go **into the room**; play **inside the garage**
19 the cup **on the table**; those women **near the tree**
20 something **behind you**; anybody **in this class**
21 keen **on football**; interested **in swimming**

Prepositional phrases are often used for place (» **100**) and time (» **101**).

A **for** *phrase* is a *prepositional phrase* with *preposition* **for**, e.g. **for her, for the doctor**, etc. An **of** *phrase* is a *prepositional phrase* with *preposition* **of**, e.g. **of England, of her friends**, etc.

68 The **tall** girl is my daughter. My daughter is **tall**.

Tall is an *adjective*. *Adjectives* have one form for *gender* and *number*, e.g. **a tall girl, a tall boy, a tall tree, the tall girls, the tall boys, the tall trees**. Most *adjectives* can both *premodify* a *noun* (1, 3; called *attributive* use) and can also be *complement* of **be** (2, 4; called *predicative* use):

1 I like this hot soup.
2 This soup is hot.
3 Wild animals should not be in zoos.
4 Those animals aren't wild.

However, there are certain *adjectives* that have only one of these possibilities, including these common ones, which are only used as *complements*:

5 Mrs Bryant is alone. (*Not* x an alone woman x)
6 That insect's alive. (*Not* x an alive insect x)
7 My father's very well. (*Not* x a well man x)

8 Her sister was ill. (*Not* x an ill girl x)
9 I was really afraid. (*Not* x an afraid boy x)
10 The baby's asleep. (*Not* x an asleep baby x)
11 The two pictures are alike. (*Not* x two alike pictures x)

There are other *adjectives* that have only one possibility; students should consult a good dictionary.

Adjectives do not normally *postmodify nouns*, but there are a few exceptions including, e.g. **the people present, the members absent, the boys involved, the papers concerned.** All these cases mean the same as a *restrictive relative clause* (« **58**), e.g. 'the people that were present', 'the boys that are involved', etc.

When an *adjective* is itself *postmodified*, it must go after the *noun*, e.g.

12 I'd like a chicken large enough to serve six people.

69 An **attractive young Welsh** girl sang the first song.

Two or more words – *adjectives* or *nouns* – can *premodify* a *noun*. Although the ordering of these words is not absolutely fixed, the most usual order is:

a)	**both, all** or **half**	**both**
b)	*determiner*	**the**
c)	*ordinal number*[1]	**last**
d)	*cardinal number*[2]	**two**
e)	judgement[3]	**nice**
f)	measurement[4]	**big**
g)	age or temperature	**old**
h)	shape	**round**
i)	colour	**red**
j)	*verb* form[5]	**carved**
k)	origin	**French**
l)	material	**wooden**
m)	noun[6]	**card**
n)	*head noun*	**tables**

Naturally, there is often only one *premodifying* word and it is rare for there to be more than three or four to a *head noun*. In most cases these words do not have **and** and need not have commas (,), although if there are two or more *adjectives* from categories (*e*) to (*j*), they may be separated by commas (1,4,6):

Descriptive *adjectives* that do not fall into one of the categories (*e*) to (*l*) e.g. **general, natural, systematic,** etc. tend to go between (*g*) and (*h*).

1 two large (,) oval mirrors (*d,f,h,n*)
2 all those handsome tennis players (*a,b,e,m,n*)
3 the only antique pewter jug (*b,c,g,l,n*)

4 an enormous (,) steaming pressure cooker (*b,f,j,m,n*)
5 her new Austrian skiing boots (*b,g,k,m,n*)
6 some attractive (,) round (,) black beads (*b,e,h,i,t,n*)

Every *adjective modifies* the *head noun*, so **some attractive round black beads** are some beads that are attractive, round and black, (« » **9**). Colours have **and** if there are two, e.g. **a black and red flag**; they have a comma (,) and **and** if there are three, e.g. **a red, white and blue flag**.

---

[1] (» **254**), and also **next, last** and **only**.
[2] (» **254**), and also expressions of quantity, e.g. **(a) few, (a) little, a lot of**.
[3] e.g. **pretty, lovely, awful, terrible**, etc.
[4] e.g. **wide, fast, little, thick**, etc.
[5] i.e. a *past participle* (as in the example above), or an **-ing** form used to describe what the *head noun* is doing (« **4**).
[6] i.e. a *premodifying noun*, including **-ing** forms used as *nouns*, (« **5**, and **9c**).

70 Our house is about **as** big **as** that one.

We use **as . . . as** with an *adjective* (1, 2), with an *adverb* (3, 4), and with **much** (5), **many** (6), **little** and **few**. With a *negative* there is an alternative form with the same meaning, e.g. **not as big as**, or **not so big as**. The *personal pronoun* after **as . . . as** is either the *subject* form plus the appropriate *auxiliary verb*[1], e.g. **I am** (1), **they are** (3) or, in informal style, the *object* form alone, e.g. **me** (1), **them** (3).

We use **as . . . as** to express that somebody or something has a quality or a quantity to the same extent as somebody or something else, e.g.

1 My brother is as tall as I am. (or as me)
2 These instruments aren't as accurate as my old ones.
3 Are we working as fast as they are? (or as them)
4 Does George play tennis as well as his father?
5 I think this jar holds as much as that one.

I think this jar holds as much as that one.

Notice the use of **possible** in such sentences as 6b:

> 6a Send as many samples as you can.
> 6b Send as many samples as possible. (*Not* x̶ ̶p̶o̶s̶s̶i̶b̶l̶y̶ ̶x̶)

---

[1] The *subject* form alone, e.g. **as I** in 1, **as they** in 3, is rare.

71 Fred **is taller than** Kate.

Taller is a *comparative*. We make *comparative* and *superlative* (» **72**) forms in two ways:

a) for *adjectives* and *adverbs* with one syllable, e.g. **strong, small, bright, fast, hard** (but not words ending in -ed, e.g. **bored**), and also for *adjectives* with two syllables[1] that end with the vowel sounds /ə/, e.g. **clever**, or /ɪ/, e.g. **pretty**, we use the endings -**er** and -**est**:

	strong	fast	clever	pretty
comparative	stronger	faster	cleverer	prettier
superlative	strongest	fastest	cleverest	prettiest

b) for all other *adjectives* and *adverbs*, including all *adjectives* ending in -**ing** and -**ed**, e.g. **boring, bored**, we use **more** and **most**:

	delicious	quickly[2]	bored	boring
comparative	more delicious	more quickly	more bored	more boring
superlative	most delicious	most quickly	most bored	most boring

Comparatives can be *premodified*, with various meanings, by e.g. **a little, much** (1), **far, a lot** (2), **rather** and **somewhat**, but not **very, quite, fairly** or **pretty**.

We use *comparatives* with **than** to compare people, things, etc. **Than** can go with a *comparative adjective* (1, 2), a *comparative adverb* (3, 4), and also with **more** (« **27**), **less** (« **28**) and **fewer** (« **29**). The *personal pronoun* after **than** is either the *subject* form plus the appropriate *auxiliary*[3], e.g. **I am** (1), **they do** (3) or, in informal style, the *object* form alone, e.g. **me** (1), **them** (3):

> 1 Jack is much stronger than I am. (or than me)
> 2 Is football a lot more exciting than cricket?

3   We always work faster than they do. (or than them)
4   Mrs White talks more quickly than her husband.

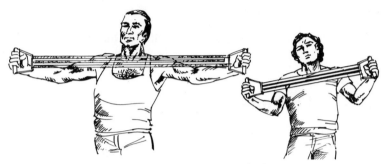

Jack is much stronger than I am.

We can omit the phrase with **than** when we can understand the comparison from the context, e.g.

5   I'm strong, but Jack is much stronger. (« » 1)

We can also use **the** with a *comparative* to select between two things, e.g.

6   I'm older than my sister, but she is the taller. (« » **72**.9)
7   Which is the bigger, London or New York? (« » **72**.10)

Notice the use of **usual** in such sentences as 8b:

8a The water is hotter than it usually is.
8b The water is hotter than usual. (*Not* x than usually x)

Note: Sentences like **She knows you better than me** have two possible meanings, either 'She knows you better than she knows me' or 'She knows you better than I know you'. Normally the context will make it clear which is intended, but if there is a possibility of confusion, we use the longer form to make it clear.

For the spelling of regular *comparatives* and *superlatives* » **256**; for irregular *comparatives* and *superlatives* » **258**.

---

[1] The situation with two-syllable *adjectives* and *adverbs* is in fact confused. For example, **noble, subtle, often, common, polite** and **quiet** usually take **-er** and **-est**. But even words that normally take **-er** and **-est** sometimes take **more** and **most**. In general, if learners are unsure about two-syllable words, they should use **more** and **most**.

[2] In informal style we can also make the *comparative* and *superlative* forms of *adverbs* in **-ly** like the corresponding *adjectives*, i.e. **quicker, quickest**.

[3] The *subject* form alone, e.g. **than I** in 1, **than they** in 3, is rare.

72 That's **the oldest** restaurant in the town.

Oldest is a *superlative*; (for the forms « **71**). A *superlative* normally goes with **the**, e.g. **the cheapest, the most useful**[1].

We use the *superlative* of an *adjective* to express that nobody or nothing has more of the quality. We can limit the scope of the comparison with **of** and a number etc. (1, 2), with **in** and a place (3, 4), or with a *restrictive relative clause* (5):

  1   These flowers are the prettiest (of all).
  2   That is the most comfortable of the three chairs.
  3   London is the biggest city in Britain.
  4   Is it the most exclusive club in the world?
  5   Which is the longest book (that) you have ever read?

Certain short *adverbs* also have *superlatives*, e.g.

  6a Of all my relatives my sister works the hardest.

However, we often avoid the *superlative* of *adverbs* and instead use the *comparative* with **than anybody, than anything, than all**, etc., e.g.

  6b My sister works harder than all my other relatives.
  7   Jenny eats faster than anyone I know.
  8   He expresses himself more subtly than any other contemporary writer.

The *superlative* is always used when three or more people or things are involved, and in informal style you will also meet the *superlative* when only two people or things are involved[2], e.g.

  9   I'm older than my sister, but she's the tallest.[2] (« » **71**.6)
  10 Which is the biggest, London or New York?[2] (« » **71**.7)

However, a *superlative* can never be used with **than,** so *Not* x oldest than x in 9.

---

[1] We can use **most** without **the** to mean 'very', but this is not very frequent, e.g.

  11 It was a most interesting visit. (i.e. very interesting)

[2] Some people consider this incorrect usage.

73 It's **the same** colour but a **different** shape.

Same and **different** are *adjectives*. We use **the same** to talk about identity and **different** to talk about non-identity. We can make the relation explicit with **the same . . . as** and **different . . . from**[1], e.g.

  1   Is that the same make of car (as yours)?

2   These are different pears (from the ones I bought on Friday).

---

[1] Instead of **from** you may hear and read **to** or **than,** with the same meaning, but some people consider this incorrect usage.

74 The clothes should be **completely dry**.

Completely is an *adverb*. Some *adjectives* (1–4) and *adverbs* (5, 6) refer to qualities that can have different degrees; these words can be *premodified* by *adverbs* that indicate the degree, e.g. **perfectly** (2), **completely, terribly, awfully, very** (5), **really** (3), **quite** (6), **rather** (1), **fairly, pretty** (4):

1   Don't you think he's rather young for the part?
2   He seemed perfectly normal before his illness.
3   He told us some really funny stories.
4   We made pretty good progress.
5   We had to work very hard.
6   Molly comes to see us quite often. (i.e. fairly often; « » 7)

When they are followed by a *singular count noun*, **quite, rather, fairly** and **pretty,** which all mean 'to some extent, but not very', do not all go in the same position:

> **quite** goes before **a(n)**, e.g. **quite a slow dance;**
> **rather** goes before or after **a(n)**, e.g. **a rather slow dance,** or **rather a slow dance;**
> **fairly** goes after **a(n)**, e.g. **a fairly slow dance;**
> **pretty** goes after **a(n)**, e.g. **a pretty slow dance.**

Pretty is informal style.

Quite has a different use with *adjectives* that refer to qualities that can be complete, e.g. **full, empty, finished, perfect, ready;** here **quite** usually means 'completely', e.g.

7   The barrel seems to be quite empty. (i.e. completely empty; « » 6)

75 She's **so** clever **(that)** she doesn't need to study.

We use **so** with an *adjective* alone (1, 5), with an *adverb* (2, 6), and with **much, many** (3), **few** (4) and **little**. These phrases go with a **that** *clause*, with optional **that.**

We use this structure to express that somebody or something has a quality, etc., that has a certain consequence, e.g.

1 This food is so salty (that) I can't eat it. (i.e. it is too salty for me to eat)
2 He lied so obviously (that) no one believed him.
3 Susan made so many mistakes (that) I could hardly read her letter.
4 There are so few music lovers round here (that) we can't start a record club.

Without the **that** *clause*, the **so** has the sense of an exclamation, e.g.

5 Jill was so helpful! (« » **40**.4, **41**.1, **76**.2)
6 They ski so badly! (» **76**.3)

For other uses of **so** » **236, 251.**

76 **How** stupid we were!

We use *adverb* **how** with an *adjective* alone (1, 2) or an *adverb* (3) for exclamations, which have an exclamation mark (!). They do not have the *verb* form or word order of a *question* (2, 3), e.g.

1 How nice of them!
2 How helpful Jill was! (*Not* x was Jill x; « » **40**.4, **41**.1, **75**.5)
3 How badly they ski! (*Not* x do they ski x; « » **75**.6)

When there is a *verb* (2, 3), we often prefer to express these exclamations with **so** (« **75**). We cannot use **how** with a *noun*; instead we use **what** (« **41**).

For other uses of **how** » **163–168.**

77 These shoes are **too** small for Brian.

Adverb **too** can *premodify* an *adjective* (1, 2) or an *adverb* (3, 4). We use **too** to express that a quality is excessive in a particular situation; the relation to the situation is expressed with a **for** *phrase* (1), a **to** *clause*[1] (2), or both (3). If the situation is clear from the context, then the relation can be omitted (4). **Too** can be *premodified* (for emphasis) by **far** (1) and **much** (2); **rather** ('not much') can also *premodify* **too** (5):

1 The jacket was far too expensive for my brother.
2 It is much too cold to sit outside.
3 The guide spoke too quickly for us to understand.
4 You're driving too fast!

These shoes are too small for Brian

Too does not necessarily mean 'very'; in the picture the shoes are not very small, but they are too small for Brian, because he has enormous feet.

We avoid **too** plus an *adjective* before a *noun*, so:

5   We used some paper that was rather too thin. (*Not* x some rather too thin paper x)

---

[1] When the **to** *clause* is a **to** *infinitive* alone, it has two possible functions in the sentence. For example, in 6 **we** is the unmentioned *subject* of **eat**, and in 7 **Sara** is the unmentioned *subject* of **read**:

6   We were too hot to eat. (i.e. we could not eat because we were too hot; « » 8, 10)
7   Sara was too tired to read. (i.e. Sara could not read because she was too tired; « » 9, 11)

In these cases, if the *verb* can have an *object*, then an *object* can follow the **to** *infinitive*, e.g.

8   We were too hot to eat the food. (« » 6, 10)
9   Sara was too tired to read the letter. (« » 7, 11)

On the contrary, in 10 **the food** is the unmentioned *object* of **eat**, and in 11 **the books** is the unmentioned *object* of **read**. Consequently, in these cases the **to** *infinitive* cannot have another *object*, e.g.

10   The food was too hot to eat. (*Not* x to eat it x; i.e. the food could not be eaten because it was too hot; « » 6, 8)
11   The books were too difficult to read. (*Not* x to read them x; i.e. the books could not be read because they were too difficult; « » 7, 9)

In sentences like 10 and 11, a *verb* that needs a *preposition* before an *object* (**191, 224**) also needs the *preposition* here, e.g.

12   The talk was too boring to listen to. (*Not* x to listen x)
13   His jokes are too stupid to laugh at. (*Not* x to laugh x)

Also « **31**.

66

78 This coat isn't big **enough** for Sara.

Adverb **enough** *postmodifies* an *adjective* (1, 2) or an *adverb* (3, 4). We use **enough** to express that a quality is sufficient for a particular situation; the relation to the situation is expressed with a **for** *phrase* (1), a **to** *clause* (2), or both (3). If the situation is clear from the context, then the relation can be omitted (4):

1. This spot is quiet enough for a picnic.
2. Henry isn't old enough to have known your father.
3. Does this·machine dry quickly enough for me to dry all the clothes this morning?
4. You aren't writing carefully enough.

For **enough** with *nouns* « **32**.

79 Mrs Norton is always **lucky at cards**.

Certain *adjectives*, e.g. **lucky**, can be *postmodified* by *prepositional phrases*, e.g. **at cards**; certain *past participles*, e.g. **interested**, can also be used in these phrases. The only *verb* form that can follow a *preposition* is an ·-**ing** *form*. Here are some typical examples:

with a *noun*	with an -**ing** *form*
good at chess	good at making salads
keen on football	keen on collecting stamps
used to the weather	used to¹ getting up early
interested in music	interested in listening
bored with the speech	bored with working

The *preposition* depends on the *adjective* or *participle*; students should consult a good dictionary for each combination.

The *past participles*, which are here used as *adjectives*, do not relate the sentence to time; the form of **be** or **get** relates the sentence to past (1–2), present (3–6) or future time (7, 8):

1. My father was happy with the results. (« » **80**.1, **81**.1)
2. After Jack started his new job, he quickly got used to meeting new people all the time.
3. Are they justified in having mentioned our name?
4. Are you afraid of thunder? (« » **80**.4, **81**.4)
5. She is delighted at having been chosen. (i.e. delighted that she has been chosen)
6. My brother is not used to¹ getting up early, so he finds it rather difficult.

7   She'll get tired of waiting.
8   I'll never get used to working at night.

Adjective **worth,** without a *preposition,* can be *postmodified* by a *noun* (9) or an **-ing** *form* (10); *adjective* **busy** can be *postmodified* by an **-ing** *form* (11):

9   It took a long time to scrape the old paint off, but it was worth the trouble.
10   The new model will be worth waiting for.
11   The manager's busy arranging the exhibition.

Preposition **to** goes after certain other *past participles,* including **accustomed, opposed** and **given;** the only form of a *verb* that can follow it is an **-ing** *form* (» **195**[1], **199**[1]).

---

[1] For another use of **used** » **121.**

80 Our children were **sure (that) we would agree.**

Certain *adjectives,* e.g. **sure,** can be *postmodified* by a **that** *clause,* with optional **that.** These *adjectives* include *past participles* that are used as *adjectives:* **afraid, alarmed, amazed, amused, angry, annoyed, anxious, ashamed, astonished, aware, careful, certain, confident, conscious, delighted, depressed, determined, disappointed, disgusted, distressed, disturbed, fortunate, frightened, glad, grateful, happy, hopeful, horrified, irritated, jealous, keen, lucky, mad, optimistic, pleased, positive, proud, relieved, sad, satisfied, shocked, sorry, sure, thankful, upset, worried.** These *adjectives* need a *preposition* if they are followed by a *noun* (« **79**), but not here because a **that** *clause* can never follow a *preposition:*

1   My father was happy (that) I had passed. (« » **79**.1, **81**.1)
2   We were very pleased (that) we met her. (« » **81**.2)
3   The manager was annoyed (that) the sales were so poor.
4   Are you afraid (that) there might be a storm? (« » **79**.4, **81**.4)

81 Pat was **content to let the others talk.**

Certain *adjectives,* e.g. **content,** can be *postmodified* by a **to** *clause.* These *adjectives* include *past participles* that are used as *adjectives.* These *adjectives* need a *preposition* if they are followed by a *noun* (« **79**), but not here because a **to** *clause* can never follow a *preposition.*

There are different groups of these *adjectives*. One group is of *adjectives* that express a feeling, and the **to** *clause* gives the cause of the feeling, i.e. the action is previous to the feeling, and so the **to** *clause* often has a *perfect infinitive* (1, 2). These *adjectives* include: **amused, angry, annoyed, ashamed, astonished, bored, concerned, content, delighted, depressed, disappointed, disgusted, dissatisfied, embarrassed, excited, fascinated, furious, glad, happy, irritated, lucky, pleased, proud, puzzled, sad, satisfied, surprised, upset, worried,** e.g.

1   My father was happy to have passed the exam. (or to pass the exam; i.e. happy that he himself passed; « » **79**.1, **80**.1)
2   We're very pleased to have met her. (i.e. pleased that we have met her; « » **80**.2)
3   I'm very pleased to meet you. (i.e. now; « » 2)

Another group is of *adjectives* that express an attitude towards the action of the **to** *clause*, i.e. the attitude is previous to the action, so a *perfect infinitive* is not possible here. These include: **afraid, apt, anxious, curious, determined, eager, free, impatient, inclined, keen, prepared, ready, reluctant, unwilling, willing,** e.g.

4   Are you afraid to go out in the storm? (« » **79**.4, **80**.4)
5   My mother is prepared to lend us the money.

Adjectives **prompt, quick** and **slow** can also be *postmodified* with a **to** *clause*, but with a different meaning, e.g.

6   They were quick to complain. (i.e. they complained immediately)
7   Our teacher is slow to notice. (i.e. does not notice immediately)
8   The villagers were prompt to offer help. (i.e. offered help immediately)

82 The boys are **sure to break something**.

Structure:

A *subject*	B be	C *adjective*	D **to** *clause*
1 Their son	is	certain	to find out.
2 Fred	is	likely	to fail the test.
3 Her sisters	are	liable	to turn up without any warning.

Adjectives that can go in Column C are: **bound, certain, liable, likely, sure, unlikely**[1]. The *subject* (A) is really the unmentioned *subject* of the **to** *clause* (D), and the *adjective* (C) expresses the probability of the whole sentence, e.g.

> 4 The inspector is liable to ask some awkward questions. (i.e. it is probable that the inspector will ask)
> 5 Mrs Bright isn't likely to come this afternoon. (i.e. it is not probable that Mrs Bright will come)
> 6 They are unlikely to have been arrested. (i.e. it is unlikely that they have been arrested)

---

[1] We cannot use **possible, impossible, probable** or **improbable** in this structure although they are related in meaning.

83 **On Saturday** we worked **quickly to get home early**.

Adverbials can be *adverbs*, e.g. **quickly, here, always,** or *prepositional phrases*, e.g. **on Saturday, by car, with a knife,** or *clauses*, e.g. **to get home early, when we see him.** Many *adverbs* end in -ly, e.g. **quickly, happily, interestingly, confidentially,** and these usually correspond to an *adjective*, e.g.

> 1 She works quickly. (*adverb*)
> 2 She is a quick worker. (*adjective*)
> 3 They told the story interestingly. (*adverb*)
> 4 They told the story in an interesting way. (*adjective*)

In a few cases this correspondence does not apply:

a) with *adjectives* that end in -ly, e.g. **friendly, cowardly**; from these we make *adverbials* with **way** or **manner** (» **85**), e.g.

> 5 The chemist is friendly. (*adjective*)
> 6 He treats you in a friendly way. (**in a friendly way,** *adverbial*)

b) with **fast** and **hard,** which are both *adjectives* and *adverbs*:

> 7 Ann is a fast swimmer. (*adjective*)
> 8 Ann can swim fast. (*adverb*)
> 9 The builders were hard workers. (*adjective*)
> 10 The builders worked hard. (*adverb*)

For the spelling of words ending in -ly » **256**; for **hardly** » **98**.

84 They worked **hard yesterday.**
Yesterday they worked **hard.**

Adverbials do not have only one fixed position in the *clause*, but most *adverbials* tend to go in one of three positions:

a) first in the *clause*, i.e. before the *subject*. This does not change the word order of the rest of the sentence, e.g.

> 1a Last week we had a lot of rain. (*Not* x had we x)
> 2a On the train there were a lot of soldiers. (*Not* x were there x)

b) last in the *clause*, i.e. after the *object* (3), after the *complement* (4), or, when there is no *object* or *complement*, after the *verb* (5a):

> 3 Henry studies English in the evenings.
> 4 The colours look different in daylight.
> 5a The temperature rose slowly.

Adverbials of manner (» **85**) normally go last, but a short *adverb* of manner can go in *mid-position* (« » **c** below), e.g.

> 5b The temperature slowly rose.

Adverbials of place (» **88**) and *adverbials* of time (» **89**) can usually go first (1a, 2a) or last (1b, 2b):

> 1b We had a lot of rain last week.
> 2b There were a lot of soldiers on the train.

When there are two or three *adverbials* at the end of the sentence, the most frequent order is: *a)* manner *b)* place *c)* time, e.g.

> 6 Mrs Biggins walked quietly to the door. (**quietly:** manner; **to the door:** place)
> 7 We're going to the zoo this afternoon. (**to the zoo:** place; **this afternoon:** time)
> 8a Everybody worked quite well in the lab this morning. (**quite well:** manner; **in the lab:** place; **this morning:** time)

When there are two or three *adverbials* of time at the end of a sentence, the order tends to be: *a)* duration *b)* frequency *c)* when, e.g.

> 9a They stayed for a short while quite often last year. (**for a short while:** duration; **quite often:** frequency; **last year:** when)

However, we often avoid three *adverbials* at the end by putting one first, e.g.

> 8b This morning everybody worked quite well in the lab.
> 9b Last year they stayed for a short while quite often.

c) Frequency *adverbs* and certain other short *adverbs*, including **almost, also, even, hardly, just, nearly, quite, soon, still,** and also **regularly,** usually go in *mid-position.*

The most common *frequency adverbs* are:

more frequent ←				→ less frequent	
A	**B**[1]	**C**[1]	**D**[1]	**E**	**F**
always	usually	often	sometimes	rarely	never[2]
constantly	normally	frequently	occasionally	seldom	
continually	generally				
continuously					
ever[2]					

With *main verbs* **am, is, are, was, were,** *mid-position* means that the *adverb* goes before the *complement*, e.g.

	adverb	complement
10a The teachers were	sometimes	cruel.
11 Are you	still	tired?
12 Our neighbours are not	usually	so stupid.
13 Weren't they	ever	out of bed?

With all other *verbs*, *mid-position* means that the *adverb* goes before the *main verb*[3] in positive *statements* (14, 16, 18, 19), *questions* (15, 21, 22) and *statements* with **not** (17, 20), e.g.

	adverb	main verb	
14 Mary	almost	broke	her arm.
15 Did Mary	almost	break	her arm?
16 We	often	walk	to school.
17 We don't	often	walk	to school.
18 Snakes can	sometimes	be	dangerous.
19 Snakes can	sometimes	attack	you.
20 Jack isn't	even	trying	to help.
21 Are they	still	sitting	there?
22 Have you	ever	been	in a cave?
23 Jim has	never	seen	an elephant.

---

[1] Words in Columns B, C and D can also go first in *statements* (10a) and occasionally last (10b):

> 10b Sometimes the teachers were cruel.
> 10c The teachers were cruel sometimes.

[2] **Never** is *negative*; **ever** is an **any** *word* (» **253**)

[3] When there are two or more *auxiliary verbs*, *mid-position* means that the *adverb* goes after the first *auxiliary*, e.g.

> 24 These mistakes have never been corrected.
> 25 The house must still have been standing in 1914.

85 She dresses very **smartly**.

Smartly is an *adverb*; it is an *adverbial* of manner, i.e. it corresponds to a *question* with **how** (» 163). *Adverbials* of manner are *adverbs* (1, 2) or *prepositional phrases*, often with **way**, **manner** or **fashion** (3, 4); they often go last (but « » 84.5–8), e.g.

1   The boys speak French very well. (*Not* ~~xvery well Frenchx~~; » **190**.3, 4)
2   Did they send the order immediately?
3   She talks about her work in an interesting way.
4   Yvonne was dressed in the latest fashion.

For *adverbials* of manner with *prepositional verbs* and *phrasal verbs* » **191, 194, 221**.

86 You can obtain a free poster **by sending 50 pence**.

By sending 50 pence is an *adverbial* of means, i.e. it says how something is done. It is a *prepositional phrase* with **by** and an -**ing** *form* (1, 2) or a *noun phrase* (3); these *adverbials* usually go last:

1   A: How did they get into the flat?
    B: (They got into the flat) by breaking a window.
2   We finally persuaded them by not paying the bill.
3   The authorities tried to avert the strike by a show of force.

For **by** with means of transport » **103**.

87 They smashed the glass **with a brick**.

With a brick is an *adverbial* of instrument, i.e. it refers to the thing that you use in order to do something; it is a *prepositional phrase* with **with** and a *noun phrase*. These *adverbials* go last:

1   A: What did you cut the flowers with?
    B: (I cut them) with these scissors.
2   We mended the chair with some special glue.
3   These young gangsters attack people with broken bottles.

88 They ran **down towards the factory**.

Down and **towards the factory** are *adverbials* of place, i.e. they correspond to questions with **where** (» **171**). *Adverbials* of place, both for position (1, 3) and movement (2, 4), can be *adverbs*, e.g. **here, in**[1], **south**, etc., or *prepositional phrases*, e.g. **across the street, near the garage, up the hill**. These *adverbials* usually go last (1a, 2–4); *prepositional phrases* of position (1b), but not of movement (2) sometimes go first, (but also » 5–8):

1a The post office is across the street.
1b Across the street is the post office.
2a The old ladies walked across the street. (*Not* x Across the street the old ladies walked x; but « » 2b)
3 Peter is going to stay here for two weeks.
4 Peter came here yesterday.

Certain short *adverbs* of place, e.g. **here, there, off, away, up, down, in, out, back,** can go first to give a lively or surprising emphasis to the sentence. When the *subject* is a *pronoun*, it must go before the *verb* (5, 6); when the *subject* is not a *pronoun*, it usually goes after the *verb* (7):

5 'In,' he said to the dog, and in it came.
6 Mother kissed them goodbye and away they went.
7 Away went the children.

These *adverbs* can also go before **you** and an *imperative* (» **136**), and this gives a lively emphasis to the command, e.g.

8 Everybody ready? Right, off you go!

Occasionally you will also meet a *prepositional phrase* of place + the *verb* + the *subject*, e.g.

2b Across the street walked the old ladies.

But this is unusual style and students should avoid using it.

---

[1] Many *adverbs* of place, e.g. **in, on, out, off, up, down**, etc., have the same form as *prepositions*. The distinction is their use in the sentence: a *preposition* always goes with a *noun phrase* to make a *prepositional phrase* (9; » **99**), but without a *noun phrase* the word is an *adverb* (10; » **193, 194**):

9 They put the eggs in the box.
10 They opened the box and put the eggs in.

89 We'll call **again tomorrow**.

Again and **tomorrow** are *adverbs* of time. There are different groups of these *adverbs*:

a) **yesterday, today** and **tomorrow**, like other *adverbials* that tell us when something happened, e.g. **last night, in 1978**, etc., can go first or last, e.g.

> 1a Yesterday we went to the circus.
> 1b We went to the circus yesterday.

b) Frequency *adverbs* and certain others (« **84c**) go in *mid-position*.

c) *Adverbs* showing relative position in time, e.g. **before, previously, first, next, then, later, lastly, afterwards, eventually, finally**, usually go first in the *clause*, e.g.

> 2 First they prepared the food, and then they went for a swim.

For **once, twice**, etc. » **168**; for **already, yet** » **94**; for **still** » **95**; for relative order of *adverbials* of time « **84c**.

90 They **only** dance in the evenings.

Only is an *adverb* that normally goes in *mid-position*, but in meaning it can point to different parts of the sentence. In speech we use stress to show the word(s) that **only** points to, e.g. if we stress **dance**, it means 'All they do in the evenings is dance'; if we stress **evenings**, it means 'The only time they dance is in the evenings.' In writing we cannot use stress to make this clear, so it it is not clear from the context, we can put **only** immediately before the word(s) that it points to. For example, if the context does not make 1 clear, then we can use 2 or 3, where the position of **only** shows that it refers to the words immediately after:

> 1 The police only wanted to talk to my father about the march.
> 2 The police wanted to talk only to my father about the march.
> 3 The police wanted to talk to my father only about the march.

Sentences like 1 are all right providing it is clear from the context which meaning is intended.

If **only** points to the *subject*, then **only** goes first (4), and if **only** points to a number, it often goes immediately before the number (5):

> 4 Only Mrs Pring understood what was happening.
> 5 We have room for only five more people.

91 Jim **also** plays billiards on Saturdays.

Also is an *adverb* that normally goes in *mid-position*, but in meaning it can point to different parts of the sentence. In speech we use stress to show the word(s) that **also** points to, e.g. if we stress **billiards**, it means 'Billiards is not the only game that Jim plays on Saturdays'; if we stress **Saturdays**, it means 'Saturday is not the only day that Jim plays billiards'. In writing we understand from the context which word(s) **also** points to, e.g.

> 1 The chief constable had discussed the dangers of the meeting with the organisers. The police also wanted to talk to my father about the meeting. (Here, **also** points to **my father**, i.e. as well as the organisers)
> 2 My father went to the police station to discuss the protest march. The police also wanted to talk to my father about the meeting. (Here, **also** points to **the meeting**, i.e. as well as the protest march.)

If **also** points to the *subject*, it goes after the *subject* and between commas (,):

> 3 My father had already discussed the meeting with teachers and politicians. The police, also, wanted to talk to my father about the meeting.

Also occurs rarely at the end of a sentence; we usually prefer **as well** or **too** in this position (» **92**).

92 This is pretty, and that is, **too**.

Here, **too** is an *adverb* that normally goes last; it has the alternative **as well**, with the same meaning. We use **too** when a sentence adds information similar to a previous sentence; both sentences must be *positive*, (« » **93**).

> 1 Tom's impolite, and he's boring, too. (« » **93**.1)
> 2 I've been to Spain, and I've been to Portugal, too. (« » **93**.2)
> 3a Terry can swim, and his sister can, too. (i.e. can swim; « » **93**.3)
> 4a A: They always buy fruit in the market.
>   B: I do, too. (i.e. I always buy fruit in the market; « » **93**.4)

When the only new thing is the *subject* (3a, 4a), we use the *auxiliary verb*, e.g. **can, do**, to replace the rest of the sentence. In these cases, but not in 1 and 2, there is an alternative structure with **so** plus the *auxiliary* plus the new *subject*, e.g.

> 3b Terry can swim, and so can his sister.
> 4b A: They always buy fruit in the market.
>   B: So do I.

93 This isn't long enough, and that isn't, either.

Here, **either** is an *adverb* that normally goes last. We use it when a sentence adds information similar to a previous sentence; both sentences must be *negative* (« » **92**).

1 Tom isn't polite, and he isn't interesting, either. (« » **92**.1, **228**.6)
2 I haven't been to Italy, and I haven't been to Greece, either. (« » **92**.2, **228**.5)
3a Pat can't swim, and her brother can't, either. (« » **92**.3)
4a A: They never buy fruit in the supermarket.
    B: I don't, either. (« » **92**.4)

When the only new thing is the *subject* (3a, 4a), we use a short *negative auxiliary*, e.g. **can't, don't,** to replace the rest of the sentence. In these cases, but not in 1 and 2, there is an alternative structure with **neither** or **nor** plus the *auxiliary* plus the new *subject*, e.g.

3b Pat can't swim, and neither can her brother. (or and nor can her brother)
4b A: They never buy fruit in the supermarket.
    B: Nor do I. (or Neither do I)

94 Fred's **already** here, but Penny hasn't come **yet**.

Already and **yet** are *adverbs*; **already** is a **some** *word*, **yet** is an **any** *word* (» **253**). **Already** normally goes in *mid-position*; **yet** normally goes last. We use these *adverbs* with a *verb* in the *present* (1, 3) or the *perfect* (2, 4–7; » **147**).

In a *positive statement*, **already** emphasises 'sooner than expected', e.g.

1 We expected our guests to come later, but they're already here.
2 Mrs Aston thought the workmen would be in the house all day, but they've already finished.

In a *negative statement*, **yet** emphasises 'by now', e.g.

3 The machines aren't working yet.
4 The programme hasn't started yet.

In *questions* **already** emphasises 'sooner than expected' and expects a *positive* answer (5); **yet** has no expectation (6), or assumes a *negative* answer (7):

5 Have you already done your homework? That was very quick.

6 Have you seen that new film yet?
7 A: I'm going to clean the car.
   B: Haven't you cleaned it yet? (i.e. I am surprised that it is still not cleaned)

For another use of **yet** » 237 *Note*.

95 We're **still** waiting for the delivery.

Still is an *adverb*; it emphasises that a situation continues from a previous time. In *positive statements* (1) and *questions* (2), it goes in *mid-position*; in *negative statements* (3, 4), it goes after the *subject*, e.g.

1 When I called this morning, they were cleaning the flat, and this afternoon they were still cleaning it.
2 I know Ann used to live in Soho. Does she still live there?
3 They said they would tell us about the exams last week, but we still don't know the results.
4 Jim said he would give me the money a month ago, but he still hasn't given me it.

When I called this morning, they were cleaning the flat, and this afternoon they were still cleaning it.

96 She doesn't sing **any longer**.
She **no longer** sings.

Any longer and **no longer** are *adverbials*; **any longer** has the alternative **any more**, but **no more** cannot mean 'no longer'. **Any longer** and **any more** are **any** *words* (» 253); they emphasise that a previous situation does not continue. In *statements* **any longer** normally goes last (1, 3); **no longer** normally goes in *mid-position*. They do not normally go in *questions*[1], (2):

1   She used to study French, but she doesn't study it any longer. (or any more)
2   A: Does Ann still live in Soho?
     B: No, she no longer lives there. (*Not* ~~she no more lives~~; « » **95**.2)
3. C: Could I speak to Mrs Price, please?
     D: I'm afraid she doesn't work here any longer. (or any more)

---

[1] When **any longer** means 'more time', it can go in *questions*, e.g.

4   We've been here for two hours. Do you want to stay any longer?

97 We moved into this flat about a year **ago**.

We use *adverb* **ago** to separate a point in past time from the present moment. **Ago** goes with the *past simple* (1, 2) and sometimes with the *past progressive* (3), but never with the *present perfect*, e.g.

1   Your father went to work about half an hour ago.
2   A: How long ago was Cologne Cathedral completed?
     B: (It was completed) only a hundred years ago.
3   Ten years ago I was working as a junior clerk.

We join points in past time to the present moment with **since** and **for**, which go with *perfect verb* forms, but these words and **ago** are never interchangeable. Consider the following situation:

In 1970 Jane met Peter for the first time at a party. After the party they met several times, but their last meeting was at a wedding in 1975. It is now 1978.

Based on this situation, we can make the following statements:

4   Jane first saw Peter eight years ago. (» **150** *Note*)
5   Jane last saw Peter three years ago. (» **150** *Note*)
6   Jane hasn't seen Peter for three years.
7   Jane hasn't seen Peter since 1975.
8   Jane hasn't seen Peter since the wedding.
9   Jane hasn't seen Peter since they met at the wedding.
10   C: How long is it since Jane saw Peter? (« » 2)
      D: It's three years since Jane saw Peter.

For **since** and **for** » **148**; for **for** » **101e**.

98 We could **hardly** see anything.

Hardly is an *adverb*; *adverbs* with similar meaning are **scarcely** and **barely**. They all mean 'almost not'; they normally go in *mid-position*, and they go with **any** *words* (2–5; » **253**):

1   I've walked so far (that) I can hardly stand. (i.e. can almost not stand)
2   There are scarcely any ripe apples. (i.e. almost no ripe apples)
3   They have barely started (yet). (i.e. have only just started)

These words can go first before an *indefinite pronoun* (« **50, 51**) as *subject*, e.g.

4   Hardly anyone understood the speaker. (i.e. Almost no one)

We use **hardly ever** (i.e. almost never) in *mid-position*, e.g.

5   Their children hardly ever visit them.

For *adverb* **hard** « **84b**.

99 **On** Friday they were **on top of** those boxes.

Prepositions are either simple, i.e. one word, e.g. **on**, or compound, i.e. more than one word, e.g. **on top of**. The most common simple ones are: **about, above, across, after, against, along, alongside, among(st), around, as, at, before, behind, below, beneath, beside, besides, between, beyond, but, by, despite, down, during, except, for, from, in, inside, into, like, minus, near, of, off, on, onto, opposite, out, outside, over, past, per, plus, round, since, than, through, throughout, till, to, towards, under, underneath, unlike, until, up, via, with, within, without.** Certain -ing *forms* are also used as *prepositions*: **barring, concerning, considering, excepting, pending, regarding, respecting.**

There are too many compound *prepositions* (and similar *prepositional phrases*) to list here; some of the most common ones are: **according to, in addition to, along with, apart from, as for, as from, as to, away from, because of, in case of, due to, except for, in favour of, in front of, instead of, on the left of, on the right of, by means of, near to, in need of, next to, on to, out of, owing to, in place of, with regard to, for the sake of, by the side of, in spite of, together with, on top of, in touch with, in view of, up to,** etc.

A *preposition* is, by definition, part of a *prepositional phrase*, which consists of a *preposition* and a *noun phrase* (or a *noun clause* » **181, 182**). The *noun phrase* normally goes immediately after the *preposition*[1], and the only form of a *verb* that can follow a *preposition* is an **-ing** *form*[2], e.g.

preposition	*noun phrase*	*preposition*	*noun phrase* (**-ing** *form*)
in	her bedroom	in	accepting the prize
after	the storm	after	hearing the news
without	any trouble	without	having written first
regarding	your income	regarding	your spending
instead of	a knife	instead of	being invited

Many *prepositional phrases* are used to talk about position, e.g. **on the box, in the box, under the box.** When they are used for position, *prepositions* have a fixed, regular meaning, and they have different meanings from each other, so **on the box** and **in the box** are both good English but they mean different things.

When *prepositions* are not used for position, there are certain cases, especially with regard to time (» **101**), where different *prepositions* are possible, with different meanings, e.g.

> **on Tuesday, by Tuesday, after Tuesday, before Tuesday**
> **in the way, on the way**
> **look after him, look for him**

These phrases are all good English, but the different *prepositions* change the meaning of the phrase.

However, *prepositions* also have many idiomatic uses, where they do not have a fixed regular meaning, but only one *preposition* is correct in a particular phrase. A different *preposition* does not mean something different in these cases; it is simply wrong. For example, we say **good at English**, *Not* x good on English x, and we say **listen to me**, *Not* x listen at me x.

Learners need to learn the different meanings of the *prepositions* of position and also of other phrases where different *prepositions* change the meaning. In all other cases, it is not a question of meaning, and students should learn which *preposition* goes in which phrase, because there are no rules to explain why we say, e.g. **good at** (*Not* x good on x), or **listen to** but **look at**, or **on purpose** but **by accident**.

Prepositional phrases can act as *complement* of **be** (1; » **107**.17–20), *adverbials* (2; « **83, 86–88**), as *postmodifiers* of *nouns* (3; « **55**) and of *adjectives* (4; « **79**):

    1   Have the children been on the roof?
    2   She was driving at top speed.
    3   Ask the man behind that desk.
    4   Marjory wasn't very pleased with her new job.

---

[1] The only exceptions are when a sentence process moves the *noun*

phrase to the front of the *clause*. This can happen in *questions* (» **169**), in *relative clauses* (« **60, 63**), in *noun clauses* (» **181, 182**) *passives* (» **173**), and in *to clauses* (« **65, 77**).

² **But** and **except** are exceptions. They are folowed by a *plain infinitive* when they contrast with another *plain infinitive* (5), but by an -**ing** *form* when they contrast with a *noun phrase* (6):

    5   They don't do anything except watch TV. (or but watch; **watch** contrasts with **do**)

    6   He doesn't like any exercise except taking the dog for a walk. (or but taking; **taking** contrasts with **any exercise**)

100 It's **on** the table **in** that room.

On and **in** are *prepositions* of place. There is a basic system of these *prepositions*; the choice depends on the relation between the two things: **on** (opposite **off**) is for a relation to a line or surface; **in** (opposite **out**) is for a relation to an enclosed area or volume; **at**¹ is used when the exact relation is unimportant, i.e. we do not consider the place as line or surface or area or volume, but simply as a point, e.g. we say someone is **at the bus-stop** because it does not matter if he or she is next to it, behind it or in front of it. Similarly, we say that someone is **at home** because it does not matter if he or she is in the garden, on the roof, or in the kitchen; in every case he or she is still **at home**.

Here are two examples:

    1   These people are all at a restaurant. The children are at a table in the garden; the older people are in the restaurant itself. There are some birds on the roof.

2 These people are all at a swimming pool. Some are in the pool itself, others are lying on the grass. One or two are waiting at the entrance for their friends.

Corresponding to these *prepositions* of place, there are *prepositions* of movement: **onto** (opposite **off**) for movement to a line or surface; **into** (opposite **out of**) for movement to an enclosed area or volume; **to** (opposite (**away**) **from**) when we do not consider the destination as a line or surface or area or volume, but simply as a point:

3 We moved the papers off the table onto the desk.
4 Sally took the plants out of the greenhouse into the kitchen.
5 At the weekend they went to the coast; they get away from home whenever they can.

Put, although it involves movement, normally goes with **on, in, at,** (and also other *prepositions*) e.g.

6 Put the flowers on the table and the basket in the kitchen.

There are many other *prepositions* of place and movement; learners should consult a good dictionary for their different meanings.

---

[1] For the opposite of **at,** we normally use **not at,** but we use **away from** for an extended absence from home or work, e.g.

7 The Jacksons weren't at the restaurant.
8 Fred is working away from home this month.

Also » **104.**

101 Sara was born **at 2 o'clock on the seventeenth of July.**

Here, **at** and **on** are *prepositions* of time. For points and periods of time that correspond to a *question* with **when** we use:

a) at with times of the clock (» 255), e.g. **It starts at six o'clock;** similarly, **at midday, at midnight, at lunchtime,** etc., which are equivalent to specific times.

We also use **at** in **at the weekend, at Christmas, at Easter,** and also **at night, at the time, at that time.**

b) on with days, e.g. **on Tuesday,** etc., also **on Friday morning,** etc; **on Christmas Day, on Easter Sunday,** etc; **on 5th September,** etc; **on your birthday,** etc.

We do not use **on** with **last, this** and **next,** e.g. **last Monday, this week, next month,** etc., except when the *noun* is *postmodified,* e.g. **on the last Monday in March.**

c) in for months, seasons and years, e.g. **in May, in (the) autumn, in 1939,** etc. We also use **in** with parts of the day, e.g. **in the morning, in the afternoon, in the evening, in the daytime,** (but **at night**), and notice also **on** in **on Thursday afternoon,** etc., and **on the morning of 21st March,** etc.

d) during for a specific period (1) or an event that implies a period (2); **during** does not normally indicate duration (» **e** below), it corresponds to a *question* with **when,** e.g.

    1   A: When did the shed blow down?
          B: It blew down during the night.
    2   We didn't go out much during the strike.

For duration, i.e. corresponding to a *question* with **How long (for)** we use:

e) for in past, present and future time; **for** can sometimes be omitted, e.g.

    3   Last year we stayed (for) two weeks; this year we're staying (for) three weeks, and next year we're going to stay (for) longer if we can.

For is not omitted in *negative statements* (4) or when a period is not *premodified* (5):

    4   I haven't played tennis for six months.
    5   I've been writing this for months and months.

If the period is already specific, then we can refer back to it with **during,** e.g.

    6   We stayed for three weeks. During those three weeks we didn't have a drop of rain.

f) in for a point in future time measured from the present moment, e.g.

    7   Come back in half an hour. (i.e. half an hour from now)
    8   In three years all these houses will have disappeared. (i.e. three years from now)

g) **by** to mean 'at a certain time, or before', e.g.

    9   You must be home by 5. (i.e. before or at 5, but not later)
    10   I'll finish it by Monday. (i.e. not later than Monday)

h) **till** or **until** for a period that finishes at a point of time, e.g.

    11   We played cards until 2 o'clock. (i.e. we stopped playing cards at 2 o'clock)

Till and **until** can also be *conjunctions,* with the same meaning; on the other hand, *conjunction* **as soon as** means 'immediately after'. Consider the situation:

> Mrs Lee is ill. Her son Jack stays with her during the morning. Her daughter Jill comes at 12 o'clock, and Jack immediately leaves. Jill stays with her mother during the afternoon.

Here we can say:

    12   Jack stays till Jill comes. (or until)
    13   Jack leaves as soon as Jill comes.

102 Reports of the incident are still coming in.

Of is the most frequent *preposition;* it has a variety of uses, including possession, (« **10**). There are no absolutely clear lines to distinguish the use of the following three forms:

a) the club's policy, (i.e. *premodification* by a *possessive* « **10**);

b) the club policy, (i.e. *premodification* by a *noun* « **9**);

c) the policy of the club, (i.e. *postmodification* by an **of** *phrase*).

In all three cases **policy** is the *head noun.*

The following represents guidance, not strict rules:

We tend to use **a)** especially when the modifying *noun* is animate, in particular for specific humans, e.g. **Tom's brother, the teacher's books, my sister's room, the cat's food,** and also **the committee's decision;** but compare with **library books, cat food** (i.e. food for cats in general; « **9b**).

We tend to use **b)** when the *head noun* is an integral part of the modifying *noun,* which is concrete and inanimate (« **9d**), e.g. **shop window, chair legs, car door, shirt collar,** but compare with **ship's funnel.**

We tend to use c) in other cases, e.g. **the customs of the natives, the strength of the materials, a margin of error, tolerance of religious differences,** etc.

103 Did you come **by bus** or **by train**?

With *verbs* of travelling, e.g. **arrive, come, go, leave, travel,** we talk about means of transport with the following *prepositional phrases*: **by air[1], by bicycle, by boat[1], by bus, by canal, by car, by land, by plane[1], by rail[1], by river, by sea[1], by taxi, by train[1], by tram,** but **on foot** and **on horseback,** e.g.

    1a They go to school by train.
    2   A: Did you go by car?
          B: No, we went on foot.

We can also use **on the boat, on the bus, on the plane** and **on the train** with the same meaning, e.g.

    1b They go to school on the train.

When we talk about a specific car, we use **in** with a *determiner* or *possessive* (3); when we talk about a specific **bicycle, bus, plane,** etc., we use **on** (4, 5):

    3   We can all go in my car. (*Not* x by my car x)
    4   My grandparents arrived on the overnight train.
    5   The engineer came on the plane that arrives after lunch.

---

[1] For goods we usually use **air, rail** and **sea**; for people we usually use **boat, plane** and **train**.

104 Peter isn't **at school** today.

Certain *nouns* for places can go without **the** both for situation and for movement. For situation we say: **at church, at college, at home, at school, at university, at work,** but **in bed, in hospital, in prison, in town.** For movement we use **to** with all, e.g. **to school, to bed,** etc., except **home,** which has no *preposition* with *verbs* of movement, e.g. **arrive, come, get, go, reach, travel** (3).

We use these phrases without **the** for the normal users of a place, e.g. **to bed** (1) for a sleeper, **to work[1]** (2) for a worker, **home** (3) for one's own home, etc., e.g.

    1   Mary has just gone to bed. (i.e. to sleep; *Not* x to the bed x)
    2   How do you get to work? (*Not* x to the work x)
    3   We went home early. (*Not* x to the home x)
    4   Her sister is in prison for stealing a car. (*Not* x in the x)

For people (and things) that are not the normal users, we use a *determiner*, e.g.

    5   They found a snake in the bed. (« » 1)
    6   Our teacher gives lessons in the prison. (« » 4)

---

[1] **Mary is going to work** has two possible meanings: either **work** is a *noun* and it means 'Mary is (now) going to her job'; or **work** is a *verb*, and it means 'Mary is going (in the future) to do some work', (» **going to** *future* **145**). However, **Mary goes to work** can only mean 'Mary goes to her job', i.e. **work** is a *noun*.

105 I'm speaking **as** a friend.
You talk **like** my boss.

Here **as** and **like** are *prepositions*. **As** means 'in the capacity or role of', e.g.

    1   As your lawyer I advise you to wait. (i.e. In my capacity of lawyer)
    2   We need people to act as guides. (i.e. to be guides)
    3   Mrs Tate spoke as an actress. (i.e. in her capacity as an actress; i.e. she is an actress; « » 6)

As in this sense is used in a *prepositional phrase* after the *object* of certain *verbs*, including **accept, acknowledge, characterise, claim, class, count, define, describe, intend, interpret, look on, recognise, regard, see, think of, treat** and **use**, e.g.

    4   At one time we regarded emigration as our only solution. (i.e. we thought emigration was our only solution)
    5   He intended his remarks as a compliment.[1] (i.e. he wanted his remarks to be a compliment)
    6   I often have to use a knife as a screwdriver. (i.e. use a knife to do the job of a screwdriver)

Like means 'similar to' or 'in the manner of', e.g.

    7   Tom sings like his father. (i.e. in a similar way)
    8   She is quite like her sister. (i.e. similar to)
    9   Mrs Coope spoke like an actress. (i.e. similar to the way actresses speak, but she was not an actress; « » 3)

Subordinator **as** corresponds to *preposition* **like**, i.e. it means 'in a way similar to', e.g.

    10   Tom sings as his father sings. (or his father does; « » 4)
    11   Mrs Coope spoke as an actress speaks. (or an actress does; « » 6)

You will also meet **like** instead of **as** in these sentences, e.g. **like his**

father sings (7), but some people consider this incorrect.

---

[1] The corresponding *passive* is:

> 12   His remarks were intended as a compliment.

For another use of **as** » **235**.

106 We changed our plans **because of** his late arrival.
We changed our plans **because** he arrived late.

Because of is a *preposition*; **because** is a *subordinator* (» **234**). Several *prepositions* have *subordinators* that correspond in meaning; in some cases the forms are the same, in others they are different:

	prepositional phrase	*subordinate clause*
same form	after his arrival before his arrival since his arrival till his arrival until his arrival	after he arrived before he arrived since he arrived till he arrived until he arrived
different form	because of his arrival during his stay on his arrival	because he arrived (» **234**) while he stayed (» **233**) when he arrived (» **231**)

Prepositions **after** and **because of** can also go with a *noun clause* (» **181**), e.g. **after what she said, because of what she said.**

Prepositions **despite** and **in spite of** can be followed by a *noun phrase* (1), a *noun clause* (2, » **181**) or **the fact** plus a **that** *clause* (3):

> 1   She is energetic despite her weight.
> 2   She is energetic in spite of how much she weighs.
> 3   She is energetic despite the fact that she weighs so much.
>   (*Not* x despite that she x)

Preposition **according to** can be followed by a *noun phrase* (4) or a *noun clause* (5; » **181**), e.g.

> 4   According to his letter he'll arrive tomorrow.
> 5   According to what he wrote he'll arrive tomorrow.
>   (*Not* x according to (that) he wrote x)

Prepositions **due to** and **owing to** can be followed by a *noun phrase* (6) or **the fact** plus a **that** *clause* (7):

> 6   The delay was due to a strike.
> 7   Everything came late owing to the fact that there had been a strike. (*Not* x owing to (that) there x)

PART 3

Verb phrase

Introduction

A *verb phrase* consists of a *main verb* alone (1) or a *main verb*, which is in **bold** type, with one or more *auxiliaries* (2):

1 **is; takes; went; wrote; walk**
2 can **be**; has **taken**; is **reading**; must have **walked**; might have been **painted**

For the different structures of the *verb phrase*, » Table 4 on p 93.

Main verbs

Main verbs have three principal parts:

a) a *plain infinitive*, e.g. **walk, call, go**, etc., which has the same form as the *present simple* (» **141**) and the *imperative* (» **136**); it is used after most *modals* (» **112–135**) and in other structures (» Index). A **to** *infinitive* is a *plain infinitive* preceded by **to**, which is not a *preposition* here, e.g. **to walk, to call, to go**, etc. A **to** *infinitive* is used after *modal* **ought** (» **120**) and in other structures (» Index).

b) a *past simple*, e.g. **walked, called, went**, etc. (» **150**).

c) a *past participle*, e.g. **walked, called, gone**, etc., which is used for *perfect verb phrases* (» **146, 153, 156**) and *passive verb phrases* (» **173**).

For regular *verbs*, the *past simple* and the *past participle* are the same form.

Main verbs also have a form with ending -(e)s, e.g. **walks, calls, goes**, etc. (» **141**).

Main verbs also have an -**ing** form, e.g. **walking, calling, going**, etc., which is used in various *verb phrases* and structures (» below and also » Index).

For the spelling of regular *verb* forms » **256**; for *verbs* with irregular *past simple* and *past participle* » **259**.

Table 2 *Modal* system for obligation, permission and prohibition

present or future time			past time	
personal¹	general¹		action happened, i.e. he went	action did not happen, i.e. he did not go
he **must** go (» **124**)	he **has**² (**got**) to go (» **125**)	obligation or necessity	he **had**² **to** go (» **126**)	
he'd **better**² go (» **123**)	he **should** go (» **119**)	advice for		he **should have** gone (» **132**)
he **may** go (» **115**)	he **can** go (» **112**)	permission	he **was allowed**² **to go**	he **could have** gone (» **130**)
he **doesn't have**² to go (» **125**)	he **doesn't have**² to go (» **125**)	absence of obligation		he **didn't have**² to go (» **126**)
	he **doesn't need**² to go (» **134**)	absence of necessity	he **needn't**² **have** gone (» **135**)	he **didn't need**² to go (» **134**)
he'd **better**² not go (» **123**)	he **shouldn't** go (» **119**)	advice against	he **shouldn't have** gone (» **132**)	
he **mustn't** go (» **124**)	he **mustn't** go (» **124**)	prohibition		

¹ For the explanation of this difference, » individual sections.
² These are not *modals*, but they help to complete the system.

90

Table 3 *Modal* system for assumption

present time		past time
it **must be** him (» **124**)	certain	it **must have been** him (» **128**)
it **might be** him it **may be** him (» **116**)	possible even probable	it **might have been** him it **may have been** him (» **131**)
it **could be** him (» **116**)	possible	it **could have been** him (» **130, 131**)
it **can't be** him it **couldn't be** him (» **112**)	impossible	it **can't have been** him it **couldn't have been** him (» **129**)

Modal verbs

The *modal verbs*, often simply called *modals*, are: **can, could, will, would, shall, should, may, might, must** and **ought to**. All *modals* have only one form (« » *main verbs* above).

Modals have various meanings but in particular they help to form two systems to express *a*) obligation, permission and prohibition (« Table 2 on p 90), and *b*) assumption (« Table 3 above). **Will** and **would** are used in *conditionals* (» **240–242**). *Modals* belong to the *auxiliary verbs*.

Auxiliary verbs

The *auxiliary verbs*, often simply called *auxiliaries*, are:

a) **can, could, will, would, shall, should, may, might, must,** and **ought to,** but » also **used** (**120**), **dare** (**133**) and **need** (**134**)

b) **have, has, had, having**

c) **am, is, are, was, were, be, being, been**

d) **do, does, did**

These *verbs* are called *auxiliaries* ('helping') because they help to make certain *verb phrases* (A–D; » Table 4, p 93) and they help in certain sentence processes (p 94).

A *Modal verb phrases*

An *auxiliary* from group **a**) is followed by a *plain infinitive*, except **ought**, which goes with a **to** *infinitive*, to make *modal verb phrases* (» Table 4, examples 5, 6, 15–17, 20). For the uses of *modal verb phrases* » **112–135**.

B *Perfect verb phrases*

An *auxiliary* from group **b**) is followed by a *past participle* to make *perfect verb phrases* (» Table 4, examples 7–10, 15, 16, 18–20, 23, 24, 26, 29, 30). For the uses of *perfect verb phrases* » **146–149, 153, 154, 156, 157.**

C *Progressive verb phrases*

An *auxiliary* from group **c**), except **being**, is followed by an **-ing** *form* to make *progressive verb phrases* (» Table 4, examples 11–14, 17–20, 25, 26). These are sometimes called *continuous*. For the uses of *progressive verb phrases* » **138, 149, 151, 157**. All *verb phrases* that are not *progressive* are called *simple* (» Table 4, examples 1–10, 15, 16, 21–24). For the uses of *simple verb phrases* » **141, 146, 150, 156**.

D *Passive verb phrases*

An *auxiliary* from group **c**) is followed by a *past participle* to make *passive verb phrases* (» Table 4, examples 2, 4, 6, 8, 10, 12, 14, 16, 22, 24, 28, 30). For the uses of *passive verb phrases* » **173–176**.

When a *verb phrase* has more than one *auxiliary* from groups **a**)–**c**), then the order is always A B C D (» Table 4).

Notes to Table 4

[1] In *statements* the *simple present* (1) and the *simple past* (3) have no *auxiliary*; these need *auxiliaries* **do, does** or **did** for the sentence processes, p 94. All the other *verb phrases* in 1–20 have *auxiliaries*; in every case the first one, which is in **bold** type, is used for the sentence processes, p 94.

[2] or **can, could, might, will, would, shall, should, must** or **ought to.**

[3] The corresponding *passive* forms are rare.

Passive forms are dealt with in **173**.

The various *infinitives* (21–26) and *-ing forms* (27–30) are not treated separately in the grammar (» Index for structures that use these forms.) The *progressive infinitive* (25) forms a part of *modal progressives* (17); the *perfect progressive infinitive* (26) forms a part of

Table 4 The *verb phrase:* its different structures

	auxiliaries				*main verb*	
	A *modal*	**B** **have** *perfect*	**C** **be** *progressive*	**D** **be** passive		
1					take (s)¹	**141**
2				**am/is/are**	taken	*passive* of 1
3					took¹	**150**
4				**was/were**	taken	*passive* of 3
5	**may²**				take	**112–124**
6	**may²**			be	taken	*passive* of 5
7		**have/has**			taken	**146**
8		**have/has**		been	taken	*passive* of 7
9		**had**			taken	**153**
10		**had**		been	taken	*passive* of 9
11			**am/is/are**		taking	**138**
12			**am/is/are**	being	taken	*passive* of 11
13			**was/were**		taking	**151**
14			**was/were**	being	taken	*passive* of 13
15	**may²**	have			taken	**128–132, 156**
16	**may²**	have		been	taken	*passive* of 15
17	**may²**		be		taking³	**112, 124, 155**
18		**have/has**	been		taking³	**149**
19		**had**	been		taking³	**154**
20	**may²**	have	been		taking³	**128, 129, 157**
21					(to) take	
22				(to) be	taken	*passive* of 21
23		(to) have			taken	
24		(to) have		been	taken	*passive* of 23
25			(to) be		taking³	
26		(to) have	been		taking³	
27					taking	
28				being	taken	*passive* of 27
29		having			taken	
30		having		been	taken	*passive* of 29

modal perfect progressives (20). Examples of the other compound *infinitives* and **-ing** *forms* will ˙be found as follows: 22, « **67**.3, » **189**.2; 23, « **78**.2, **81**.2; 24, « **82**.6, » **176**.3; 28, » **200**.3, **205**.2; 29, « **79**.3, « **207**.7; 30, « **79**.5.

Sentence processes

The first *auxiliary* in a *verb phrase* is used for various sentence processes; for these processes, a *verb* in the *present simple* uses **do** or **does** (» **141**), and a *verb* in the *past simple* uses **did** (» **150**). *Main verbs* cannot perform the following processes, except *main verbs* **be** (» **107**) and **have** (» **110**).

Consider the three *statements*:

1 Mary can swim. (*auxiliary*: **can**; *main verb*: **swim**)
2 Jim has been waiting. (or Jim's; first *auxiliary* **has**; *main verb*: **waiting**)
3 Ann works. (no *auxiliary*; *main verb*: **works**)

a) *Direct questions*

In *direct questions*, the *auxiliary* goes before the *subject*; if there is a *question word*, that goes first, e.g.

4 Can Mary swim?
5 Has Jim been waiting?
6 Does Ann work?

7 How far can Mary swim?
8 Where has Jim been waiting?
9 When does Ann work?

Also » **158** for *questions* when the *question word* is *subject*.

b) *Statements* and *questions* with **not**; short *negative* forms

Not goes after the first *auxiliary* to form *negative statements* and *questions*. **Not** can make a short form with the first *auxiliary*:

full form	cannot	could not	may not	might not	must not	
short form	can't	couldn't	(» **115**)	mightn't	mustn't	
full form	ought not	shall not	should not	will not	would not	
short form	oughtn't	shan't	shouldn't	won't	wouldn't	
full form	have not	has not	had not	am not	are not	is not
short form	haven't	hasn't	hadn't	(» **107**)	aren't	isn't
full form	was not	were not	do not	does not	did not	
short form	wasn't	weren't	don't	doesn't	didn't	

In formal style, we avoid these short forms.

10 Mary cannot swim. (or can't)
11 Jim has not been waiting. (or hasn't)
12 Ann does not work. (or doesn't)

13 Can't Ann swim?
14 Hasn't Jim been waiting?
15 Doesn't Ann work?

Also » Note on *answers* to *negative questions*, p 96.

c) Question tags

Question tags are short *questions* that are added to the end of a *statement*, usually to ask for confirmation of the *statement*. If the *statement* is *positive*, the tag is usually negative; if the *statement* is *negative*, the tag is always *positive*, e.g.

16 Mary can swim, can't she?
17 Jim has been waiting, hasn't he?
18 Ann works, doesn't she?

19 Mary can't swim, can she?
20 Jim hasn't been waiting, has he?
21 Ann doesn't work, does she?

Also » Note on *answers* to *negative questions*, p 96.

d) Contrast

An *auxiliary*, which must be written in full and in speech is stressed, is used in a *positive statement* to contrast with a *negative*, e.g.

22 A: Mary can't swim.
    B: You're wrong. Mary **can** swim.
23 C: Jim hasn't been waiting.
    D: You're wrong. Jim **has** been waiting. (*Not* x Jim's x)
24 E: Ann doesn't work.
    F: You're wrong. She **does** work. (« » the normal she works, 3a)

e) Substitution for the whole *verb phrase*

Instead of repeating a whole *verb phrase* (plus *object*, etc.), we can use the *subject* with the *auxiliary* alone (which cannot here be a short form) in a *positive* sentence, or the short *negative* form (« b) in a *negative* sentence. Short answers:

25 A: Can Mary swim?
    B: Yes, she can./No, she can't.
26 C: Has Jim been waiting?
    D: Yes, he has. (*Not* x he's x)/No, he hasn't.
27 E: Does Ann work?
    F: Yes, she does./No, she doesn't.

Change of *subject* only, with a *positive statement* (« **92**):

28   Mary can swim, and I can, too.
29   Jim has been waiting, and I have, too. (*Not* x I've x)
30   Ann works, and I do, too.

Change of *subject* only, with a *negative statement* (« **93**):

31   Mary can't swim, and I can't, either.
32   Jim hasn't been waiting, and I haven't, either.
33   Ann doesn't work, and I don't, either.

Change of *subject*, with contrast:

34   Mary can swim, but I can't.
35   Jim has been waiting, but I haven't.
36   Ann works, but I don't.

37   Mary can't swim, but I can.
38   Jim hasn't been waiting, but I have. (*Not* x I've x)
39   Ann doesn't work, but I do.

f) Short *positive* forms

Certain *auxiliaries* have short forms that join with a *pronoun subject* in *positive statements*, e.g. **we'll, they've, you're**, etc. They are sometimes also used when the *subject* is not a *pronoun*, e.g. **Jim's been waiting** (« » 2). The forms are:

full form	will	would	have	has	had	am	is	are
short form	'll	'd	've	's	'd	'm	's	're

Notice that the short forms of **has** and **is** are both **'s,** and the short forms of **would** and **had** are both **'d.**

We cannot use these short forms when the *auxiliary* stands alone, i.e. without the rest of the *verb phrase* (« » 26, 29, 38). In formal style we avoid these short forms.

Note on *answers* to *negative questions*

As *answers* to any *question, positive* or *negative,* **yes** implies a *positive statement,* and **no** implies a *negative statement,* e.g.

  6   Does Ann work?   ⎫ **Yes** always means
15   Doesn't Ann work?   ⎪ 'Ann works
18   Ann works, doesn't she? ⎬ **No** always means
21   Ann doesn't work, does she? ⎭ 'Ann doesn't work'

In other words, to *questions* like 15, 18 and 21, we cannot answer x Yes, she doesn't x or x No, she does x.

107 Her mother **is** a good cook.

Here, **is** is the *present* of *main verb* **be**. The forms are:

statement forms without **not** or **n't**		*statement* forms with **not** or **n't**		
A full form	**B** short form	**C** full form	**D** short form	**E** short form
I am	I'm	I am not	——	I'm not
you are	you're	you are not	you aren't	you're not
he is	he's	he is not	he isn't	he's not
she is	she's	she is not	she isn't	she's not
it is	it's	it is not	it isn't	it's not
we are	we're	we are not	we aren't	we're not
you are	you're	you are not	you aren't	you're not
they are	they're	they are not	they aren't	they're not

question forms without **not** or **n't**	*question* forms with **not** or **n't**	
F	**G** full form	**H** short form
am I?	am I not?	aren't I?
are you?	are you not?	aren't you?
is he?	is he not?	isn't he?
is she?	is she not?	isn't she?
is it?	is it not?	isn't it?
are we?	are we not?	aren't we?
are you?	are you not?	aren't you?
are they?	are they not?	aren't they?

The short forms (**B, D, E, H**) are normal in conversation and also in writing that is not formal style, but they cannot be used at the end of a *clause* (3, 7, 11, 19). The *question full forms* (**G**) are rare.

Is goes with any *singular noun phrase* except **I** and **you**; **are** goes with any *plural noun phrase* and also *singular* **you**.

The *imperative* forms are **be** (13) and **don't be** (14).

In the *present simple* of *main verb* **be**[1], i.e. **am, is, are,** and also the *past simple*[1] (» **108**, i.e. **was, were**) the word order of a *statement* is: *subject* plus **be** plus *complement* (1, 2, 5, 6, 9, 10, 15, 17, 18, 21, 22); and the word order of *questions*[2] is: **be** plus *subject* plus *complement* (3, 4, 7, 8, 11, 12, 16, 19, 20).

The *complement* of **be** can be a *noun phrase* (1–8), an *adjective* (9–16), an *adverbial* of place (17–20), or a **to** *clause* (« **4**.8,9).

We use a *proper noun* or a definite *noun phrase* as *complement* to identify people and things, e.g.

1   I'm Jane Brown. (or I am)
2   This village isn't Matlock. (or is not)
3   A: Are those tents ours?
    B: Yes, they are. (*Not* x they're x)
4   Isn't Sheffield your home town?

We use a *count noun* or a *mass noun* as *complement* to classify people and things, e.g.

5   Connie's one of my friends. (or is)
6   Oranges aren't my favourite fruit. (or are not)
7   C: Is milk a good drink?
    D: Yes, it is. (*Not* x it's x)
8   Aren't birds animals?

We use *adjectives* as *complement* to talk about permanent characteristics (9–11) or temporary states (12–14), e.g.

9   My sister's very tall. (or is)
10   Scotland isn't flat. (or is not)
11   E: Is that book heavy?
     F: Yes, it is. (*Not* x it's x)
12   Aren't you happy?
13   We haven't got much time, so be quick!
14   Don't be so stupid!

When the *subject* includes an *adjective* and the *complement* is also an *adjective*, the *statement* and *question* forms are, e.g.

15   That big book is heavy.
16   Is that big book heavy? (« » 11)

We use an *adverbial* of place (« **88**) as *complement* to talk about position, e.g.

17   Cardiff's in Wales. (or is)
18   Mr and Mrs Croft aren't here. (or are not)
19   G: Are we near home now?
     H: Yes, we are. (*Not* x we're x)
20   Aren't they in the country today?

Main verb **be** cannot have as *complement* an *adverbial* of movement, so e.g. *Not* x Aren't they to the country? x, x I was to the cinema x, but » **146** *Note*.

¹ *Main verb* **be** can have *progressive* forms only when it means 'behave, act', and this is rare, e.g.

> 21   The children are being naughty. (i.e. acting naughtily)

² When *main verb* **be** has any other form, the word order for *questions* is the same as for every other *main verb*, e.g.

> 22   Has Mary been at home today?
> 23   Can you be quicker?

108 Where **were** you yesterday?

Here, **were** is the *past simple* of *main verb* **be**. In *statements* without **not** the forms are: **I was, you were, he was, she was, it was, we were, you were, they were.** There are no short forms without **not**, (1, 3; « » the *present* of be, 107), but there are short *negative* forms: **wasn't** and **weren't** (2, 4), e.g.

> 1   Connie was one of my friends. (« » **107**.5)
> 2   Mr and Mrs Croft weren't there. (or were not; « » **107**.18)
> 3   Was that big book heavy? (« » **107**.16)
> 4   Weren't you happy? (« » **107**.12)

109 The children **are** cold.

We use **be** in several idiomatic expressions with *adjectives* (1–6) or a number (7) as *complement*; the *adjectives* can be *premodified* by e.g. **very** (2), **rather, quite** (5), e.g.

> 1   Jane was cold. (i.e. was feeling cold)
> 2   They boys are very hot. (i.e. feeling very hot)
> 3   We're thirsty. (i.e. we need a drink)
> 4   They were hungry. (i.e. they needed some food)
> 5   You are quite right. (i.e. what you say is quite correct)
> 6   Mike was wrong. (i.e. what Mike said was wrong)
> 7   A: How old is Jack?
>   B: He's nineteen (years old). (or nineteen years of age)

110 I have (got) two sisters.

Here, **have** is a *main verb*; it sometimes has the alternative form **have got**. There are two ways to make *statements* with **not** (or **n't**) and *questions*:

without **do** and with optional **got**		with **do** and without **got**	
statements without **not** or **n't**			
A full form	**B** short form	**H** full form	**I** short form
I have (got) he has (got)	I've (got) he's (got)	I have he has	I've[1] he's[1]
statements with **not** or **n't**			
C full form	**D** short form	**J** full form	**K** short form
I have not (got) he has not (got)	I haven't (got) I've not got[2] he hasn't (got) he's not got[2]	I do not have he does not have	I don't have he doesn't have
questions without **not** or **n't**			
E full form		**L** full form	
have I (got)? has he (got)?	—— ——	do I have? does he have?	—— ——
questions with **not** or **n't**			
F full form	**G** short form	**M** full form	**N** short form
have I not (got)? has he not (got)?	haven't I (got)? hasn't he (got)?	do I not have? does he not have?	don't I have? doesn't he have?

You, we, they and *plural noun phrases* also go with **have**; **he, she, it** and *singular noun phrases* also go with **has**. The short forms are normal in conversation and informal writing; the full forms of Columns F and M are rare.

There are various meanings of *main verb* **have**. When there is a possible difference between a temporary state or feature and a more permanent state or feature, then the forms with **got** are used for the former (1, 3) and those without **got** and with **do** are used for the latter (2, 4), e.g.

1 That shop's got some good cheese. (i.e. now)
2 That shop usually has good cheese.
3 Have you got a headache?[3] (i.e. now)
4 Do you ever have headaches?

There is a corresponding difference with **have** ('be obliged' » **125**), e.g.
e.g.

5 Have you got to get up early tomorrow?[3]
6 Do you often have to get up early?

In general the forms of Columns A–G are more common, e.g.

7a A: Have you (got) a car?
    B: Yes, I have./No, I haven't.[3]
8 We haven't (got) much money.[3]
9 She's got blue eyes. (or She has blue eyes)

There is also the common use of **have** for certain activities, e.g. **have a wash, a bath, a shower; have breakfast, lunch, tea, dinner, supper; have a lesson; have a cigarette; have a cup of tea, coffee; have an argument**, etc. Here, **have** behaves like every other *verb* that refers to an activity, i.e. it uses *auxiliary* **do** (10, 11) and it also has *progressive forms* (12):

10 What time do you normally have supper? (*Not* x have you got x)
11 They don't often have arguments. (*Not* x haven't often got x)
12 They're having lunch at the moment.

---

[1] These forms are normally only used when **have** is an *auxiliary*.

[2] These short forms must have **got** or, when **have** is an *auxiliary*, a *past participle*.

[3] In these uses some speakers, including most Americans, use forms with **do** (Columns H–N), with the same meaning. e.g.

7b A: Do you have a car?
    B: Yes, I do./No, I don't.

111 Mr Dobson **had** a motorbike when he was young.

Here, **had** is the *past simple* of *main verb* **have** (« **110**); there is only one form. In all uses we normally use *auxiliary* **did** to make *statements* with **not** and *questions*, e.g.

1 Did you have a headache at the time? (« » **110**.3)
2 Did you ever have headaches before the accident? (« » **110**.4)

3   She had blue eyes. (« » **110**.9)
4   What time did you have supper? (« » **110**.10)
5a We didn't have much money. (« » **110**.8)

For possession (e.g. 5a) you will also meet alternative forms without **did** and with optional **got**, e.g.

5b We hadn't (got) much money.

112 **Can** you speak English ?

Can is a *modal*. It has only one form; it goes with a *plain infinitive*, e.g. **I can go, can he come**? etc. The full *negative* form is usually written as one word, i.e. **cannot**. The short *negative* form is **can't**.

We use **can** to express general ability (1, 2a) or ability on a particular occasion in present (3) or future time (4a). When an activity does not need strength (e.g. 1), **can** means 'know(s) how to':

1   Your son can speak German, can't he?
2a Some people can walk for hours.
3   Can you mend that vase?
4a I can't finish the housework by 12 o'clock.

We sometimes use **be able to** to express general ability (2a), but not for knowledge (1), e.g.

2b Some people are able to walk for hours.

We can use **will be able to** to express ability in future time, e.g.

4b I won't be able to finish the housework by 12 o'clock.

We also use **can** for general permission, (« » **may 115**), e.g.

5   A: Can we smoke in here? (i.e. Are we allowed to smoke)
    B: Yes, you can./No, you can't. (« » **115**.1)
6   My sister can stay out until midnight now. (i.e. is allowed to stay out)

We also use **can** for offers (7) and for requests (8), e.g.

7   Can we help you? (« » **113**.4, **115**.3)
8   Can you help me? (*Not* x~~May you~~ x; « » **113**.5, **117**.12, **122**.1)

We also use **can** for general possibility that is based on previous experience of this possibility, e.g.

9   Too much sun can be dangerous. (i.e. Too much sun is sometimes dangerous)
10 Even specialists can be wrong. (i.e. Even specialists are sometimes wrong)

Can cannot be used for the possibility of a future event (» **116**).

We use **can't,** or sometimes **couldn't,** for the speaker's assumption that something is impossible in present time, e.g.

11   That man can't be English because he speaks with a foreign accent. (i.e. I assume that he is not English; « » **124**.6)

12   Janet's upstairs and Wendy's in the kitchen, so they can't be playing a game. (i.e. I assume that they are not playing a game; « » **124**.7)

Verbs of perception **feel, hear, see, smell** and **taste** normally go with **can** for present perceptions (13, 14) and with **could** for past perceptions (15), e.g.

13   Look out of the window! What can you see?

14   Mary says she can hear a dog.

15   When I got home yesterday, I could smell gas.

113 I **could** swim when I was six.

Could is a *modal*. It has only one form[1]; it goes with a *plain infinitive*, e.g. **I could go, could she come?** etc. The short *negative* form is **couldn't.**

We use **could** to talk about general ability in past time (1, 2), but we cannot use **could** for ability on a specific occasion in past time (» **114, 130**).

1   My grandmother could speak German. (« » **112**.1)

2   Roman soldiers could walk for hours. (« » **112**.2a)

We also use **could** for general permission in past time, e.g.

3   When my sister was 15, she could only stay out until 9 o'clock. (« » **112**.6)

We also use **could** for tentative or polite offers (4) or requests (5):

4   Could we help you? (« » **112**.7, **115**.3)

5   Could you help me? (« » **112**.8, **117**.12, **122**.1)

We also use **could** to express the possibility of something in present or future time (» **116**).

---

[1] Historically, **could** is the *past form* of **can**; their meanings do not always correspond, (but » *reported speech* **177**).

114 The sailors **managed to** swim to the island.

We use *main verb* **managed** with a **to** *infinitive* to talk about a particular occasion in past time when ability resulted in successful action. We sometimes express this meaning with **was** or **were able to**:

1a The driver managed to avoid an accident. (i.e. there was no accident)
1b The driver was able to avoid an accident. (*Not* x~~could avoid x~~; « » **130**.1)
2a We managed to get home before it rained. (i.e. we got home before it rained)
2b We were able to get home before it rained. (*Not* x~~could get x~~; « » **130**.2)
3a Jim's parents managed to talk to his teacher. (i.e. they talked to his teacher)
3b Jim's parents were able to talk to his teacher. (*Not* x~~could talk x~~; « » **130**.3)

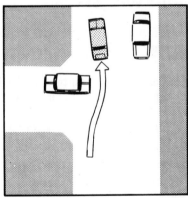

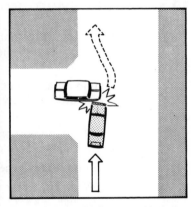

The driver was able to avoid an accident.   The driver could have avoided the accident. (» **130**.1)

For **able** in present and future time « **112**.2b, 4b; for **could** « **113**; for **could have** » **130**.

115 **May** I come in?

May is a *modal*. It has only one form; it goes with a *plain infinitive*, e.g. **you may go, may we come?** etc. The short *negative* form, **mayn't**, is rare.

We use **may** in *questions* to ask for the listener's personal permission (1) and in *statements* to give the speaker's personal permission (2):

1 A: May we smoke in here? (i.e. Do you give us your permission?)
   B: Yes, you may./No, you may not. (« » **112**.5)
2 You may go home now. (i.e. I give you permission to go)

For permission we often use **can**, which implies that the permission is general, not personal, (« **112**).

We also use **may** for polite offers, e.g.

3 May we help you? (« » **112**.7, **113**.4)

We also use **may** to agree with one aspect of something before introducing a contrary aspect, e.g.

4 C: He's very clever.
   D: He may be clever, but he's not very helpful. (i.e. I agree that he is clever, but)

Also » **116**.

116 Joe **might** come tomorrow.

Might is a *modal*. It has only one form[1]; it goes with a *plain infinitive*, e.g. **he might go, might she be**? etc.

We use **might**, and also **may**, for something that is possible, or even probable, in present (1, 2) and future time (3):

1 A: Where's Jill?
   B: I don't know, but she might be at work. (or she may be; i.e. perhaps she is; « » 4)
2 C: What's Terry doing?
   D: I don't know, but he might be having a bath. (or may be; i.e. perhaps he is having)
3 Peter might go to London this weekend. (or may go; i.e. perhaps he will go; « » 5)

We use *modal* **could** (« **113**) for something that is possible in present (4) or future time (5):

4 Jill could be at work, but I doubt it. (i.e. it is possible; « » 1)
5 Peter could go to London this weekend, but I don't think he will; « » 3, and **241**.9)

———
[1] Historically, **might** is the *past form* of **may**; their meanings do not usually correspond (but » *reported speech* **177**).

117 Will Robin go to the match?

Will is a *modal*. We very often use the short forms **'ll** (only in *statements*) and **won't**, but we use **will** and **will not** for emphasis and in formal style. **Will** goes with a *plain infinitive*, e.g. **I'll go, will she come?** etc.

In *statements* and *questions*, when the *subject* cannot influence the events, **will** concerns a fact (1, 2) or a prediction (3, 4) about future time:

    1   Ann'll be five next birthday, but I'll be six, won't I?
    2   A: Will James be five next birthday?
           B: Yes, he will./No, he won't. (*Not* x Yes, he'll. x)
    3   Those birds won't come back before next winter.
    4   Will those birds come back to the same place?

We also sometimes use **will I** and **will we** in *questions* about future time that nobody can answer, e.g.

    5   Will I ever speak English as well as you do?
    6   Where will we all be in 20 years' time?

In *statements*, when the *subject* can influence the event, **will** expresses willingness or a promise (7, 8) and **will not** expresses refusal (9):

    7a   C: We need some salt.
           D: I'll get some today. (i.e. I promise at this moment; « » **145**.4)
    8   E: I can hear the telephone.
        F: It's all right. Jim'll answer it.
    9   I've asked her to come, but she won't.

We sometimes use **won't** with a thing as *subject*, as if the thing refused, e.g.

    10   The window won't open. (i.e. can't be opened)
    11   Won't your car start? (i.e. Can't your car be started?)

In *questions*, when the listener can influence the event, **will you** is a request for the listener to act (12) or to express a promise (13):

    12   Will you help me? (« » **112**.8, **113**.5, **122**.1)
    13   Will you keep my secret?

In *statements* and *questions*, when other people (not the speaker and the listeners) could influence events, **will** can express either prediction about somebody's behaviour before asking the person (14, 16), or the willingness that somebody has already expressed (15, 17), but the context will usually make it clear, e.g.

    14   Susan'll lend us her guitar. (i.e. She hasn't said so, but I predict that she will lend us her guitar)
    15   Susan'll lend us her guitar. (i.e. She has already said that she is willing; we simply need to ask.)
    16   My brother won't help us. (i.e. He hasn't said so, but I predict that he won't help us)
    17   My brother won't help us. (i.e. He has already refused)

In these cases we can make it clear that a *statement* is about willingness by using **say(s)**, e.g.

18   Susan says (that) she'll lend us her guitar. (« » 15)

We can also use **will** for assumptions about present time, e.g.

19   G: There's a man with red hair waiting to see you.
      H: Oh, that'll be Robin. (i.e. I assume that it is Robin)

Note: In *statements* you will sometimes meet **I shall** and **we shall** instead of **I will** and **we will**, with the same meaning, e.g.

7b   D: I shall get some today.
20   I shan't be happy until you come. (i.e. I won't)

For **shall** in *questions* » **118**.

118 Shall I make some tea ?

Shall is a *modal*. It has the short *negative* form **shan't** (« **117**.20); it goes with a *plain infinitive*, e.g. **shall I come?**, **shall we go?** etc.

We use **shall I** and **shall we** to ask the listener for a decision that affects the speaker; the *question* may ask for instructions (1), or offer to do something (2), or make a suggestion (3), or ask for a suggestion (4):

1   Shall we put on our warm coats?
2   A: Shall I help you with the dishes?
      B: Yes, please./No, thank you.[1]
3   Shall we go to the cinema tonight? (i.e. Do you agree to my suggestion that we go?)
4   What shall we do this evening?

———

[1] This is an offer, so *Not* x Yes, you shall x or x No, you shan't x

For **shall** in *statements* « **117** *Note*.

119 People **should** be more careful.

Should is a *modal*. It has only one form[1]; it goes with a *plain infinitive*, e.g. **I should go, should he come?** etc. The short *negative* form is **shouldn't**.

We use **should** to talk about the right thing to do, or the best thing to do, and to give and ask for advice, both in general (1, 2) and for a particular person (3, 4), e.g.

1   People who get bad service should complain, shouldn't they? (i.e. that is the right thing to do; « » **120**.1)
2   If one has a cold, one should stay in bed. (i.e. that is the best thing to do for oneself; « » **120**.2)
3   A: Should I give the waiter a tip?
      B: Yes, you should./No, you shouldn't.
4   He shouldn't talk about his wife all the time, should he?

We also use **should** to mean that something will happen if things go as we expect (5) or according to a plan (6), e.g.

> 5   My husband should be home soon. (i.e. I expect him soon)
> 6a The match should start at 3 o'clock.

When there is a plan (6a), we can also use **supposed to**, with similar meaning, e.g.

> 6b The match is supposed to start at 3 o'clock.

---

[1] Historically, **should** is the *past* form of **shall** (« **118**); their meanings do not usually correspond, but » *reported speech* **177**. For **had better** » **123**.

Also » **240, 241**.

120 You **ought to** report the matter to the police.

Ought is a *modal*. It has only one form; it goes with a **to** *infinitive*, e.g. **you ought to go, ought we to go?** etc., but occurs mostly in *statements*.

Its meaning is similar to **should** (« » **119**), but it often suggests that something is one's duty, not simply that it would be the right thing to do, e.g.

> 1   People who get bad service ought to complain. (i.e. it is their duty to complain; « » **119**.1)
> 2   If one has a cold, one ought to stay in bed. (i.e. it is one's duty; it is the best thing for other people; « » **119**.2)
> 3   If you think she cheated you, you ought to tell her.

Ought to goes alone if we can understand the rest of the sentence, e.g.

> 4   We haven't telephoned her yet, but we ought to. (i.e. we ought to telephone her)

121 Kate **used to** be really thin.

Here, **used** is a *verb*. The usual way[1] to form *statements* with **not** and *questions* is with **did** (2–4). **Used** goes with a **to** *infinitive*, e.g. **I used to go, she didn't use to come, did he use to be?** etc.

We use the *verb* **used** only about past time; it is for an activity that was repeated many times (1, 2) or for a state that lasted a long time (3, 4). **Used** implies that the activity or state does not continue at the present time, e.g.

> 1   I used to play bridge a lot; now I hardly ever play.
> 2   We didn't use to watch television very much.
> 3   They used to live in Wales, didn't they?

Kate used to be really thin.

4   A: Did Jackie use to have long hair?
     B: Yes, she did./No, she didn't.

Used to goes alone if the rest of the sentence can be understood, e.g.

5   They don't live in Wales now, but they used to.

We express the corresponding activity or state in present time with the *present simple* (» **141**), e.g.

6   Now we watch television quite a lot. (« » 2)
7   They live in Scotland now. (« » 3)

---

[1] In formal style **used** can be an *auxiliary*, with the same meaning, i.e. it can form *statements* with **not** and *questions*, e.g. **she usedn't to come, used he to be?** etc.

For *adjective* **used** « **79**.

122 **Would** you open the door, please ?

Would is a *modal*. It has only one form[1]; it goes with a *plain infinitive*, e.g. **I would go, would you like?** etc. We often use the *forms* -**'d** (only in *statements*) and **wouldn't**, but we avoid these forms in formal writing.

We use **would** (like **will**) in polite requests, e.g.

1   Would you help me? (« » **112**.8, **113**.5, **117**.12)
2   A: Would you close the window, please?
     B: Certainly./I'm afraid I can't.

These *questions* are requests, so *Not* x~~Yes, I would~~x or x~~No, I wouldn't~~x here.

We also use **would** with **like** to ask about (3) and to express wishes (4–6) at the present moment:

> 3   C: Would you like a cup of tea?
>   D: Yes, please./No, thank you.
> 4   I'd like a lemonade, please.
> 5   We'd like to see some cotton shirts, please.
> 6   I'd like him to go to the post office. (» **216**.4)

In wishes like sentences 4–6, **want** instead of **would like** sometimes sounds abrupt and impolite.

In formal style we can use **should** instead of **would** with I and **we**, e.g.

> 7   I should like to apply for the post that you have advertised.

We use **would not** to express refusal in past time, e.g.

> 8   I asked her to come, but she wouldn't. (« » **117**.9)
> 9   The window wouldn't open. (« » **117**.10)

We also sometimes use **would** for a repeated event in past time; we more usually use **used to** (« **121**) in this sense. e.g.

> 10   As a young woman she would read for hours without a break. (i.e. she used to read)

We use **would** with **rather** for a present wish for something in preference to something else; we can make explicit the thing that is not preferred with **than** (11a, 12a), e.g.

> 11a   A: Would you like some tea, or would you rather have coffee?
>   B: I'd rather have coffee (than tea).
> 12a   C: Daddy says he'll take you to the park or to the zoo.
>   D: We'd rather go to the zoo (than to the park).

We can use **would sooner**, with the same meaning, e.g.

> 11b   B: I'd sooner have coffee (than tea).

We can also express the same meaning with **would prefer**, which is followed either by a *noun phrase* (11c) with *preposition* **to** to show the preference, or by a **to** *clause* (12b) with **rather than** to show the preference, e.g.

> 11c   B: I'd prefer coffee (to tea).
> 12b   D: We'd prefer to go to the zoo (rather than to the park).

We can also use **would rather** to politely disagree with a suggestion. Notice the two possible *negative* forms, e.g.

> 13   E: Would you like to go to the cinema?
>   F: I'd rather not go today. (*Not* x wouldn't rather x)
> 14   G: Is it all right if I put the TV on?
>   H: I'd rather you didn't (put it on). (*Not* x wouldn't rather x)

Didn't in 14 is *past* in form but refers to present time (» **241, 245**).

———

[1] Historically, **would** is the *past* form of **will**; their meanings do not usually correspond, but » *reported speech* **177**.

For **would** in *conditionals* » **241, 242**.

123 You **had better** go today.

Had better is an expression that goes with a *plain infinitive*. We often use the short form -**'d better** in *statements* (1, 2, 4). *Questions* are formed with **had** (3); *negative statements* are formed with **not** after **better** (4).

We use **had better** to express personal advice or recommendation for a particular occasion, but not for advice in general. The speaker may use it for himself (2):

1   You'd better go to the police.
2   I'd better post the letter myself, hadn't I?
3   A: Had we better leave early?
     B: Yes, you should./No, you don't need to.[1]
4   You'd better not swim if you've just eaten.

If the advice is general or not for a particular occasion, we use **should** (« **119**), e.g.

5   People in trouble should go to the police. (« » 1)
6   Nobody should swim just after a meal. (« » 4)

———

[1] **Yes, you had** is also possible here, but we avoid the short *negative* answer **No, you hadn't**.

124 You **must** get there before nine o'clock.

Must is a *modal*. It has only one form; it goes with a *plain infinitive*, e.g. **you must go, must I come?** etc. The short *negative* form is **mustn't**.

In *statements* we use **must** and **must not** (or **mustn't**) to express obligation (1), necessity (2), prohibition (3), or strong recommendation (4). This can be personal obligation or necessity i.e. it either comes from the speaker, or at least the speaker agrees with it[1], (» **have (got) to 125**), e.g.

1   You must sit and wait.
2   I must get up early tomorrow. (e.g. because there are many things that I want to do; « » **125**.1)
3   You mustn't go in there. Your mother's sleeping.
4   Children mustn't play with knives because they're dangerous.

In *questions* we use **must** to ask for the listener's decision regarding obligation, etc., e.g.

> 5   A: Must I go immediately?
> B: Yes, you must. (i.e. you are obliged to) / No, you don't have to. (or No, you haven't got to; i.e. you are not obliged to; » **125**)

We also use **must**, but not **must not**, for the speaker's assumption that something is true in present time, e.g.

> 6   That man must be a foreigner because he speaks with a strong foreign accent. (i.e. I assume that he is foreign; « » **112**.11)
> 7   The girls are very quiet. They must be playing a game. (i.e. I assume that they are playing a game; « » **112**.12)

There is no *past* form of **must** (» **126, 128**).

———

[1] However, in many situations there is little difference in meaning between **must** and **have (got) to**.

125   You **have (got) to** send the papers this week.

Here, **have (got)** means 'be obliged'; it goes with a **to** *infinitive*. There are two ways to make *statements* with **not** and *questions* (« **110**), e.g. **you have (got) to go, have I (got) to come?, do we have to stay?** etc. There is a tendency to use the forms of Columns A–G in the table in **110**, often with **got**[1], for a specific occasion (1, 3, 5), but the forms of Columns H–N for other cases (2, 4, 6).

In *positive statements* we use **have (got) to** to express obligation or necessity that is general, i.e. the speaker is not responsible for it (« **must 124**), e.g.

> 1   I've got to get up early tomorrow.[1] (or I have to; i.e. because I'm obliged to start work earlier than usual; « » **124**.2)
> 2   My brother has to get up early every day. (i.e. because he starts work early)

In *questions*, **have (got) to** asks for general obligation or necessity for which the listener is not responsible, e.g.

> 3   A: Has he (got) to take any medicine?[1]
> B: Yes, he has./No, he hasn't.
> 4   C: Does he always have to take this medicine?
> D: Yes, he does./No, he doesn't.

In *negative statements* **have (got) to** expresses absence of obligation or necessity, e.g.

5 She hasn't (got) to do anything special today.[1] (i.e. she is not obliged to do anything special)
6 She doesn't usually have to wake the children. (i.e. it is not usually necessary)

Have (got) to goes alone if we can understand the rest of the sentence, e.g.

7 I might go tomorrow, but I haven't got to. (i.e. to go)

Modals can go with **have to**, but always without **got**, e.g. **will** for future time (8), **must** for assumption (9), and **might** or **may** for possibility (10), e.g.

8 You'll have to work hard if you want to pass the exam.
9 E: Terry starts work at six o'clock.
   F: He must have to get up early. (i.e. I assume he has to)
10 I might have to go to London next week. (or may; i.e. perhaps I will be obliged to go)

_____

[1] Some people avoid **got** in e.g. sentences 1, 3, 5.

126 Jane **had to** go to prison.

Here, **had** is the *past* of **have (got)** (« **125**). We normally use **did** for *statements* with **not** and *questions*, e.g. **she didn't have to go, did you have to come?** etc.

We use **had to** for obligation and necessity in past time when the event in fact took place (« » **should have 132**); the meaning corresponds to both **must** (« **124**) and **have (got) to** (« **125**), e.g.

1 Yesterday we had to sit and wait, didn't we? (i.e. we sat and waited; « » **124**.1)
2 I had to get up early yesterday. (i.e. I got up; « » **124**.2, **125**.1, **132**.3)
3 A: Did you have to go to the police station?
   B: Yes, we did./No, we didn't.

Had to goes alone if we can understand the rest of the sentence, e.g.

4 C: Why did you go?
   D: Because I had to. (i.e. had to go)

We use **did not have to** (5), or **had to** with a *negative* word (6), to express that something was not necessary or obligatory in past time. This normally implies that the event did not take place, e.g.

5 The policeman warned us, but we didn't have to pay a fine. (i.e. we did not pay a fine)
6 They never had to work hard when they were young. (i.e. **they never worked hard.**)

127 You **are to** follow the instructions to the letter.

In formal style, we can use the *present* of **be** with a **to** *infinitive* for obligation (1) and prohibition (2), e.g.

    1   We are to report again tomorrow. (i.e. We have to report)

    2   They are to speak to no one. (i.e. They mustn't speak to anyone)

This structure is also used in formal style for official announcements about future events, e.g.

    3   The chief officer is to make a full investigation.

    4   The wedding is to take place on 25 March.

We also use the *past* of **be** with a **to** *verb*, but this suggests that the speaker does not know whether the event took place or not, e.g.

    5   The wedding was to take place on 25 March.

128 It **must have rained** during the night.

We use **must have** plus a *past participle* in *statements* to express the speaker's present assumption that something was true in past time, e.g.

    1   The man must have been a foreigner because he spoke with a strong foreign accent. (i.e. I now assume that he was foreign; « » **124**.6, **129**.1)

    2   The girls were very quiet. They must have been playing a game. (i.e. I now assume that they were playing; « » **124**.7, **129**.2)

Note: For present assumptions about past events we cannot use **will**, **should** or **have (got) to,** although **will** (« **117**.19) is used for assumptions about present time, and **should** (« **119**.5) for expectations about present or future time.

129 She **can't have loved** him very much.

We use **can't have,** or sometimes **couldn't have,** plus a *past participle* , in *statements* to express the speaker's present assumption that something was not true in past time, e.g.

    1   That man can't have been English because he spoke with a strong foreign accent. (or couldn't have; i.e. I assume that he was not English; « » **112**.11, **128**.1)

2   Janet was upstairs and Wendy was in the kitchen, so they can't have been playing a game. (or couldn't have; i.e. I now assume that they were not playing; « » **112**.12, **128**.2)

130 My sister **could have been** a lawyer.

We use **could have** plus a *past participle* to talk about ability or possibility (1–3), or permission in past time (4), when the event did not in fact take place, e.g.

1   The driver could have avoided the accident. (i.e. it was possible, but he did not avoid it; « » **114**.1b and picture)
2   We could have got home before it rained. (i.e. it was possible but we did not get home; « » **114**.2b)
3   Jim's parents could have talked to his teacher. (i.e. they had the opportunity but they did not talk to him/her; « » **114**.3b)
4   A: Did you stop your daughter going to the demonstration?
     B: No, she could have gone as far as we were concerned.

We use **could not have** to express that there was not enough ability and so the event did not take place, e.g.

5   We couldn't have won the match even if we had tried harder. (i.e. it was impossible for us)

Also » **131**.4, 5.

131 They **might have taken** a later train.

We use **might have**, or sometimes **may have**, plus a *past participle*, for something that possibly, or even probably, happened in past time, e.g.

1   A: Where was Jill at 8 o'clock yesterday?
     B: I don't know but she might have been at work. (or may have been; i.e. perhaps she was at work; « » **116**.1)
2   C: What was Terry doing when you called?
     D: I don't know, but he might have been having a bath. (or may have; i.e. perhaps he was having; « » **116**.2)
3   Peter might have gone to London last weekend. (or may have; i.e. perhaps he went; « » **116**.3, **242**.2)

We use **could have** for past time for something that possibly happened, e.g.

4   Jill could have been at work, but I doubt it. (« » **116**.4)
5   Peter could have gone to London last weekend, but I don't think he did. (« » 3, **116**.5, **242**.6)

132 You **should have taken** an umbrella.

We use **should have** plus a *past participle*, for something that did not happen in past time (« » **had to 126**), but the speaker says, or asks if, it would have been the right thing to do, e.g.

1   If they got bad service, they should have complained. (i.e. they did not complain, but it would have been the right thing to do; « » **119**.1)

2   Should I have given the waiter a tip? (i.e. I did not, but would it have been the right thing to do?; « » **119**.3)

We also use **should have** when there was a previous plan or arrangement that was not fulfilled, e.g.

3   I should have got up early yesterday. (i.e. I did not get up; « » **126**.2)

4a The match should have started at 3 o'clock, but there was a delay. (« » **119**.6a)

In sentences like 3 and 4, we can also use **supposed to,** with similar meaning, e.g.

4b The match was supposed to start at 3 o'clock, but there was a delay. (« » **119**.6b)

We also use **should have** to express an assumption that something has happened, but only if nothing unusual has taken place, e.g.

5   They left here early and it isn't far to their house, so they should have arrived by now.

For a more certain assumption that something has happened, we can use **must have,** e.g.

6   They left here an hour ago and their house is only ten minutes away, so they must have arrived by now.

Ought to have has similar meaning to **should have,** but often suggests that the action, which did not happen, was someone's duty (« **120**), e.g.

7   If they got bad service, they ought to have complained. (i.e. they did not, but it was their duty; « » 1, **120**.1)

8   If he had a cold, he ought to have stayed in bed. (i.e. it was his duty, but he did not stay in bed; « » **120**.2)

133 We don't **dare (to)** open it.

We usually treat **dare** as a *main verb,* i.e. we use **dares** for **he, she** and **it** (1) and we use **do** or **does** for *statements* with **not** (2a) and *questions* (3a) in the *present,* and **did** in the *past* (4). *Main verb* **dare** goes with a *plain infinitive* or a *to infinitive*.

Dare means 'be courageous enough', e.g.

   1 I'll be surprised if she dares (to) speak.
  2a They don't dare (to) contradict Nicholas.
  3a Do we dare (to) sleep in that house?
   4 Did she dare (to) ask for a rise?

In the *present*, **dare** is sometimes used as an *auxiliary*, i.e. it has only one form and goes with a *plain infinitive*. Auxiliary **dare** can make *statements* with **not** (2b) and *questions* (3b), but it is rare in *positive statements*, e.g.

  2b They daren't contradict Nicholas.
  3b Dare we sleep in that house?

Also » **216.**

134 This company **needs** some new ideas.

We usually treat **need** as a *main verb*, i.e. we use **needs** for **he, she** and **it** (1), and we use **do** or **does** for *statements* with **not** (2, 5a) and *questions* (3, 6a). *Main verb* **need** goes with a **to** *infinitive*.

We use **need** with a *noun phrase* as *object* (1–3) to talk about something that is lacking or necessary, e.g.

  1 The kitchen needs a new light bulb.
  2 This machine doesn't need a lot of attention.
  3 Do we need anything from the supermarket?

We use *main verb* **need** with a **to** *infinitive* to express the necessity of an action, e.g.

  4 We need to wash these walls before we paint them.
  5a The children don't need to shout.
  6a A: Do I need to shave?
       B: Yes, you do./No, you don't.

In the *present*, when **need** is followed by a *verb*, **need** is sometimes used as an *auxiliary*, i.e. it has only one form, and **need** is used to make *statements* with **not** (5b) and *questions* (6b); *auxiliary* **need** goes with a *plain infinitive*; it is rare in *positive statements*.

  5b The children needn't shout.
  6b A: Need I shave?
       B: Yes, you must./No, you don't have to. (or No, you needn't.)

Note: Although they have similar meaning, **do not need to** and **do not have to** have different emphases, e.g.

  7 I don't need to go. (i.e. it is not necessary)
  8 I don't have to go. (i.e. nobody forces me)

The weather forecast was very good, so I didn't need to take my umbrella.

In past time, when an action did not happen, we can express absence of necessity with **did not need to**, e.g.

    9   We didn't need to send any money. (i.e. it was not necessary, so we didn't send any; « » **135**.2)

    10   The weather forecast was very good, so I didn't need to take my umbrella. (i.e. I didn't take my umbrella; « » **135**.3)

135 You **needn't have brought** a towel with you.

We use **need not have** with a *past participle* to talk about something that happened in past time but was not necessary, e.g.

    1a   You needn't have come at 5 o'clock; we don't start till about 6. (i.e. you came at 5, but it was not necessary)

    2   We needn't have sent any money. (i.e. we sent some money, but it was not necessary; « » **134**.9)

    3   It didn't rain after all, so I needn't have taken my umbrella. (i.e. I took my umbrella, but it was not necessary; « » **134**.10)

It didn't rain after all, so I needn't have taken my umbrella.

Note: You will sometimes meet **did not need to** (**do**) instead of **need not have** (**done**), with the same meaning, e.g.

1b You didn't need to come at 5 o'clock.

However, some people consider this incorrect and reserve **did not need to** for events that did not take place (« » **134**.9, 10)

136 **Open** the door, please.

Here, **open** is an *imperative*. The *positive* form is the same as the *plain infinitive*, e.g. **come, go**; we make the *negative* form with **do not**, usually in the short form **don't** (3, 5).

We use an *imperative* to talk to one person (1) or to more than one (2); it can express a command (1–3) or a request (4, 5)[1]. With a command we usually use an exclamation mark (!):

1 Tom, stand up!
2 Children, stand up!
3 Don't touch those things!
4 Mary, pass the salt, please.
5 Don't give me many potatoes, Mummy.

We sometimes use **you** before an *imperative*, e.g. speaking to three people:

> 6   You bring the plates; you get the knives and forks, and you help me with the food.

---

[1] We recognise whether an *imperative* is a command or a request either from the situation, or from other words, e.g. **please** (4), or from the tone of voice.

137 **Let's** go to the cinema.

Let's goes with a *plain infinitive*, e.g. **let's go, let's sit**, etc. When **let's** is a suggestion, it does not have a full form, so *Not* x let us go x in this sense[1]. With **not** there are two alternative forms, e.g. **let's not go, don't let's go**. There is no corresponding *question*; instead we use **shall we** (1, 3).

We use **let's** to suggest an activity for the speaker and his or her listener(s); the speaker knows what he or she wants to do and **let's** tries to persuade the other(s), e.g.

> 1   Let's have a game of cards, shall we?
> 2   A: What can we do this evening?
>   B: Let's go and see your mum and dad.

The *negative* is usually in reply to a previous proposal, e.g.

> 3   C: Shall we go to the park this afternoon?
>   D: No, let's not go to the park. (or don't let's go)

---

[1] However, we can use the *imperative* **let** as a request to allow someone to do something, e.g.

> 4   Let me go early! (i.e. Allow me to go early!)
> 5   Let Jane go early! (i.e. Allow Jane to go early!)
> 6   Let us go early! (i.e. Allow us to go early!)

In 6 **us** does not include the listener; here **let us** cannot have a short form, so *Not* x let's x in this sense.

138 Mrs Jones **is talking** to a customer.

Is talking is a *present progressive*; we make it with the *present* of **be**, which is here the *auxiliary*, and an -ing *form*. We make *statements* and *questions* with the same word order as for *main verb* **be** (« 107).

We use the *present progressive* for an action that is incomplete at the present moment; it is used for an activity that is in progress at the moment of speaking (1–3) and also for a temporary state of affairs that is perhaps not in progress at the moment of speaking (4–6):

1 Look! It's snowing. (i.e. at this moment)
2 A: What's Bill doing at the moment?
  B: He's making some soup.
3 The children are playing in the garden. (i.e. at this moment)
4 I'm reading a very interesting book about animals and men. (i.e. I have started it but not finished it)
5 I'm sleeping badly, doctor. (i.e. implies that I normally sleep well, but this is not true of recent nights)
6 Alan's working overtime this week. (i.e. a temporary situation)

For the spelling of -ing *forms* » **256**; for *verbs* that in certain meanings do not have *progressive* forms » **142**; also » **139, 140**.

139 I am playing football on Saturday.

We use the *present progressive* (« **138**) to talk about future time, either with an *adverbial*, e.g. **on Friday** (1), **next weekend** (2), or when it is clear from the context that reference is to future time (3).

We use the *present progressive* to express a previous commitment to do something[1], i.e. it is the kind of thing that people write in advance in their diary, and so we often use this form to give a reason for not doing something else (1, 3):

1 A: Would you like to go to the cinema on Friday?
  B: I can't. I'm having supper with Ken on Friday.
2 C: What's Chris doing next weekend?
  D: She's going hiking with Robin. (» **223**)

I'm having supper with Ken on Friday.

3   You mustn't go out tonight, Bill, because Tom and Kate
    are coming to see us.

---

[1] The idea of commitment means that we do not usually use this form
for routine activities. For example, in 1, B could not reply simply **I'm
having supper on Friday**, and in 2, D could hardly say **She's listening to some records**, although **She's going to listen to some
records** would be possible (» **145**).

140 They **are always asking** for money.

We use **always**[1] with the *present progressive* (**2, 3**) or the *past
progressive* (**4, 5**). Here, **always** does not mean literally 'all the time,
on every occasion; it means 'more than we expect, more than is normal'.
Consider these sentences:

1   They always come late.
2   They are always coming late.

1 means that they literally come late on every occasion; 2 means that
they come late more often than the speaker thinks that they should, or
more often than normal, although they do not come late on every occasion.

3   She's always borrowing something from me. (i.e. she
    borrows more than she should)
4   Peter was always working in his garden. (i.e. more than
    most people do)
5   My parents were always travelling abroad. (i.e. they were
    not at home as much as most parents)

---

[1] Or synonyms, e.g. **continually, constantly**.

141 I **work** in that office.

Here, **work** is *present simple*. We use *auxiliaries* **do** and **does**[1] to make
statements with **not** and *questions*. The forms are:

full forms	short forms	full forms	short forms
you work you do not work do you work? do you not work?	you don't work don't you work?	he works[2] he does not work[2] does he work?[2] does he not work?[2]	he doesn't work[2] doesn't he work[2]
We use these forms with **I, you, we, they** and *plural noun phrases*.		We use these forms with **he, she, it** and *singular noun phrases*.	

I work in that office.

The short forms are less formal; the full forms **do you not work?** and **does he not work?** are rare.

The *present simple* is used to describe an activity or state that is considered as a whole, i.e. not considered as incomplete and in progress at the moment of speaking, (« » *present progressive* **138**). We use the *present simple* without an *adverbial* of time (« **89**) to talk about activities or states in general time, i.e. present time but also including past time and future time, e.g.

1   A: Do you smoke?
    B: Yes, I do./No, I don't.
2   C: Mrs Bradley works in a shoe shop, doesn't she?
    D: Yes, she does./No, she doesn't.
3   Wet wood doesn't burn very well.
4   Roses grow well in heavy ground.
5   They don't live near here, do they?
6   I don't do much homework. (The first **do** is *auxiliary*; the second **do** is the *main verb*)
7   What does your sister do for a living? (**Does** is *auxiliary*: **do** is the *main verb*)

We also use the *present simple* with *frequency adverbs* (« **84c**) to talk about general time, e.g.

8   Connie often works late.
9   E: Do they ever go out in the evening?
    F: No, they never go out.
10   I don't usually take my umbrella to work.

---

[1] *Auxiliaries* **do** and **does** have no real meaning, but they are necessary in *questions*, etc., in the *present simple*.

[2] There is only one -**s** ending in each case, either **works** or **does**, but

123

not both, and it is always on the *verb* that goes first, so *Not* x he does not works x, *Not* x does he works? x, *Not* x he don't works x, *Not* x do he works? x.

142 Now I **understand**.

Here, **understand** is a *present simple* although it refers to the present moment. **Understand** is one of a number of *main verbs* which, when used in certain meanings, do not have *progressive* forms[1]. In these meanings, we use the *simple present* both for general time, i.e. the same as with all *main verbs* (« **141**), and also to refer to the present moment, when other *verbs* normally use the *present progressive* (« **138**). Consider the following examples, which all refer to the present moment:

	A	**B**
1	Maura is watching a play.	She thinks it's very good. (*Not* x she is thinking x)
2	Dr Coe is examining the girl.	She seems to be quite well. (*Not* x she is seeming x)
3	Ken's riding a bicycle.	It belongs to my daughter. (*Not* x it is belonging x)

If the meaning of the *verb* refers to an activity (A), then the *verb* can have *progressive* forms in that meaning; if the *verb* does not refer to an activity (B), then the *verb* cannot have *progressive* forms in that meaning. In other words, if the meaning is not about what someone or something does, then the *verb* in that meaning can only go in the *present simple* (« **141**), the *past simple* (» **150**), the *perfect simple* (» **146, 153**) and the *future simple* (» **156**), but not *progressive* forms.

Verbs that have at least one meaning that cannot have *progressive* forms are:

a) *Verbs* with meanings connected with knowledge, belief, appearance, emotions and the senses: **appear, believe, care, consider, envy, expect, fear, feel** (9)**, forget, guess, hate, hear, hope, intend, interest, know, like** (4)**, love, mean** (5)**, mind, notice, please, prefer, realise, regret, remember, resemble, see, seem, smell, sound, taste** (10, 11)**, think** (12, 13)**, understand, want, wish**, e.g.

4   I like that picture. (*Not* x I am liking x)
5   What did the sign mean? (*Not* x was the sign meaning x)

b) *Relational verbs*, i.e. *verbs* that refer to relations, qualities or capacities: **be** (« **107**)**, belong, concern, contain** (6)**, cost, depend, deserve, equal, exist, fail, fit** (14, 15)**, have** (« **110**)**, hold** (16,

17), **include, lack, matter, measure** (18, 19), **need, owe** (7), **own, possess, stand for, weigh,** e.g.

    6   That box contains socks. (*Not* ~~x is containing x~~)

    7   Now you owe me three pounds. (*Not* ~~x you are owing x~~)

Here, for comparison, are some of these *verbs* that have both possibilities:

A Meaning that is an activity, so *progressive* forms are possible.	**B** Meaning that is not an activity, so there are no *progressive* forms
8 The man is feeling in the boy's pockets. (i.e. searching with his hands)	9 The sun feels warm. (i.e. appears warm to the skin)
10 The chef is tasting the soup. (i.e. sampling it)	11 The soup tastes perfect. (i.e. has a perfect taste)
12 Susan is thinking about the problem. (i.e. examining with her mind)	13 I think you are stupid. (i.e. it is my opinion)
14 My father is fitting some shelves. (i.e. putting them in the right place)	15 The dress fits you very well. (i.e. is the right size)
16 Mary is holding the baby. (i.e. supporting the baby)	17 This jar holds two kilos. (i.e. is big enough for two kilos)
18 The tailor is measuring his customer. (i.e. taking his measurements)	19 The customer's waist measures 105 centimetres. (i.e. has the measurement)

The tailor's measuring his customer.

The customer's waist measures 105 centimetres.

---

[1] All *main verbs*, whatever their meanings, have an **-ing** *form*, which is used as a *noun* (« **4, 79,** » **199, 200**).

143 Their train **leaves** at 9.20 this evening.

We use the *present simple* (« **141**) with a future *adverbial* for events in future time that are fixed and practically unchangeable, e.g. for the times of trains, planes, boats, concerts, sports events, etc., e.g.

1   What time does your plane leave?
2   I think the concert starts at 8.
3   That programme about whales begins in ten minutes.

Compared with many languages, we use the *present simple* very rarely for future time, only in fact in these special circumstances. For more frequent ways of referring to future time « **will** (**117**), the *present progressive* (**139**), and » the **going to** *future* (**145**).

144 Keegan **beats** the back and **crosses** the ball to the far post.

We use the *present simple* (« **141**) for an action at the moment of speaking when we are simply interested in the complete action, not in the action as something in progress. The *present simple* is often used in this way in radio and TV commentaries (1), in descriptions of demonstrations (2), and in commentaries and reviews of books, plays, films, etc., (3):

1   Jones serves. A good one. Bradley returns well. Jones runs back and hits the ball into the far corner.
2   First I draw a simple body, like this. Then I put on a round head, and then I draw the arms and legs, like this.
3   When the hero senses the danger, he arranges for the rest of the party to get to safety.

145 We **are going to** see a play on Friday.

Are going to see is the **going to** *future*; it is made with the *present progressive* of **go** and a **to** *infinitive*, e.g. **I am going to play, is he going to come?** etc.

We use the **going to** *future* about future time to indicate that someone intends to do something because he or she has made a previous decision. It can go without a time *adverbial* (1, 2) or with one (3, 4), and in most cases it refers to the near future, but e.g. the new office (2) may be in the distant future.

1   My sister is going to buy a new car. (i.e. she has decided)
2   Our company is going to open a new office. (i.e. the decision has been made)
3   I can't go hiking because I'm going to wash some clothes on Saturday. (i.e. I have decided; « » **139**.2)
4   A: We need some salt.
     B: I know. I'm going to get some today. (i.e. I had decided before you spoke; « » **117**.7a)

We cannot use **will** to express that a previous decision has been made. Consequently, sentences like **My sister will buy a new car** (« » 1) are grammatically correct, but rare.

We also use the **going to** *future* when the present situation contains the cause of something in the future, e.g.

5   My wife's going to have a baby. (i.e. she is now pregnant)
6   The sun's going to come out. (i.e. the clouds are now moving away.)

Going to goes alone if we can understand the rest of the sentence, e.g.

7   I haven't mended it yet, but I'm going to. (i.e. to mend it)

Also « **104**[1].

146 Tom **has broken** a cup.

Has broken is a *present perfect simple*; it is made with the *present* of **have**, which is here the *auxiliary*, and a *past participle*. The word order for *statements* and *questions* is the same as for *main verb* **have** without **do** (« **110** Columns A–G) e.g. **I have taken, I have not taken, have I taken?, haven't I taken?** etc.

We use the *present perfect* to connect the present moment with a past event[1]. Without a time *adverbial* the *present perfect* emphasises the present consequences or relevance of the past event, e.g.

1   Look! We've painted the kitchen. (i.e. the kitchen is now completely painted; « » **149**.1)
2   A: Has Paul broken his arm? (i.e. is it now broken?)
     B: Yes, he has./No, he hasn't.
3   C: What have you done today? (i.e. interest in results)
     D: I've written some letters. (« » **149**.5)
4   Sally's visited Moscow, hasn't she? (i.e. she has that experience.)
5   Have you read any stories by Damon Runyan? (i.e. at any time in your life)

We also use the *present perfect* with *adverb* **just** in *mid-position* (« **84c**) to talk about an event in very recent past time, e.g.

6   Your letter has just arrived. (i.e. in the last few minutes)
7   They've just returned from holiday.
8   Have you just had a shave? (i.e. you look freshly shaved)

Note: *Past participles* **been** and **gone** with *preposition* **to** can both correspond to **go**, but with different meanings, e.g.

9   Jim's gone to London. (i.e. and not returned yet)
10   Mary's been to London. (i.e. she is not there now)

---

[1] The exact time of the event is unimportant, so we cannot use the *present perfect* for completed past time, e.g. with expressions like **yesterday, in 1978, when I was a child,** etc. For this relation to past time we use the *past simple* (» **150**.9–16).

147 My grandfather **has never visited** London.

We can use the *present perfect* with *frequency adverbs* (« **84c**), to refer to all (relevant) past time up to the present moment, e.g.

1   My father has very rarely had to see a doctor. (i.e. implies that father is still alive; « » **150**.15)
2   Ken has never met his American cousins. (i.e. in his life up to now)
3   The company has always treated me well. (i.e. implies that I still work for the company; « » **150**.16)

When something happens for the first time, we use the *present perfect* to express that it has not happened before, e.g.

4   Hello! I don't think we've met before.
5   This is the first time that I've eaten mussels. (i.e. while eating them; *Not* x that I eat x)

For the *present perfect* with **already** and **yet** « **94**.

148 I haven't seen her since we left school.

The *present perfect* always refers to a period of time up to the present moment (« **146, 147**). We can specify the period in one of three ways:

a) with a phrase such as **today, this morning, this afternoon, this week, this month, this year, this century,** which includes the present moment, (but » **150**.13, 14), e.g.

1   We haven't worked very hard today, have we?
2   How many really cold winters have there been this century?
3   Those boys have broken three windows this week.

b) with a **for** *phrase* (« **101e**), which always goes last. This corresponds to the *question* phrase **How long** (» **167**), and is for a situation that has remained constant (4–6) or an event repeated regularly during the period (7):

4   A: How long has she been ill (for)?
     B: She's been ill (for) several weeks.
5   I haven't seen Ann for months.
6   Mr West has worked for that firm (for) 15 years.
7   We've been to Brighton every summer for years.

For a situation that has not remained constant (8) or has not been repeated regularly (9) we use **during the last** or **during the past** with **month, year,** etc:

8   There has been a gradual increase in accidents during the last year. (or the past year)
9   C: Have you seen Ann during the last year? (or the past year)
     D: Yes, I've seen her twice (during the last year).

c) with **since** (« **106**) either with a point of time (10) or with an event (11a, b):

10   I haven't seen Bill since 1976.
11a I haven't seen Bill since his wedding.
11b I haven't seen Bill since he got married. (*Not* x since that x; *Not* x since he gets married x)

For **since, for** and **ago** also « **97**.

149 Fred **has been cleaning** his car.

Has been cleaning is a *present perfect progressive*; it is made with **have been** (or **has been**) + an **-ing** *form*, e.g. **we have been working, has she been waiting?** etc.

We use the *present perfect progressive* to join the present moment to past time. The *present perfect simple* (« **146**) emphasises the completed results or consequences of an action; in contrast, the *progressive* emphasises either an incidental consequence (1, 2) or the activity itself (3, 5) or its unbroken duration (6, 7):

1 A: I think I can smell paint.
   B: Yes, we've been painting the kitchen. (i.e. the kitchen may or may not be completely painted; « » **146**.1)
2 C: Why are your hands dirty?
   D: I've been mending my bike. (i.e. the bike may or may not be mended)
3 Who's been eating my porridge? (i.e. there's some missing)
4 Who's eaten my porridge? (i.e. there's none left)
5 E: What have you been doing today? (i.e. interest in activity)
   F: I've been writing some letters. (« » **146**.3)
6 We've been waiting for this bus for half an hour.
7 Mrs Brown has been baking her own bread for years.

150 Yesterday Mrs Turner **went** to Plymouth.

Went is a *past simple*. We use *auxiliary* **did**[1] to make *statements* with **not** and *questions*, e.g.

full forms	short forms
she went[2] she did not go[2] did she go?[2] did she not go?[2]	she didn't go[2] didn't she go?[2]

The full form **did she not go?** is rare.

We use the same forms for all *subjects*.

We use the *past simple* to refer to events in completed past time, i.e. when there is a time *adverbial* that puts the event at a definite time previous to the present moment (1–5). The events can be short (1, 2), long (4) or repeated (5):

1 A: When did Chaplin die?
   B: He died in 1977.
2 C: Did you go to the match last Saturday?
   D: Yes, I did./No, I didn't.
3 They built their garage years ago, didn't they?
4 As a young woman she worked for a long time as a model.
5 When I was a teenager, I played football almost every Saturday.

We also use the *past simple* when a definite past occasion is given or implied by the context or situation, e.g.

6   (I've read one book by Dickens.) I didn't like it very much.
7   That's a nice sweater. Where did you buy it?
8   E: Hello, dear. Any news today?
    F: Yes, Mrs Aston phoned to tell me that her daughter's had a baby.

Without a time *adverbial*, the *past simple* always implies that the period is finished, i.e. it does not continue to the present moment, so the situation described cannot now be changed (9, 11, 13, 15, 16). In contrast, the *present perfect* implies a period that continues to the present moment, and so leaves a possibility that the situation may still change (10, 12, 14):

9   Dorothy didn't invite Peter to the party. (i.e. implies that the party has already taken place)
10 Dorothy hasn't invited Peter to the party. (i.e. implies that the party has not yet taken place)
11 Did you see the Henry Moore exhibition? (i.e. implies that it is not still on)
12 Have you seen the Henry Moore exhibition? (i.e. implies that it is still on)
13 What did you do this morning? (said e.g. at 5pm)
14 What have you done this morning? (said e.g. at 11am)
15 My father very rarely had to see a doctor. (i.e. implies either that he is dead, or that this concerns a part of his life that is now finished, e.g. as a young man; « » 147.1)
16 The company always treated me well. (i.e. implies that I no longer work for the company; « » 147.3)

When we do not hear or understand something, we usually comment on it with the *past simple*, even though this is immediately after the event, e.g.

17 Sorry! What did you say?
18 I didn't quite understand that. Can you say it again?

Note: **Last** ('the last time') and **first** ('the first time') go in *mid-position* (« **84c**) with the *past simple*, e.g.

19 G: When did you last see your sister?
    H: (I last saw her) about three weeks ago.
20 I: When did you first hear about the discovery?
    J: (I first heard about it) years ago.

For a comparison with the *past progressive*, » **151**.

———

[1] *Auxiliary* **did** has no real meaning, but it is necessary in *questions*, etc., in the *past simple*.

[2] There is only one *past* form in each case, either **went** or **did**, but not both, and it is always the first *verb*, so *Not* x~~she did not went~~x, *Not* x~~did she went?~~x, *Not* x~~she doesn't went~~x, *Not* x~~does she went?~~x.

151 We **were listening** to the radio.

Were listening is a *past progressive*. It is made with **was** or **were** + an -ing *form*, e.g. **I was going, was he talking?** etc.

The *past progressive* refers to a state or activity that was incomplete or in progress at a particular moment in past time. Both the *past simple* (« **150**) and the *past progressive* can be used for events that last a short or a long time; it is not the duration that is important. What is important is that we see the event as complete (*past simple*) or as something unfinished and in progress at the moment in question (*past progressive*), e.g.

1   A: Were you at home yesterday?
    B: Yes, I got up quite late, and then I cleaned my car in the afternoon.
    A: Oh, I phoned at about 3 o'clock, but you didn't answer.
    B: I didn't hear the phone. That's when I was cleaning my car.

I didn't hear the phone ring. That's when I was cleaning my car.

Obviously, **I cleaned my car** and **I was cleaning my car** refer to the same activity, which perhaps lasted for one hour. The first sentence sees the activity as a complete event; the second sees it as in progress at the time when A telephoned; also » 5–10.

2   C: Were you working at 10 o'clock yesterday?
    D: Yes, I was./No, I wasn't.
3   Last week at this time we were lying on the beach, weren't we?
4   A year ago this factory was producing only half its present output.

We often use the *past progressive* in contrast with the *past simple* to show that something was in progress when something else happened (» **232, 233**), e.g.

> 5 When Sarah arrived, they were playing the National Anthem.
> 6 When the Queen arrived, they played the National Anthem.

Sarah arrived while the anthem was in progress, but the National Anthem followed, and was because of, the Queen's arrival.

With two actions that lasted some time simultaneously, we can choose to emphasise that they were in progress at the same time, i.e. *past progressive* (7, 9), or we can describe them as completed events, i.e. *past simple* (8, 10); our emphasis changes, although the events themselves remain the same, e.g.

> 7 While the others were collecting firewood, we were preparing the food.
> 8 While the others collected firewood, we prepared the food.
> 9 The children were waiting patiently while the teacher was speaking to the parents.
> 10 The children waited patiently while the teacher spoke to the parents.

For *verbs* that sometimes do not have *progressive* forms « **142**.

152 They **were going to** have a party last Saturday.

Were going to have is the *past form* of the **going to** *future* (« **145**). We use it to talk about an intention in past time; usually either we do not know whether the event took place (1) or we know that it did not take place (2):

> 1 Bill was going to buy the tickets yesterday. (i.e. that was his intention, but I do not know if he did buy them)
> 2 I was going to write some letters last night, but my cousins came to see me, so I couldn't.

We also occasionally use this form for something that did take place later, e.g.

> 3 The carnival was going to start the following day, so everybody was making last-minute preparations. The carnival turned out to be a great success.

153 When Mr Trent arrived, Val **had** already left.

Had left is a *past perfect simple*. It is made with **had** + a *past participle*, e.g. **we had walked, had she taken?** etc. In *statements* **had** can have the short form **'d**.

The *past perfect* emphasises that one event was earlier than another event, both in past time. The *past perfect* can correspond to the *present perfect* (« **146**–**8**), so it can go with *adverbials* **just** (1), **never** (2), **ever, already** (3), **yet,** and phrases with **since** (4). In this use, the *past simple* cannot replace the *past perfect*:

1 They had just returned from holiday when the telegram arrived. (« » **146**.7)
2 Ken had never met his American cousins before they visited him last summer. (« » **147**.2)
3 When Mr Aston came home at 3 o'clock, the workmen had already finished. (« » **94**.2)
4 Until your party last Saturday, I hadn't seen Bill since his wedding. (« » **148**.11a)

The *past perfect* can also correspond to the *past simple* (« **150**), but we often use the *past simple* instead in these cases if the relation of the two events remains clear from the context, e.g.

5 A: It took me ages to get home on Saturday because of the football crowds leaving the match.
   B: Had you been to the match yourself? (or Did you go; « » **150**.2)
6 We built our garage a long time ago, but our neighbours had built theirs years before that. (or our neighbours built; « » **150**.3)
7 Before she became an actress, she had worked for a long time as a model. (or she worked; « » **150**.4)

When the context does not indicate the opposite, we assume that *statements* with the *past simple* are in the same order as the events that they describe, e.g.

8 Tom called to Kay, but she went into the garden.
9 Kay went into the garden, but Tom called to her.

However, if the sentences are not in the same order as the events, and this is not clear from the context, then we must use the *past perfect* to make it clear, e.g.

10 Tom called to Kay, but she had gone into the garden. (i.e. she went before he called)

We avoid a series of sentences that all have the *past perfect*. When it is established that we are describing events that were previous to another event, then it is normal to continue with the *past simple*, e.g.

11 Before the day of the concert, the organisers had made elaborate preparations. They distributed leaflets to every house in the district; they arranged for hundreds of stewards; they even made announcements on local radio.

154 Tom **had been working** in the garden.

Had been working is the *past perfect progressive*; it is made with **had been** + an -**ing** *form*, e.g. **he had been going, had you been working?** etc. In *statements* we can use the short form **'d**.

This form corresponds to the *present perfect progressive* (« **149**), but here the state or activity is before a moment in past time, not the present moment, e.g.

1 When they came last Sunday, there was a smell of paint because we had been painting the kitchen. (« » **149**.1)
2 When I got to the dining room, I immediately noticed that somebody had been eating my porridge. (« » **149**.3)
3 When the bus finally arrived, how long had you been waiting? (« » **149**.6)

For *verbs* that sometimes do not have *progressive* forms « **142**.

155 In two hours I **will be doing** the exam.

Will be doing is a *future progressive*; it is made with **will be** + an -**ing** *form*, e.g. **we will be sitting, will you be coming?** etc.

We use the *future progressive* for an activity or state that will be in progress, and so incomplete, at some particular point in future time. This form has no sense of intention or willingness (« **will 117**); it is only concerned with prediction, e.g.

1 The trip starts the day before my birthday, so on my birthday I'll be sailing across the Atlantic.
2 Those girls are in their final year at school. In a few months they will be either working or looking for work.

We also sometimes use this form with a meaning similar to the *present progressive* (« **139**), e.g.

3 I'll be seeing Tim tomorrow, so I can give him the message. (i.e. I'm seeing Tim tomorrow)
4 You can go into town with my mother. She'll be going in her car. (i.e. she's going in her car)

For *verbs* that sometimes do not have *progressive* forms « **142**.

156 I **will have finished** this book by tomorrow.

I will have finished this book by tomorrow.

Will have finished is a *future perfect simple*; it is made with **will have** + a *past participle*, e.g. **he will have spoken, will you have been?** etc.

We use the *future perfect* to talk about future time. Like the *present perfect* (« **146**) it does not concern the specific time when something happens; it only emphasises that something will happen before or by a particular point in future time, e.g.

1   They will have painted the kitchen by next weekend. (i.e. by next weekend the painting will be complete)
2   Derby have won seven matches in a row, so if they win again tomorrow, they'll have won eight consecutive matches.

157 She **will have been swimming** for two hours.

Will have been swimming is a *future perfect progressive*; it is made with **will have been** + an -**ing** *form*, e.g. **he will have been working, will you have been coming?** etc.

We use this form to talk about future time. It emphasises that an unbroken state or activity will be in progress up to a particular moment in future time, e.g.

1   In five minutes I'll have been waiting for an hour. (i.e. at the moment I have been waiting for 55 minutes)
2   At the end of this year she will have been studying English for ten years. (i.e. this is the tenth consecutive year)

For *verbs* that sometimes do not have *progressive* forms « **142.**

PART 4

Sentence processes

Introduction

Here we deal with five sentence processes:

a) *Questions* with a *question word*, e.g. **who, where, how many**, etc. (» **158–172**);

b) *Passive sentences* (» **173–176**);

c) *Reported speech*, sometimes called *indirect speech* (» **177–180**);

d) *Noun clauses* (» **181, 182**);

e) Sentences with introductory *subjects* **there** (» **183**) and **it** (» **184–189**).

158 What did Fred cook ?
Who cooked the meat ?

These are *question word questions*; **what** and **who** are *question words*. We can relate both these *questions* to the *statement*:

    1   Fred cooked the meat.

The first *question* asks about something that is not the *subject* of 1, so an *auxiliary*, **did**, must go before the *subject*, **Fred**, of 2 (« p 93):

    2   A: What did Fred cook? (*Not* x What Fred cooked? x; *Not* x What cooked Fred x)
            B: (Fred cooked) the meat.

The second question asks about the *subject* of 1, **Fred**, so the *question word*, **who**, is the *subject* of 3, and there are no changes in the *verb phrase* or in the word order:

3   A: Who cooked the meat? (*Not* ~~x Who did cook the meat? x~~)
    B: Fred (cooked the meat).

Question word questions are always made in one of these two ways[1], depending on whether they ask about the *subject* or about something else. Consider the following *statements*:

	subject	verb phrase	complement
4	Connie's mother	can play	the piano.
5	All three girls	work for	Mrs Black.
6	The boy with the cap	turned on	the old radio.
7	The money	was stolen	yesterday.

Questions corresponding to 4–7 that are about the *subject*:

	subject	verb phrase	complement
8	Who	can play	the piano?
9	Whose mother	can play	the piano.
10	How many girls	work for	Mrs Black.
11	Which boy	turned on	the old radio.
12	What	was stolen	yesterday?

Questions corresponding to 4–7 that are not about the *subject*:

	question word	auxiliary	subject	main verb
13	What	can	Connie's mother	play?
14	Who	do	all three girls	work for?
15	Which radio	did	the boy with the cap	turn on?
16	When	was	the money	stolen?

---

[1] With *main verbs* **am, is, are, was, were** there is no *auxiliary*. In *questions* about the *subject*, the word order is the same as the *statement* (17, 18); in *questions* that are not about the *subject*, the *subject* goes after the *verb* (19):

    17 Mrs White is the French teacher.
    18 Who is the French teacher?
    19 What is Mrs White?

For *questions* with *main verb* **have** « **110**.

159 **What** can you do?

What is a *question word*; it can be a *pronoun* (1–5) or a *determiner* (6, 7). When *pronoun* **what** is *subject*, the *verb* is normally *singular* (3). **What** can ask about the *subject* (2, 7) or about the *complement* (1, 3–6).

We use *pronoun* **what** to ask about things, e.g.

> 1 A: What's that?
>   B: It's a German dictionary.
> 2 What is happening outside that shop?
> 3 What do those machines make?

We also use *pronoun* **what** to ask about jobs or roles of people, e.g.

> 4 C: What does Mrs Brown do?
>   D: She's a bus driver.
> 5 E: What's that man?
>   F: He's the goalkeeper.

We use *determiner* **what** to ask about things, (and only occasionally about people), e.g.

> 6 What food are we going to take?
> 7 What organisation helps blind people?

What cannot be *postmodified* by an **of** *phrase*, so *Not* x what of your books x (but » **which 161**).

Learners should notice the two **what** *questions*:

> 8 What do you call this in English? (*Not* x How x; « » **163**.4)
> 9 What is this called in English? (*Not* x How x)

Also » **169.**

160 **Who** is coming to the party?

Who is a *question word*; it is only a *pronoun*. It can ask about the *subject* (1, 2) or the *complement* (3, 4). When **who** is *subject*, the *verb* is normally *singular* (1), even if we expect a *plural* answer. In formal style **whom** replaces **who** when it refers to the object (3, 4 and « **59**).

We use **who** to ask about people, e.g.

> 1 A: Who's coming tonight?
>   B: Sally and her brothers.
> 2 C: Who scored the first goal?
>   D: Tom did.
> 3 E: Who(m) did you consult?
>   F: (I consulted) Dr Brown.

4   G: Who(m) is she going to paint?
      H: (She's going to paint) my mother.

Who cannot be *postmodified* by an **of** *phrase*, (so *Not* x who of your friends x; « » **which 161**.8).

Also » **169**.

161 Which came first, the chicken or the egg?

Which is a *question word*; it can be a *pronoun* (1, 3–5, 8) or a *determiner* (2, 6, 7). *Pronoun* **which** can be *postmodified* by an **of** *phrase* (3, 4, 8). **Which** can ask about the *subject* (1–4, 8), and then the *verb* is *singular* (1, 3) or *plural* (4) depending on our expectation; or it can be about the *complement* (5–7).

We use **which** to ask for identification of particular people and things, usually from a limited choice, e.g.

1   A: There are three hats here. Which is yours?
      B: That green one.
2   C: Which car won the race? You've mentioned four of them.
      D: ·The one driven by Fittipaldi.
3   E: Which of these books is the best?
      F: The one with the yellow cover.
4   G: Which of these books are about art?
      H: These in this bookcase.
5   I: I'll give her two of my drawings. Which would she like?
      J: I think she'd like these two.
6   K: We don't have to check all the machines. Which ones have already been checked?
      L: All the old ones.
7   M: Which authors are included in the list?
      N: Only the most famous ones.
8   Which of your friends helped you the most?

Also » **169**.

162 Whose mother is in hospital?

Whose is a *question word*; it is a *determiner* (1a, 2, 3), or a *pronoun* (1b, 4) if we can understand the *noun* from the context. **Whose** can ask about the *subject* (2) or the *complement* (1, 3, 4).

We use **whose** to ask about possession (and other relationships, « **10**), and the answer is a *possessive noun phrase*, e.g.

1a A: Whose shoes are these?
   B: (They're) mine.
1b A: Whose are these shoes?
2 C: Whose children are making that noise?
   D: Mrs White's, as usual.
3 E: Whose umbrella have you borrowed?
   F: My wife's.
4 G: We're not going to visit Bob's relatives.
   H: Whose are you going to visit then? (i.e. whose relatives)
   G: Susan's.

Also » **169**.

163 **How** do you make an omelette?

How is a *question word*; it is an *adverb*. **How** alone cannot ask about the *subject* (but » **165**). We use **how** alone to ask about manner or process, e.g.

1 A: How do you stay so slim?
   B: By not eating too much.
2 C: How are you going to travel?
   D: By train.
3 E: How was she dressed?
   F: Very simply.
4 How do you say 'very, very big' in English? (« » **159**.8, 9)

164 **How's** your sister?
What's your sister like?

Here, **how** asks about health, i.e. a temporary state only (1); **what . . . like** asks about appearance (2) or character (3), i.e. permanent features, e.g.

1 A: How's your sister?
   B: She's fine, thanks.
2 C: What's your sister like?
   D: She's tall and dark; in fact she's quite like me. (i.e. similar to me; « **105**)
3 E: What's your boss really like?
   F: Well, he's very efficient, but he's not very pleasant.

We can also use **what . . . like?** of things, e.g.

4 G: I saw that new film last night.
   H: What was it like?
   G: A bit boring, to be honest.

165 **How many** people came ?
How much can you carry ?

How many and **how much** are *question words*. **How many** goes with
a *plural count noun* (1, 3) and **how much** goes with a *mass noun* (2,
4–6); they can be alone, i.e. without a *noun*, if we can understand the
noun from the context (1, 5, 6). They can ask about the *subject* (1, 2)
or the *complement* (3–6).

We use **how many** and **how much** to ask about quantity, e.g.

    1   Twelve inches make a foot, but how many make a yard?
          (i.e. how many inches)
    2   A: How much rain fell last month?
          B: About 6 centimetres.
    3   How many sandwiches should we make?
    4   How much oil does your motorbike use?

We also use **how much**, without a *noun*, to ask about the cost of
something, e.g.

    5   B: How much are these apples? (*Not* x What are x)
          C: 45 pence a pound.
    6   D: How much did those jeans cost? (or What did)
          E: About 20 pounds.

Also » **169.**

166 **How tall** are you ?

We use *question word* **how** with *adjectives* (1a, 2) and *adverbs* (3, 4) to
ask about the degree or extent of something, e.g.

    1a   A: How high is the Eiffel Tower?
          B: 300 metres.
    2   C: How heavy are those cases?
          D: Oh, they're not heavy.
    3   E: How well do they sing?
          F: (They sing) beautifully.
    4   G: How fast can she swim?
          H: (She can swim) quite fast.

In asking about measurements, there is often an alternative structure
with **what** and the corresponding *noun*, which is more formal style, e.g.

    1b What height is the Eiffel Tower?

The common correspondences are:

How big ...?	What size ... ?	How high ... ?	What height ... ?
How long ... ?	What length ... ?	How tall ... ?	What height ... ?
How wide ... ?	What width ... ?	How thick ... ?	What thickness ... ?
How heavy ... ?	What weight ... ?	How deep ... ?	What depth ... ?
How old ... ?	What age ... ?	How fast ... ?	What speed ... ?

167 How far have you walked ?
How long did the concert last ?

We use *question word* **how far** to ask about distance, and **how long** to ask about duration. **Far** and **long** are **any** *words*, the corresponding **some** *words* are **a long way** (2) and **a long time** (3). **How long** can normally have **for** at the end of the sentence (3, 4), (but also « **101e**).

1   A: How far have you walked?
     B: Not far. About half a mile.
2   C: How far is it to Edinburgh?
     D: It's a long way.
3   E: How long have you been waiting (for)?
     F: A long time.
4   G: How long will the Johnsons be away (for)?
     H: Not long. About three or four days.

We use **how long ago** to ask about a past time measured from now, e.g.

5   I: How long ago was the Crimean War?
     J: It was over a hundred years ago, I think.

168 How often do you wash your hair ?

We use *question word* **how often** to ask about frequency. Frequency is often expressed as a number of times during a certain period, e.g. **twice a month** (1) or **three times a day** (3). We usually use **once** for 'one time' and **twice** for 'two times'. The relation to the period is expressed with **a(n)**[1] or, in formal and technical style, **per**[1] (4):

1   A: How often do you clean your shoes?
     B: About twice a month.
2   C: How often do the buses go into town?
     D: About every ten minutes. (i.e. with intervals of ten minutes)
3   E: How often do you have to take these tablets?
     F: Three times a day.
4   This wheel turns at 15,000 revolutions per minute.

If we ask about a total number of times, we use **how many times,** e.g.

    5 G: How many times did you try?
         H: Six or seven.
    6 I: How many times have you written?
         J: Only once.

----

[1] **A(n)** and **per** are also used to relate money, e.g. **£4,000 a year** (or **per**), **65 pence a pound** (or **per**), etc., and for speeds, e.g. **75 miles an hour** (or **per**), **120 kilometres an hour** (or **per**).

169 **Who(m)** would you like to speak **to** ?

Preposition **to,** although it is at the end of the sentence, in meaning goes with *question word* **who**(m). **Whom** is more formal than **who,** and in formal style there is also an alternative structure, with the same meaning:

    1 To whom would you like to speak?

Question words that can go with *prepositions* are: **what** (2, 5), **who**(m) (3, 6), **whose** (4, 8), **which** (9), **how many** (10) and **how much** (11).

In general, both simple *prepositions*, e.g. **at, with,** and compound ones, e.g. **on top of,** can go at the end of the *question* and at the beginning. However, with **be** the *preposition* can only go at the end (2); we also prefer the *prepositions* of *prepositional verbs* (» **191**) at the end (3, 4):

    2 What is this button here for? (*Not* x For what x)
    3 Who(m) are you laughing at?
    4 Whose cat are they looking for?

Here are some examples with both alternatives: the first alternative is always more frequent, the second is formal style:

    5 What do they make margarine out of? (or Out of what)
    6 A: Who(m) did John sit behind? (or Behind whom did)
         B: (John sat behind) Mary.

Who(m) did John sit behind?

Who sat behind John?

Compare 6 with 7, where **who** is *subject*:

    7   C: Who sat behind John?
          D: Nobody (sat behind John).
    8   Whose typewriter did you type it on? (or On whose)
    9   Which plant do they get sugar from? (or From which)
  10   How many are you preparing dinner for? (or For how many)
  11   How much money can you manage with? (or With how much)

We ask about origin with **from** at the end of a *question* with **where**, e.g.

  12   Where do you come from? (i.e. What is your home country or town?)

To ask about destination, **to** is optional at the end of a *question* with **where** (» **171**).

170 **When** do the shops open?

Question word **when** is an *adverb*. We use **when** to ask about time, e.g.

    1   A: When is your birthday?
          B: In March.
    2   C: When do the children come home?
          D: At about 4 o'clock.
    3   E: When are you going to Glasgow?
          F: Next week.
    4   G: When did your son have that accident?
          H: In 1977.

To ask about a specific time, we can use **what time** instead of **when**, e.g.

    5   What time do the children come home? (« » 2)

171 **Where** do you live ?

Question word **where** is an *adverb*. We use **where** to ask about situation at a place (1, 2) and **where**, with optional **to**, for destination, i.e. movement to a place (3, 4):

  1 A: Where are Susan's boots?
    B: In the cupboard.
  2 C: Where does Mrs Townsend work?
    D: At the supermarket.
  3 E: Where did you drive (to) yesterday?
    F: (We drove to) a little village in the country.
  4 G: Where are you going (to) this weekend?
    H: (We're going to) Epsom.

172 **Why** did you shout ?
What are they queuing **for** ?

Question word **why** is an *adverb*. **Why** can ask about cause (1) and about purpose or intention (2). **What . . . for** asks about purpose or intention (3, 6, 7), but not cause. **Why** *questions* about cause usually have answers with *because* (1); **why** *questions* about purpose or intention usually have answers with a **to** *clause* (2). *Questions* with **what . . . for** can have answers with a **for** *phrase* (4, 6) or a **to** *clause* (5, 7, and also » 252):

  1 A: Why is everything so wet?
    B: Because we've got a burst water pipe.
  2 C: Why did your brother go to town?
    D: (He went to town) to buy a new saw. (*Not* x̶ ̶f̶o̶r̶ ̶t̶o̶ ̶x)
  3 What is Ann saving for?

Possible answers to 3 are 4 and 5:

  4 (She's saving) for a holiday.
  5 (She's saving) to have a holiday. (*Not* x̶ ̶f̶o̶r̶ ̶t̶o̶ ̶x)
  6 E: What have you made all these cakes for?
    F: For the children's party.
  7 G: What are you going to the shops for?
    H: (I'm going to the shops) to buy some paint. (*Not* x̶ ̶f̶o̶r̶
       t̶o̶ ̶x)

173 Animals **are forbidden**.

This is a *passive* sentence. It contains a *past participle*, **forbidden**, but this does not refer to past time. We express the relation to time with a form of the *verb* **be**, (or **get**, » below). There is a *passive verb phrase* corresponding to every *active verb phrase* (« Table 4, p 93); the form of the *verb* **be** in the *passive* is the same as the form of the *verb* in the corresponding *active* sentence:

	active	*passive*	Table 4 p 93
present simple	**takes**	**is** taken	2
past simple	**took**	**was** taken	4
modal	**may¹ take**	**may¹ be** taken	6
present perfect simple	**has taken**	**has been** taken	8
past perfect simple	**had taken**	**had been** taken	10
present progressive	**is taking**	**is being** taken	12
past progressive	**was taking**	**was being** taken	14
modal perfect	**may¹ have taken**	**may¹ have been** taken	16
infinitive	**(to) take**	**(to) be** taken	22
perfect infinitive	**(to) have taken**	**(to) have been** taken	24
-ing *form*	**taking**	**being** taken	28
perfect **-ing** *form*	**having taken**	**having been** taken	30
	used² to take	**used² to be** taken	
	is going to take	**is going to be** taken	

¹ or **can, could, will, would, should, might, must** or **ought to.**

² or **have, has,** or **had.**

The *subject* of an *active* sentence, e.g. **they** in 1, **Val** in 3, corresponds to the *agent phrase* in the *passive* sentence, e.g. **by them** in 2, **by Val** in 4. The *object* of an *active* sentence, e.g. **trouble** in 1, **some pictures** in 3, corresponds to the *subject* of the *passive* sentence (2, 4). In a *passive* sentence, the *verb* is *singular* (2) or *plural* (4) depending on the *subject*:

1   They cause trouble. (*active*)
2   Trouble is caused by them. (*passive*; **is** because of **trouble**)
3   Val takes some pictures. (*active*)
4   Some pictures are taken by Val. (*passive*; **are** because of **some pictures**)

The relation of each *passive verb* form to time is the same as the corresponding *active verb* form, (see the examples below, and compare with the relevant sections given). As in an *active* sentence, we use the first *auxiliary* to make *statements* with **not** (5, 8, 13) and *questions* (7, 10, 15):

5   This can't be mended very easily. (« » **112**)
6   Strange sounds could be heard from upstairs. (« » **113**)
7   Will the work be finished by tomorrow? (« » **117**)
8   The complaints mustn't be encouraged. (« » **124**)
9   All these parts will have to be renewed. (« » **125**)
10   Is their car being mended? (« » **138**)

11 These vases are all painted by hand. (« » **141**)
12 Over 500 letters have been received. (« » **146**)
13 That house wasn't built last year. (« » **150**)
14 The men were being watched all the time. (« » **151**)
15 Had the traffic lights been installed? (« » **153**)

Every *passive* sentence contains information that corresponds to an *active* sentence, e.g.

16 Experts check our products. (*active*)
17 Our products are checked by experts. (*passive*)

Although they contain the same information, *active* and *passive* are not exactly equivalent. First, not all *passive* sentences have an *agent phrase*, e.g. **by experts.** This is particularly common in scientific and technical texts, where we want to sound objective (18), and also in those cases when the *agent* is either unknown or unimportant (5–15):

18 A sample of powder A was divided into three parts. One part was dissolved in dilute hydrochloric acid and was heated to a temperature of 85° C.

Second, when we use an *agent phrase*, which is relatively infrequent, it is usually because the *agent* is the new information in the context, e.g.

19 Have you heard about Mrs Bingham? She was knocked down by a motorbike.
20 A: What will happen to us when we get to the airport?
    B: You will be met by one of our representatives.

Adverbs of manner often go before the *past participle* (21, 22), but frequency *adverbs* go in *mid-position* (23):

21 They were generously rewarded. (or rewarded generously)
22 The luggage has been carefully checked. (or checked carefully)
23 The luggage has never been checked.

In informal style you will sometimes meet **get** instead of **be** in *passive* sentences, with the same meaning, e.g.

24 They got caught by the night watchman. (or They were caught)
25 When will this get put together? (or this be put)

However, **get** sometimes sounds strange, so when in doubt students should use **be** for all *passives*.

There is also a structure with **get** ('become' » **225**) plus a *past participle* that acts as an *adjective*, e.g.

26 Children often get tired of expensive presents. (i.e. become tired)
27 They are getting interested in reading. (i.e. becoming interested)

Notice also the expressions **get dressed** ('dress'), **get washed** ('wash') and **get married** ('marry'), which are more frequent than the simple *verb*, e.g.

> 28   You should get washed before you get dressed.
> 29   When did they get married?

Note: While almost all *passive* sentences correspond to an *active* sentence (but » **176**), there are types of *active* sentence that have no corresponding *passive*:

a) *Intransitive* sentences, i.e. *active* sentences with no *direct object* (» **219–225**), e.g.

> 30   The train arrived early.
> 31   They were working in the street.
> 32   Tom later became a pilot.

b) Sentences with the *relational verbs* **be, belong, cost, depend, exist, fail, fit, have, hold, lack, matter, measure, weigh** (« **142**), e.g.

> 33   Mrs Bryant is an expert.
> 34   Betty has a very nice flat.
> 35   This jar holds two kilos.

c) Not all *prepositional verbs* (» **191**) can appear in *passive* sentences; for individual *verbs*, learners should consult a good dictionary.

174 Susan was given a bicycle.

This is a *passive* sentence. The *subject*, i.e. **Susan**, is the *indirect object* of the corresponding *active* sentences:

> 1a   Someone gave Susan a bicycle. (» **215**)
> 1b   Someone gave a bicycle to Susan. (» **213**)

All the *verbs* in **213** can appear in *passive* sentences of this type, e.g.

> 2a   Mary has been offered a new job. (i.e. Someone has offered Mary a new job)
> 3a   You will be handed a small packet. (i.e. Someone will hand you a small packet)

There is also a *passive* sentence whose *subject* is the *direct object* of the corresponding *active* sentence, but this type is not so frequent, e.g.

> 2b   A new job has been offered to Mary
> 3b   A small packet will be handed to you.

Also » **213**.

175 I'm going to **have my hair cut** tomorrow.

Structure:

A *subject*	B **have**[1]	C *noun phrase*	D *past participle*	
1 Susan	had	her car	washed.	
2 We	must have	that clock	repaired. (« » **206**.4)	
3 She	has	her dresses	made	in Paris.

Columns C and D are equivalent in meaning to a *passive* sentence e.g. in 1 **her car was washed**, and in 3 **her dresses are made in Paris**. The *subject* in Column A decides the action of C and D, but does not do it, e.g.

4 The Smiths had their house painted. (i.e. somebody – not the Smiths – painted the Smiths' house)

5 The Browns painted their house. (i.e. the Browns painted their house themselves)

We can use the same structure, almost always with **had**, when something (usually unpleasant and unexpected) happens to the *subject* (Column A), i.e. in these cases the person does not decide the action, e.g.

6 My wife had her passport stolen. (i.e. somebody stole my wife's passport)

7 They had their flat broken into. (i.e. somebody broke into their flat)

---

[1] You will sometimes also meet **get** in this structure.

Also « **57**.

176 Her mother **is said to be** a brilliant linguist.

This is a *passive* sentence; the structure is:

	subject	**be**	*past participle*	**to** *clause*
1a	Some fish	are	believed	to navigate by sound.
2	She	is	known	to be sympathetic.
3	James	was	reported	to have been killed.

Past participles that we use in this structure include: **acknowledged, admitted, alleged, assumed, believed, considered, expected,** feared, felt, found, imagined, known, meant, presumed, reported, rumoured, said, seen, shown, stated, supposed, understood. In all cases (except **rumoured**) there is a corresponding *active* sentence with a **that** *clause*, e.g.

> 1b People believe (that) some fish navigate by sound.
> 2b People know (that) she is sympathetic.

In addition, with **believe, expect, imagine** and **show**, there is another alternative structure with similar meaning, e.g.

> 1c People believe some fish to navigate by sound.

For **supposed** also « **119, 132**.

177 Peter said, 'I like the park.'
Peter said (that) he liked the park.

'**I like the park**' is *direct speech*, i.e. these are the exact words that Peter used: **(that) he liked the park** is *reported speech*, i.e. it reports what Peter said, but does not use his exact words. Conjunction **that** is optional in *reported speech*; there is no comma (,) after the reporting word, e.g. **said**.

Reported speech must communicate the message of the original words, but the circumstances of the report will usually be different from those of the *direct speech* in three ways:

a) the speaker that reports and his or her listener(s) may be different from the speaker of the original words and his or her listener(s);

b) the place may be different;

c) the time may be different.

Each of these differences requires changes so that the *reported speech* communicates accurately the meaning of the original words.

First, if the people are different, then *personal pronouns, possessive adjectives*, etc., must change to fit the new situation, e.g. **I** cannot refer to the same person when used by different people. Second, if the place is different, then words related to the place, e.g. **here, there, this, these, that, those, come, go, bring, take**, must change, e.g. **this street** cannot refer to the same street when used in different streets. Third, if the difference in time changes the meaning of the original message, then we must change *verb* forms and *adverbials* of time, e.g. **Today is Peter's birthday** cannot refer to the same thing if it is spoken on different dates. *Reported questions* (» **178**) and *imperatives* (» **179**) also need differences in the structure of the sentence, but for *statements* the necessary changes are mostly common sense, e.g.

Example A

Speaker: Barry; Listener: Janet; Place: a cinema; Date: 18 May 1976:

    1   I love you. (*direct speech*)

Speaker: Janet; Listener: Janet's sister; Place: Janet's home; Date: 18 May 1976:

    2   Barry says he loves me. (*reported speech*; « » 1, 3)

Speakers: Janet (A) and Janet's sister (B); Place: Janet's home; Date: 25 July 1976:

    3   A: Barry has stopped going out with me.
           B: But he said he loved you. (*reported speech*; « » 1, 2)

Example B

Speaker: Robin; Listener: Lesley; Place: London; Date: Tuesday 16 June 1980:

    4   Last week I went to Bristol and next week I'm going to Cardiff. (*direct speech*)

Speaker: Lesley; Listener: Frank; Place: London; Date: Thursday 18 June 1980:

    5   Robin said he went to Bristol last week and next week he's going to Cardiff. (*reported speech*; « » 4, 6)

Speaker: Lesley; Listener: Eva; Place: Cardiff; Date: 17 August 1980.

    6   (I met Robin in London on 16 June.) He said he'd been to Bristol the week before and the week after he was coming here. (*reported speech*; « » 4, 5)

When a change in time is sufficient to require a change in the *verb* and the *adverbial* (e.g. 3, 6), then there are certain *reported* forms that correspond to *direct* forms:

Adverbials

direct speech	reported speech
now	then
today	that day, the same day
tomorrow	the next day, the following day
yesterday	the day before, the previous day
this week, month, etc.	that week, month, etc.
last week, month, etc.	the week, month, etc., before; the previous week, month, etc.
next week, month, etc.	the following week, month, etc.
a week, month, etc., ago	a week, month, etc., before

These correspondences apply when the *reported speech* is widely separated in time from the *direct speech*, but obviously **tomorrow** will become **today** if it is reported the day after, not **the next day,** and so on.

Verb forms

Present forms change to *past* forms:

direct speech	reported speech
he is	(that) he was
he is working	(that) he was working
he works	(that) he worked
he has worked	(that) he had worked
he has been working	(that) he had been working
he can work	(that) he could work
he will work	(that) he would work
I shall work	(that) he would work
shall I work?	(if) he should work
he may work	(that) he might work
he is going to work	(that) he was going to work
he has (got) to work	(that) he had to work

Past forms can change to *past perfect* forms:

he worked	(that) he had worked (or he worked)
he was working	(that) he had been working (or he was working)

Past perfect forms, *past modals*, etc., do not change:

he had worked	(that) he had worked
he had been working	(that) he had been working
he could[1] work	(that) he could[1] work
he ought to work	(that) he ought to work
he used to work	(that) he used to work

[1] or **would, should** or **might.**

Must has two alternatives:

he must work	(that) he must work, (that) he had to work

These correspondences apply when the *reported speech* is widely separated in time from the *direct speech,* but the changes must always be used with common sense (« 1–6). Notice in particular that it is often not necessary to change *past* forms to *past perfect* forms. The *past simple* and the *past progressive* can remain unchanged if the meaning is clear.

Reported speech rarely repeats everything that was in the *direct speech*. There is always a tendency to express the attitude or general meaning with the reporting word, e.g. **claim, suggest,** etc. (» **209**), **dare, urge,** etc. (» **216**), **advise, warn,** etc. (» **217**), and then keep the *reported speech* short. For example, imagine that someone makes a ten-minute speech on the advantages of a certain plan, ending with the words: 'For all these reasons I strongly recommend you to give the plan your serious consideration.' It is unlikely that the *reported speech* will take ten minutes, repeating the whole of what was said; instead we would perhaps say:

> 7 After explaining the plan's advantages, he urged us to give it serious consideration.

Exclamations and greetings are also reported with reporting words that suggest the meaning, rather than with words that correspond to the *direct speech*, e.g.

	direct speech	*reported speech*
8	A: Hullo! How are you? B: Fine, and you? A: Very well, thanks.	We exchanged greetings.
9	Merry Christmas!	She wished us a merry Christmas.
10	Thank you.	We thanked her.
11	Thank you very, very much indeed.	She thanked us profusely.
12a	She's grown so tall!	They remarked on how tall she
12b	How tall she's grown!	had grown.
13	What lovely flowers!	She commented on the lovely flowers.

178 'Where do you live?' she asked. She asked where he lived.

'**Where do you live?**' is a *direct question*; **where he lived** is a *reported question*. The changes for speakers, place and time are the same as for *reported statements* (« **177**). *Reporting* words for *questions* are **ask, enquire, want to know** and **wonder,** (but not **say** or **tell,** » **180**). *Reported questions* do not have a comma (,) after the *reporting* word, and they do not have a *question* mark (**?**), but they may be part of a *question* (3, 6).

If a *direct question* has a *question word*, e.g. **who, when,** then the *reported question* also has that word (1–6). If the *question word* is *subject* of the *direct question* (1–3; « **158**), then the word order of the *reported question* is the same, e.g.

    1   She asked who cooked the meat. (or who had cooked)
        (*direct question:* 'Who cooked the meat?'; « **158**.3)
    2   They were wondering how many would come.
        (*direct question:* 'How many will come?')
    3   Are you asking what happened?
        (*direct question:* 'What happened?')

If the *question word* is not the *subject* of the *direct question* (4–6; « **158**), then the *reported question* has the word order: *question word + subject + verb phrase*, i.e. like a *statement*, not like a *direct question*, e.g.

    4   She asked what Fred cooked. (or Fred had cooked)
        (*direct question:* 'What did Fred cook?'; « **158**.2)
    5   He wants to know how much he can take.
        (*direct question:* 'How much can I take?')
    6   Did they enquire where Ann was working?
        (*direct question:* 'Where is Ann working?')

If the *direct question* has no *question word*, then the *reported question* has **if** (or **whether**) + *subject + verb phrase*, i.e. like a *statement*, not like a *direct question*, e.g.

    7   He enquired if they worked. (or whether)
        (*direct question:* 'Do they work?')
    8   He enquired if they worked or studied. (or whether)
        (*direct question:* 'Do they work or study?')
    9   They asked if I was English. (or whether)
        (*direct question:* 'Are you English?')
   10   They asked if I was English or Scots. (or whether)
        (*direct question:* 'Are you English or Scots?')

When the *question word* is not the *subject* (4–6) or when there is no *question word* (7–10), the *reported question* cannot have the *verb* form or the word order of a *direct question*, (so e.g. *Not* x~~She asked what did Fred cook~~ x, « » 4; *Not* x~~He wants to know how much can he take~~ x, « » 5; *Not* x~~He enquired did they work~~ x, « » 7 *Not* x~~He enquired did they work or study~~ x, « » 8).

However, *main verb* **be**, especially with a long *subject*, sometimes has the word order of the *direct question*, e.g.

   11a He asked us what the most important points were.
   11b He asked us what were the most important points.

Yes and **no** are reported with the *subject* and the appropriate *auxiliary*, e.g.

   12   He enquired if they worked. I said (that) they did./I said (that) they didn't. (*Not* x~~I said (that) yes/I said (that) no~~ x)

13 They asked if I was English. I said (that) I was./I said (that)
    I wasn't.

Note: A request or an instruction may be in the form of a *question*, but
it will usually be reported as if it was an *imperative* (» **179**).

The structure of *reported questions* is the same as the structure of *noun
clauses* (» **181**).

179 'Stand up!' she said.
She told me to stand up.

'**Stand up!**' is a *direct imperative*; **me to stand up** is a *reported
imperative*. We use the *reported imperative* form to report requests,
orders, instructions, etc., whether the *direct* form is an *imperative* or a
question, etc.

Reported speech is often shorter than the corresponding *direct speech*
(« **177**.7). With requests, orders, instructions, etc., we indicate the
attitude of the *direct speech* with the reporting word, e.g. **ask, order,
beg, tell** (but not **say**, » **180**), e.g.

direct imperative	*reported imperative*
1 'Come without fail!'	He ordered me to come.
2 'Come!'	He told me to come. (*Not* x said x)
3 'You should come.'	He advised me to come.
4 'Could you come?'	He asked me to come.
5 'Please, please come.'	He begged me to come.

For the structure of *reported imperatives* » **216**.

180 She said (that) she was hungry.
She told them (that) she was hungry.

Say and **tell** have similar meaning, but go with different structures:

a) With a *noun phrase* (1–3) or a *noun clause* (4) we use **tell** with an
indirect object (1, 4) or without (2, 3):

   1 She told the class a story. (*Not* x said x)
   2 He always tells good jokes. (*Not* x says x)
   3 Did he tell the truth? (*Not* x say x)
   4 Jack told us what had happened. (*Not* x said us x)

157

Occasionally, especially referring to one piece of information, you will meet **say** without an *indirect object* (5) or with **to** and an *indirect object* (6):

  5 Jack said what had happened. (*Not* x told x; « » 4)
  6 Did Mr Mackey say anything to you? (*Not* x tell x)

b) In *direct speech* we use **say** (and other words, e.g. **shout, whisper,** etc.), but not **tell,** for *statements* (7), *imperatives* (8), greetings (9) and exclamations (10). **Say** can go before a *proper noun* (8) or after (7), but normally only after a *pronoun* (9, 10):

  7 'I'm coming,' Mary said. (*Not* x told x)
  8 'Be quiet!' said Mrs Swan. (*Not* x told x)
  9 'Hello!' she said. (*Not* x told x)
  10 'What pretty flowers!' he said. (*Not* x told x)

c) In *reported statements* we use either **tell** with an *indirect object* (11) or **say** without an *indirect object* (12):

  11 They told Kate (that) they would come. (*Not* x said Kate x)
  12 They said (that) they would come. (*Not* x told x)

d) In *reported imperatives* we can use **tell** (and other *verbs*, e.g. **ask, order,** etc.), but not **say** (« **179,** » **216**), e.g.

  13 She told her son to come home early. (*Not* x said x)

Say and **tell** cannot be used to report *questions* (« **178**).

181 Tell me **what I should do.**
Tell me **what to do.**

What I should do is a *noun clause*; the structure is the same as a *reported question* (« **178**), i.e. either the *question word* is *subject* of the *noun clause* (1, 3) or, if not, the *clause* has the word order: *question word + subject + verb phrase* (2, 4, 7, 9). These *noun clauses* can begin with any *question word*, e.g. **who, what, when, why, how,** etc., and also **whether** or **if**.

What to do is a *noun clause*; the structure is: *question word + to clause*. It has no *subject*, and we use this type of *noun clause* when we can understand the unmentioned *subject* from the context (5, 6, 8, 10). These *noun clauses* can begin with any *question word* except **why**, and also **whether**, but not **if**.

A *noun clause* does not have a question mark (**?**), but it can be part of a *question* (6, 9). *Noun clauses* can be *subject* (1, 2, 5), *object* of a *verb* in **212** or **218** (3, 4, 6), *complement* of **be** (7, 8), and can go after a *preposition* (9, 10):

1   What happens depends on the weather. (**What** is *subject* of **happens; what happens** is *subject* of **depends**)
2   What we do depends on the weather. (**What** is *object* of **do; what we do** is *subject* of **depends**)
3   We discussed who might be interested. (**Who** is *subject* of **might be; who might be interested** is *object* of **discussed**)
4   We discussed who(m) they might approach. (**Who(m)** is *object* of **approach; who(m) they might approach** is *object* of **discussed**)
5   How to do it was never considered.
6   Did they tell you who(m) to ask for?
7   The question was whether she was sane.
8   The problem is where to begin.
9   Are you interested in where she comes from?
10   We don't need to worry about how much money to take.

182 Ask **whoever you like.**

Whoever you like is a *noun clause*. **Whoever** (1) and **whatever** (2) are *pronouns*; **whichever** is a *determiner* (3a) or a *pronoun* (3b). A *noun clause* with one of these words can be *subject* (2), *object* (3), or can go after a *preposition* (1). Similarly, there are *adverbs* **wherever** (4), **whenever** (5) and **however** (6), which go in *clauses* that act as *adverbials*.

All these words go at the beginning of the *clause*; they emphasise freedom of choice, or that it does not matter which specific person, thing, place, time or manner is involved, e.g.

1   Give a list of rules to whoever comes. (i.e. it does not matter who comes; give them all a list)
2   Whatever they say has to be accepted. (i.e. it does not matter what they say; it has to be accepted)
3a   A: Which paper shall I buy?
      B: Bring whichever paper looks most interesting.
3b   B: Bring whichever looks most interesting.
4   Here are the keys to the school. Take your parents wherever you want. (i.e. choose freely where)
5   They can come whenever it is convenient for them. (i.e. they can choose freely when)
6   They'll not solve the problem, however hard they try. (i.e. it does not matter how hard they try)

183 **There** is some butter in the fridge.

Here, **there** is an *introductory subject*; it does not mean 'in that place'. It serves to introduce a sentence that expresses the existence of somebody or something, normally indefinite (10–13), at a particular place or time. **There** normally goes with a *singular verb* if the nearest *noun* is *singular* (1, 2, 5) and with a *plural verb* if the nearest *noun* is *plural* (3, 4, 6). *Question word* **what** goes with a *singular verb* (1). These sentences must have an *adverbial* of place or time except when the situation can be understood from the context (2, 4):

1. A: What is there in your room? (*Not* x What's there x; « » 29)
   B: There's a bed and two chairs (in my room). (or are)
2. C: Is there any hot water? (i.e. in this house)
   D: Yes, there is./No, there isn't.
3. How many cinemas are there in your home town?
4. D: There aren't any more cakes, are there? (i.e. in the kitchen)
   E: Yes, there are./No, there aren't.
5. There's a book and four pencils in this box. (or are)
6. There are four pencils and a book in this box.

We can use introductory **there** and *adverb* **there** in the same sentence:

7. There are some matches over there.

The *adverbial* can also be of time, e.g.

8. There are two express trains on Sundays.
9. Every summer there is a big festival.

We do not use introductory **there** to refer to the position of a definite *noun phrase* (11, 13). Compare:

10. There's a black cat in the garden.
11. Our cat is in the garden.
12. There are some brown shoes in the kitchen.
13. Molly's shoes are in the kitchen.

The *noun phrase* can be followed by an **-ing** *form*, which describes something that is in progress at the time, e.g.

14. There's a brown jacket hanging on that hook.
15. Are there some workers talking to the manager?

It is important to remember that introductory **there** goes with all forms of the *verb* **be**, except *progressives*, e.g.

16. There may be some foreign students here. (« **116**)
17. Will there be many people at the party? (« **117**)
18. There used to be just fields round here. (« **121**)
19. There must be a better way to do this. (« **124**)
20. There must have been a fire here. (« **128**)

21 This year there haven't been any strikes so far. (« **146**)
22 Was there enough petrol in the car? (« **150**)
23 There doesn't seem to be any bread left. (» **188**)
24 If there were more tea towels, I'd help you. (» **241**)

We use this structure with a number and an **of** *phrase* to talk about a number of people (or sometimes things) in a particular situation, e.g.

25 F: Is it a large class?
   G: No, there are only eight of us. (**We are only eight** is unusual here)
26 H: How many were there of you in the group?
   I: (There were) about twelve (of us).

Sentences like 27 and 28, which talk about the position of an *indefinite noun phrase* but without introductory **there**, are rare and often sound strange; learners should avoid them:

27 A bed and two chairs are in my room. (« » 1)
28 How many cinemas are in your home town? (« » 3)

However, a **what** *question* can omit **there**, e.g.

29 What's in your room? (« » 1)

184 It was very cold in Paris.

Here, **it** is an *introductory subject* in a sentence that refers to weather or light conditions. **It** does not refer to another *noun phrase*, but it cannot be omitted:

1 It's very cloudy today. (*Not* x ~~Is very~~ x)
2 It was a wonderful day for a picnic. (*Not* x ~~Was a~~ x)
3 A: Was it raining when the accident happened?
   B: No, but it was dark and foggy.
4 It was perfect weather for a country walk.

185 It's five miles to the nearest petrol station.

Here, **it** is an introductory *subject* in a sentence that refers to distance; the *verb* is *singular*. **There** is not possible in these sentences:

1 A: How far is it from here to Buxton? (*Not* x ~~is there~~ x)
   B: It's about 30 miles. (*Not* x ~~There are~~ x)
2 How many miles was it from the airport to the hotel?
3 It's a long way to Tipperary.

186 It took us two months to paint the whole flat.

Structure:

	A It	B take	C (*noun phrase*)	D period of time	E **to** *clause*
1	It	takes		ten minutes	to walk to the station.
2	It	will take	the girls	about an hour	to get everything ready.
3a	It	took	me	three months	to finish the book.

A *personal pronoun* in Column C must be in the *object* form.

We use this structure to talk about the period of time that is necessary (for someone) to do something, e.g.

4a It didn't take them long to get here.
5   A: How long does it take to boil potatoes?
     B: (It takes) about 20 minutes if they're small.

There is an alternative structure with the person as *subject*, e.g.

3b I took three months to finish the book.
4b They didn't take long to get here.

187 It's great that she's out of hospital.

That she's out of hospital is a **that** *clause*, i.e. **that** plus a *main clause*. **That** *clauses* can act as *object* of certain *verbs* (1; » **209, 217**), *complement* of **be** (2), and *complement* of an *adjective*[1] (3). **That** is usually optional, but » 4a.

1   The manager explained (that) things might get worse.
2   Our feeling is (that) he will not pass the exam.
3   We are surprised (that) Mary hasn't written.

We can also use **that** *clauses* as *subject*, and then **that** cannot be omitted (4a), but we normally prefer to use *introductory subject* **it** and put the **that** *clause* last (4b, 5, 6):

4a That they came at all was surprising.
4b It was surprising (that) they came at all.
5   It is terrible that their leader has refused.
6   It was obvious (that) they had told a lie.

---

[1] *Adjectives*, e.g. **surprised** (3), need a *preposition* if they are followed by a *noun phrase* (« **79**), but not here because a **that** *clause* can never follow a *preposition*.

188 It seems (that) they are out.

Structure:

	A It	B *verb* *phrase*	C **that** *clause*
1a	It	seems	(that) we have paid too much.
2a	It	appeared	(that) they had stolen almost everything.
3a	It	happens	that she hates fish.

Only these three *verbs* can go in Column B; **that** is optional with **seem** and **appear**.

Seem and **appear** talk about the apparent truth of the rest of the sentence, e.g.

4   It seems (that) there's going to be an election. (or appears; i.e. apparently there's going to be an election)

Happen in this structure talks about something that is important to the situation but which has not been considered, e.g.

5   A: I think I'll serve fish when Helen comes.
     B: It happens that she hates fish.

There is an alternative structure, with the same meaning:

1b   We seem to have paid too much.
2b   They appeared to have stolen almost everything.
3b   She happens to hate fish.

In this structure **happen** can also refer to something that is true by chance, e.g.

6   Do you happen to have a pen that I can borrow? (i.e. Have you by chance a pen)

189 It's easy to make a mistake.

Structure:

	A It	B be	C *adjective* or *noun phrase*	D **to** *clause*
1a	It	was	fun	to watch the programme.
2	It	will be	a pleasure	to be interviewed by her.
3a	It	is	difficult	to pronounce the words.

Words that go in Column C include: **difficult, easy, entertaining,**

fascinating, fun[1], funny[1], good, great, hard, impossible, nasty, nice, a nuisance, pleasant, a pleasure, a problem, no problem, no trouble, unpleasant, and others.

The **to** *clause* is the real *subject* of the *verb* **be** (B), but if we put the *subject* first, we use an **-ing** *clause*, e.g.

> 1b Watching the programme was fun.
> 3b Pronouncing the words is difficult.
> 4a It's often hard to accept defeat.
> 4b Accepting defeat is often hard.

In all these sentences we understand the unmentioned *subject* of the **to** *clause* (D) or the **-ing** *clause* from the situation. We can also make this *subject* explicit with a **for** *phrase*, e.g.

> 5a It's often hard for children to accept defeat. (« » 4a)
> 5b Accepting defeat is often hard for children. (« » 4b)

When the **to** *clause* has a *direct object*, there is an alternative structure, e.g.

> 1c The programme was fun to watch.
> 5c Defeat is often hard for children to accept.

---

[1] **Fun** is a *mass noun*; it goes with *determiners* and *adjectives*, e.g. **not much fun, good fun, great fun,** etc. **Funny** is an *adjective* and can be *premodified* by *adverbs*, e.g. **very funny, quite funny,** etc.

PART 5

Types of complement

Introduction

A *main clause* has a *subject* and a *verb phrase*. The *complement* is what follows the *verb phrase*, and there are different types of *complement*:

a) *Direct object*, with optional *adverbial* (» **190–212**). Sentences with a *direct object* are called *transitive* sentences.

b) *Direct object* and *indirect object*, with optional *adverbial* (» **213–218**).

c) no *object*, with optional *adverbial*, etc. (» **219–225**). Sentences without an *indirect object* are called *intransitive* sentences.

190 Wendy **reads the newspaper** after supper.

This sentence is *transitive*, i.e. there is a *direct object*, **the newspaper**. Structure[1]:

	subject	*verb phrase*	*direct object*	*(adverbial)*
1	The teacher	is reading	that magazine	again.
2	Those boys	helped	me	yesterday.
3	She	speaks	good English.	
4	She	speaks	English	well.

Adverbials do not go between the *verb phrase* and the *direct object*, so *Not* x is reading again that magazine x (« » 1); *Not* x speaks well English x (« » 4).

The *direct object* corresponds to a *question* with **what** (« **159**) or **who** (« **160**), e.g.

    5   What is the teacher reading? (« » 1)
    6   Who did those boys help yesterday? (« » 2)

---

[1] This is the *active* structure; for the *passive* structure « **173**.

191 They are **looking for a key**.

Look for is a *prepositional verb*; this is a *transitive* sentence with *direct object* **a key**. *Prepositional verbs* must have the *preposition* in *transitive* sentences, i.e. when there is a *direct object* (1, 3, 5), and the *object* corresponds to a question with **what** or **who**. Some are also used, without a *preposition*, in *intransitive* sentences, i.e. without an *object*, with the same meaning (2, 4, 6; » **224**), e.g.

   1   A: Who is Mary listening so carefully to?
        B: (She is listening carefully to) the guide.
   2   Why is Mary listening so carefully?
   3   Was Paul waiting for the bus?
   4   Was Paul waiting?
   5   C: What did the salesgirl look at?
        D: She looked quickly at the price-list.
   6   The salesgirl looked quickly.

There are other *prepositional verbs*, e.g. **look for, consist of, deal with**, etc., which only appear in *transitive* sentences.

Some *prepositional verbs*, especially when they do not refer to movement or physical activity, can go in a *passive* sentence, e.g.

   7   The children are being looked after by their aunt. (i.e. the children's aunt is looking after them)
   8   The problem will be dealt with promptly. (i.e. someone will deal with the problem promptly)

But *Not* x The station was arrived at x. Students should consult a good dictionary for each *verb*.

There is another type of two-part *verb*, called a *phrasal verb* (» **194**, **221**). It is important to distinguish between the two types because there are important differences:

prepositional verbs	*phrasal verbs*
a) Only appear in *transitive* sentences (but « 1–6).	Some occur in *transitive* (» **194**), some in *intransitive* sentences (» **221**).
b) Not all can occur in *passive* sentences.	All *transitive* ones can occur in *passive* sentences (» **194**).
c) The *preposition* goes before the *object* (1, 3, 5).	With a *pronoun* the *particle* goes after the *object*; otherwise the *particle* can go before or after the *object* (» **194**).
d) *Adverbs* can go between the *verb* and the *preposition* (1, 5).	*Adverbs* cannot go between the *verb* and the *particle* (» **194**, **221**).

There is no simple way to distinguish between the two types, but when the second word is **after, at, for, of, to** or **with**, the *verb* is almost always *prepositional*.

The most common *prepositional verbs* are in the list of two- and three-part verbs in **260**.

192 Keep Britain tidy!

Structure[1]:

A	B	C	D
subject	*verb phrase*	*direct object*	*adjective*
1 They	have painted	the chairs	blue.
2 You	should cut	the sandwiches	thin.
3 Harry	laid	it	flat.

Some other typical *verb* and *adjective* combinations that go in this structure are:

beat something flat
boil something dry
colour something red, etc.
get something clean, etc.
get somebody ready, etc.
hold something still, etc.
keep something dry, etc.

leave something dirty, etc.
make something safe, etc.
make somebody angry, etc.
set somebody free
tie something tight
wash something clean
wipe something dry

The *adjective* (D) is the *complement* of the *object* (C); it describes the state of the *object* after the action of the *verb*, e.g.

4 These new machines get the clothes very dry. (i.e. the clothes become very dry because of these new machines)
5 They painted the windows white and the doors cream. (i.e. the windows became white and the doors became cream)

We cannot normally put the *adjective* before the *object*, so *Not* x They painted white the doors x (« » 5)

---

[1] This is the *active* structure; examples of the *passive* structure are:

6 The chairs have been painted blue. (« » 1)
7 It was laid flat (by Harry). (« » 3)

193 Mike **took the glasses in**.
Mike **took in the glasses**.

There are two alternative structures[1]:

A subject	**B** verb phrase	**C** direct object	**D** adverb
1a Frances	took	her blouse	off.
2a Who	has put	the cat	out?
3a They	will bring	some soap	up.

E subject	**F** verb phrase	**G** adverb	**H** direct object
1b Frances	took	off	her blouse.
2b Who	has put	out	the cat?
3b They	will bring	up	some soap.

Object pronouns can only go in the first structure, i.e. Column C,

4   Frances took it off. (*Not* x off it x; « » 1a, 1b)
5   Who has put it out? (*Not* x out it x; « » 2a, 2b)

Adverbs that we use in these structures include: **in, out, up, down, on, off, back, forward, about, across, around, round, away, over.** Other *adverbs* of place, e.g. **here, outside, upstairs,** and *adverbials* of place, e.g. **on the chair, into the garden,** can only go in the first structure, e.g.

6   Bring the chairs here! (*Not* x here the chairs x)
7   We put the old table upstairs. (*Not* x upstairs the old table x)

In both structures the *adverb* describes the position of the *direct object* after the action of the *verb*, e.g. in 1, after the action, the blouse was off, i.e. off her body.

Adverbs of manner go either in *mid-position* (8) or last (9):

8   Frances quickly took her blouse off. (*Not* x took quickly x)
9   Frances took her blouse off quickly.

The *verb* **let** can be used in this structure, e.g.

10   There's someone at the door. Can you let him in? (i.e. let him come into the house)
11   The school let our children out early today. (i.e. let our children go out of the school)

¹ These are *active* structures; examples of the one corresponding *passive* structure are:

12   The cat has been put out. (« » 2)
13   Some soap will be brought up. (« » 3)

194 Sue **took the waist in**.
Sue **took in the waist**.

Here, **take in** is a *phrasal verb*; the sentences are *transitive*, with **the waist** as *direct object*. *Phrasal verbs* go in two alternative structures, i.e. the same two as in **193**, although an *object pronoun* can only go in the first (2, 4, 6). *Phrasal verbs* are combinations of certain short *verbs* and certain *adverbs*, which are called *particles*¹. Phrasal verbs often have several meanings, and the meanings are not a simple combination of the meanings of the *verb* and the *particle*:

1   The company turned our offer down (or turned down our offer; i.e. rejected our offer)
2   The company turned it down. (*Not* x down it x; « » 1)
3   The boys have put the fire out. (or put out the fire; i.e. extinguished the fire; « » **193**.2)
4   The boys have put it out. (*Not* x out it x)
5   Who will bring the children up? (or bring up the children; i.e. educate and care for the children; « » **193**.3)
6   Who will bring them up? (*Not* x up them x)

There is no absolutely clear line between the *verb + adverb* of **193** and *phrasal verbs*. The same two words, e.g. **put out, bring up**, can have several meanings ranging from a simple combination of their separate meanings (**193**.2, 3) to something totally different (3, 5 above). Students should consult a good dictionary.

Adverbs of manner go in *mid-position* (7a) or last (7b):

7a The company abruptly turned our offer down. (*Not* x turned abruptly x)
7b The company turned our offer down abruptly.

Sentences 1–7 are *active* structures; examples of the one corresponding *passive* structure are:

8   Our offer was turned down (by the company). (« » 1)
9   The fire has been put out (by the boys). (« » 3)

---

¹ The most common particles are: **away, back, down, in, off, on, out, over** and **up**.

For a comparison with *prepositional verbs* « **91**; for *phrasal verbs* in *intransitive* sentences » **221**.

The most common *transitive phrasal verbs* are in the list of two- and three-part *verbs* in **260**.

195 We must **face up to** the facts.

Face up to is a *phrasal-prepositional verb*. These *verbs* consist of a *verb* + a *particle* + a *preposition*; they only occur in *transitive* sentences, i.e. with a *direct object*, e.g.

1   Are you looking forward to[1] your visit?
2   We can't put up with his stupid ideas.
3   That school is going to do away with uniforms.

The most common *phrasal-prepositional verbs* are in the list of two- and three-part *verbs* in **260**.

------

[1] Since *to* is a *preposition* here, the only form of a *verb* that can follow it is an **-ing** *form* (« **79**[2], **199**[1]), e.g.

4   I'm looking forward to hearing from you.

For *prepositional verbs* « **191**; for *phrasal verbs* « **194**, » **221**.

196 Everybody **calls me Kate**.

Structure[1]:

	A *subject*	B *verb phrase*	C *direct object*	D *noun phrase* or *noun clause*
1	The committee	appointed	Miss Briggs	secretary.
2	They	have named	their boat	'Happy Days'.
3	Mr Creed	made	the club	what it is today.

Verbs that we use in this structure include: **appoint, call, crown, declare, elect, make, name.** An *object pronoun* can go in Column C, but not in Column D.

The *noun phrase* or *clause* (D) is *complement* of the *direct object* (C); they both refer to the same person or thing, and D is usually the result of the action of the *verb* (B), e.g.

4   My name is Catherine, but everybody calls me Kate. (i.e. uses the name Kate for me)
5   It was his secretary that made the business a success. (i.e. the business was a success because of the secretary)

------

[1] This is the *active* structure; examples of the *passive* structure are:

6   Miss Briggs was appointed secretary (by the committee). (« » 1)
7   Their boat has been named 'Happy Days'. (« » 2)

197 I consider your plan (to be) unwise.

Structure[1]:

	A subject	B verb phrase	C direct object	D (to be)	E adjective or noun phrase
1	They	found	his behaviour		very strange.
2	His wife	declares	her position	(to be)	impossible.
3	We	knew	them	to be	cowards.

Verbs that we use in this structure include: **believe, call, consider, declare, feel, find, guess, imagine, know, like, prefer, report, suppose, think, want. Call** and **find** go without **to be; feel, guess,** and **know** tend to go with **to be. To be** is optional with the other *verbs*.

The *phrase* (E) is *complement* of the *object* (C). The *subject* (A) expresses his or her attitude, belief, etc., regarding the relation of the *phrase* (E) to the *object* (C), e.g.

4   I have always wanted her (to be) happy.
5   Did they believe his ideas (to be) mistaken?
6   She felt it to be a waste of time.

---

[1] This is the *active* structure; examples of the *passive* structure are:

7   Her position was declared (to be) impossible. (« » 2)
8   They were known to be cowards. (« » 3)

Also « **192.**

198 We **want a rest.**
We **want to rest.**

Certain *verbs* can either have a *noun phrase* (1, 3, 5) or a *to clause* (2, 4, 6) as *direct object*. They include: **afford, arrange, attempt, (can't) bear[1], begin[1], cease, chance, choose, claim, commence[1], continue[1], decide, demand, deserve, desire, determine, dread[1], (can't) endure[1], expect, fail, hate[1], intend[1], learn, like[1], love[1], manage, mean** ('intend'), **neglect, offer, omit, plan, prefer[1], prepare, promise, propose[1], refuse, regret, remember, seek, (can't) stand[1], start[1], swear, threaten, try, undertake, want.** With a **to** *clause*, **not** goes before **to** (2).

1   A: What did she choose?
    B: She chose a blouse of pink satin.
2   C: What did she choose to do?
    D: She chose not to pay the fine.

3   Did Tony demand an interview with the manager?
4   Did Tony demand to speak to the manager?
5   Frank doesn't deserve promotion.
6   Frank doesn't deserve to be promoted.

To goes alone if we can understand the rest of the *clause* from the context, e.g.

7   E: Have you ever eaten oysters?
     F: No, but I'd like to. (*Not* x I'd like x)

---

[1] These *verbs* have an alternative structure with an -**ing** *form* (» **200**).
For **need** « **134**.

199 Don **enjoys helping people**.

Structure:

	A *subject*	B *verb phrase*	C (**not**)	D *direct object:* -**ing** *clause.*
1	Mike	stopped		smoking at New Year.
2	We	enjoy	not	having anything to do.
3	Sheila	couldn't help		hearing the argument.

Verbs that go in Column B include: **admit, avoid, consider, delay, deny, detest, discontinue, dislike, enjoy, face, fancy, finish, (can't) help, imagine, involve, keep (on), mind, miss, postpone, practise**[1], **recollect, recommend, risk, stop**[1], **suggest**. None of these *verbs* has an alternative structure with a **to** *clause*[1] as *object* (« **198**).

The -**ing** *form* (D) does not have progressive meaning; it can be a *verb* that does not normally have *progressive* forms (2, 3; « **142**). When the *verb* (B) is a *progressive* form, then there are two -**ing** *forms* in the sentence (5, 6):

4   Do you mind working in the corridor? (« » **201**.3)
5   We're thinking of going away this weekend. (*Not* x think to go x)
6   They are practising putting up their tents.

Note: **Need** and **want** ('need') are also used in this structure, but with *passive* meaning, e.g.

8   My shoes need mending. (i.e. need to be mended)
9   Do the plants want watering? (i.e. need to be watered)

> 7 Jim stopped to light his cigarette. (i.e. he stopped what he was doing in order to light his cigarette; « » 1)

For the two- and three-part *verbs* that go in this structure » **260**.

Also « **198,** » **200, 201, 202, 203, 205, 206.**

200 I love walking in the rain.

Structure:

	A *subject*	B *verb phrase*	C (not)	D *direct object:* -ing *clause*
1 2 3	Ann Dick She	hates began can't stand	not	having anything to do. drinking in the army. being told what to do.

Verbs that go in Column B include: (**can't**) **bear, begin, commence, continue, dread, endure, hate¹, intend, like¹, love¹, prefer¹, propose,** (**can't**) **stand, start.** All these *verbs* have an alternative structure with a **to** *clause* (« **198**). The -ing *form* (D) does not have progressive meaning; it can be a *verb* that does not normally have *progressive* forms (1, 4; « **142**). If the *verb* (B) is a *progressive* form, then we normally use the alternative structure with a **to** *clause* (6):

> 4 I don't like seeing children with nowhere to play. (or like to see)
> 5 Has Bill started taking an interest? (or started to take)
> 6 Is Bill starting to take an interest?

---

¹ With these *verbs* there can be a difference of emphasis: an -**ing** *clause* can emphasise the activity itself (7), while a **to** *clause* can emphasise the complete action (8):

> 7 I like washing dishes. (i.e. I like the activity)
> 8 I like to wash the dishes as quickly as possible. (i.e. I like to complete the activity)

To talk about a specific occasion in future time, we can only use a **to** *clause* with **would** and one of these *verbs* (9), although an -**ing** *clause* is possible if we refer to a general idea (10):

> 9 A: Would you like to play cards? (*Not* x like playing x)
>   B: I'd prefer to watch TV. (*Not* x prefer watching x)
> 10 In general I usually prefer watching TV to playing cards.

Also « **198, 199,** » **201.**

201 I didn't **like them whistling like that**.

Structure:

		direct object	
A *subject*	**B** *verb phrase*	**C** *noun phrase*	**D** -ing *clause*
1a The boss	understands	him	wanting to leave.
2a They	resented	my sister	insisting on a vote.
3 Do you	mind	them	working in the corridor? (« » **199**.4)

Verbs that we use in Column B include: **appreciate, (can't) bear, dislike, fancy, favour, hate, (can't) help, imagine, intend, justify, like, love, mind, miss, prefer, resent, (can't) stand, understand.** You will sometimes meet a *possessive* instead of a *noun phrase* (C), with the same meaning, e.g.

    1b The boss understands his wanting to leave.

    2b They resented my sister's insisting on a vote.

The -**ing** *form* (D) does not have *progressive* meaning; it can be a *verb* that does not normally have *progressive* forms (1, 4; « **142**). The *verb* (B) expresses an attitude towards the action (D) of someone (C):

    4   She hated them knowing her secrets. (i.e. hated the fact they they knew her secrets)

    5   I can't imagine Mrs Johnson helping us. (i.e. imagine a situation where Mrs Johnson helps us)

For the two- and three-part *verbs* that go in this structure » **260**.

Also « **200**, » **202**, **203**.

202 We **found my brother dancing in a nightclub**.

Structure[1]:

A *subject*	**B** *verb phrase*	**C** *direct object*	**D** -ing *clause*
1 This photo	shows	me	picking strawberries.
2 The police	caught	the boys	changing the numbers.
3 The Smiths	have kept	us	waiting an hour already.

Verbs that go in Column B include: **catch, depict, describe, find, keep, leave, paint, show, talk about, write about**. The **-ing** *form* (D) has *progressive* meaning here, i.e. the action (D) was in progress at the time of the action (B), e.g.

> 4   He painted her lying on a couch. (i.e. while she was lying)
> 5   We can't leave Sally working on her own. (i.e. while she is working)

He painted her lying on a couch.

---

[1] This is the *active* structure; examples of the *passive* structure are:

> 6   The boys were caught changing the numbers (by the police). (« » 2)
> 7   Sally can't be left working on her own. (« » 5)

Also « **199, 201,** » **203**.

203 My wife soon **got the fire going**.

Structure[1]:

A *subject*	B *verb phrase*	C *direct object*	D *-ing clause*
1 We	must stop	the news	leaking out.
2 The idea	started	everybody	talking at once.
3 The dog	sent	the glasses	flying.

Verbs that go in Column B are: **get, prevent, send, start** ('cause') and **stop**. **Stop** and **prevent** have optional **from** before the -**ing** *clause* (1, 5; « » **211**). **Get** has an alternative structure with a **to** *clause* (4). All the *verbs* mean 'cause to happen' or 'cause not to happen', e.g.

4   See if you can get the clock working. (or the clock to work)
5   Nobody can prevent him running away. (« » **211**.6)

___

[1] This is the *active* structure; the *passive* structure is possible only with **send**, e.g.

6   The glasses were sent flying (by the dog). (« » **3**)

204 I watched my cousin arrange some flowers.

Structure[1]:

	A *subject*	B *verb phrase*	C *direct object*	D *plain infinitive clause*
1	You	will see	the cuckoo	pop out.
2	They	didn't hear	the door	close.
3	Lucy	noticed	a woman	steal some gloves.

Verbs that go in Column B are: **feel, hear, notice, see, watch**. This structure emphasises a complete event, not the action in progress (» **205**), e.g.

4   We felt the table move. (i.e. the movement of the table; « » **205**.4)
5   The parents watched the children demonstrate their invention. (i.e. watched a complete demonstration; « » **205**.5)

___

[1] This is the *active* structure; only **see, hear** and **feel** can have a *passive* structure, which has a **to** *infinitive*, e.g.

6   The cuckoo will be seen to pop out. (« » **1**)
7   The table has been felt to move. (« » **4**)
Also » **206**.

205 We **watched a policeman directing traffic**.

Structure[1]:

A subject	**B** verb phrase	**C** direct object	**D** -ing clause
1 We	could hear	the girls	singing in the bathroom.
2 The crowd	watched	the lions	being fed.
3 Brian	has seen	someone	carrying a ladder.

Verbs that go in Column B include: **feel, hear, notice, observe, see, smell, watch**. The -ing *form* (D) has *progressive* meaning, i.e. the action was in progress when it was seen, heard, etc. (B) (« **204**), e.g.

> 4 Can you feel the train slowing down? (i.e. feel that the train is getting slower; « » **204**.4)
> 5 For a few minutes the parents watched the children demonstrating their invention. (i.e. while the children were demonstrating; « » **204**.5)

---

[1] This is the *active* structure; examples of the *passive* structure, which is usual only with **see, hear, notice** and **observe**, are:

> 6 The girls could be heard singing in the bathroom. (« » **1**)
> 7 Someone has been seen carrying a ladder. (« » **3**)

206 Onions always **make me cry**.

Structure[1]:

A subject	**B** verb phrase	**C** direct object	**D** plain infinitive clause
1 The teacher	made	everybody	write it again. (« » **216**.5)
2 They	will let	us all	bring a friend. (« » **216**.6)
3a I	was helping	Kate	clean the shoes.
4 We	must have[2]	someone	repair that clock (« » **175**.2)

Make, let and **have** cannot have a **to** *clause* after the *object*, although synonyms for **let**, e.g. **permit, allow,** and words with similar meaning to **make** and **have**, e.g. **get, force, cause,** must all have a **to** *clause*, (» **216**). A *passive* corresponding to **let** must have **allowed** or **permitted** (» **216**.10). **Help** can have a **to** *clause*, with the same meaning, e.g.

3b I was helping Kate to clean the shoes.

---

[1] This is the *active* structure; the *passive* structure is normally only used with **make**, and it then has a **to** *clause*, e.g.

    5   Everybody was made to write it again (by the teacher). (« » 1)

[2] **Have** is more frequent in a related structure, « **175**.

Also « **204**.

207 They **tried to open the door**.
They **tried opening the door**.

Try can go with a **to** *infinitive* or an **-ing** *form*, with different meanings. **Try to open** means 'see if you can open or not', i.e. it suggests that the thing is difficult and, in the *past*, that it was unsuccessful; **try opening** means 'open, and see if that produces the desired result', i.e. there is no difficulty in the thing itself, but there is doubt about whether it will solve another problem, e.g.

    1   They tried to open the door but it was impossible.
    2   A: How can we get rid of this smoke?
          B: Try opening the door. (i.e. open the door and then see if the smoke disappears)
    3   We tried to send them a telegram, but the post office was already closed.
    4   We couldn't contact them by phone, so we tried sending them a telegram. (i.e. we sent them a telegram to see if we could contact them)

They tried to open the door but it was impossible.

"How can we get rid of this smoke?"
"Try opening the door."

Remember and **forget** also have both these structures, with different meanings. **Remember to visit** means that memory leads to action; **forget to visit** means that bad memory leads to no action. **Remember visiting** and **forget visiting** refer to presence or absence of a memory of a previous event. **Forget** plus an **-ing** *form* is usually in a *negative* sentence (8).

> 5 I remembered to post the letter this morning. (i.e. my memory was good this morning, and I posted the letter)
> 6 I remember posting letters for my mother when I was only three or four years old. (i.e. I now have a memory of that)
> 7 I'm sure that Jack will forget to come. (i.e. he will not come because of his bad memory)
> 8 I'll never forget seeing their car disappear over the edge. (i.e. I will always have a memory of that event)

If we have no memory of a previous event, we use **not remember** plus an **-ing** *form*, e.g.

> 9 I don't remember giving her any money. (i.e. I have no memory now of that event; *Not* x I forget giving x)

Regret also has both these structures, with different meanings, e.g.

> 10 I regret to say that she is unsuitable. (i.e. I am sorry but I must now say that she is unsuitable)
> 11 I regret saying that she was unsuitable. (or having said; i.e. I am sorry now that I said that she was unsuitable)

Go on also has both these structures, with different meanings, e.g.

> 12 Before the coffee break we were talking about pollution, and after the coffee break we went on talking about pollution. (i.e. continued the same thing)
> 13 Before the coffee break we were talking about pollution, and after the coffee break we went on to talk about multinational companies. (i.e. we moved on to a different subject)

208 Would you **like a book to read**?

Structure:

	A *subject*	B *verb phrase*	C *direct object*	D **to** *infinitive*	E *(noun phrase)*
1	I	would like	a magazine	to look at.	
2	Barry	hasn't had	anything	to eat.	
3	Jack	brought	his brother	to help	us.
4	She	wants	one of us	to clean	the windows.

Verbs that go in Column B include: **bring, fetch, give (someone), have (got), like, love, need, prefer, send, take, want.**

If there is no *noun phrase* (E), then the *direct object* (C) is also the *object* of the **to** *verb*, e.g.

> 5 I need somebody to love. (i.e. somebody that I[1] can love; « » 8)
>
> 6 Sally didn't bring any warm clothes to wear. (i.e. clothes that she[1] could wear)

[1] We understand the unmentioned *subject* of the **to** *infinitive* from the context. If this *subject* is not clear, then we make it explicit with a **for** *phrase*, e.g.

> 7 Sally didn't bring any clothes for the girls to wear. (i.e. clothes that the girls could wear)

If there is a *noun phrase* (E), then the *direct object* of the sentence (C) is the unmentioned *subject* of the **to** *infinitive*, then the *noun phrase* (E) is the *object* of the **to** *infinitive*, e.g.

> 8 I need somebody to love me. (i.e. somebody that can love me; « » 5)
>
> 9 They sent a man to mend the boiler. (i.e. a man that was going to mend the boiler)

209 I realised (that) it was too late.

Many *verbs* can have a **that** *clause*, with optional **that**, as *direct object*. They include: **accept, acknowledge, add, admit[1], agree, allege, announce[1], answer, argue, arrange, ask, assume, beg, believe[2], boast, calculate, claim, complain[1], confess[1], consider, decide, declare, demand, demonstrate[1], deny, discover, doubt, dream, expect[2], explain[1], fear, feel, find (out), forget, gather, guess, hear, hold, hope, imagine[2], insist, judge, know, learn, mean, note, notice, observe, presume, promise, propose, prove[1],**

realise, regret, remark, remember, reply, report[1], request, say, see, show, suggest[1], suppose[2], suspect, swear, think[2], understand, whisper, wish. Many of these *verbs* are used to report statements (1, 2; « **177**):

> 1 The young man admitted (that) he had stolen.
> 2 Our neighbours claim (that) the fence belongs to them.
> 3 Chris hadn't forgotten (that) he had already mentioned it.
> 4 Did he prove (that) he could do it quicker?

---

[1] These *verbs* can also have **to** + an *indirect object*, i.e. a person, immediately after the *verb*, e.g.

> 5 The young man admitted to us (that) he had stolen. (« » 1)
> 6 Did he prove to the inspectors (that) he could do it quicker? (« » 4)

[2] These *verbs* are often used with **not** when the meaning is really that the **that** *clause* is *negative*, e.g.

> 7 I don't expect (that) I'll pass. (i.e. I expect that I won't pass)
> 8 He doesn't think (that) they went. (i.e. he thinks that they didn't go)

For two-part *verbs* that can be followed by a **that** *clause* » **260**. Also « **188**, » **217**.

210 I think **so**.
We hope **not**.

Here, *adverbs* **so** and **not** replace a **that** *clause* (« **209**), so when it is *positive* (1, 2), **not** when it is *negative* (3, 4). The *subject* is often I or another *personal pronoun*. *Verbs* that have two *negative* forms are: **believe, expect, imagine, suppose** and **think**, e.g.

I believe so.	I don't believe so.	I believe not.
I expect so.	I don't expect so.	I expect not.
I imagine so.	I don't imagine so.	I imagine not.
I suppose so.	I don't suppose so.	I suppose not.
I think so.	I don't think so.	I think not.

The first *negative* form is more frequent; the second is formal style. *Verbs* that have only one *negative* form are: **assume, guess, hope,** and **presume**, e.g.

I assume so.		I assume not.
I guess so.		I guess not.
I hope so.		I hope not.
I presume so.		I presume not.

Notice also the expression with **be afraid,** and also **it seems** and **it appears:**

I'm afraid so.		I'm afraid not.
It seems so.	It doesn't seem so.	It seems not.
It appears so.	It doesn't appear so.	It appears not.

1 A: Are they coming tomorrow?
   B: I hope so. (i.e. I hope (that) they're coming tomorrow)
2 They're not sure whether the film is tonight, but they think so. (i.e. they think (that) it is tonight)
3 C: Will they get here early?
   D: I don't expect so. (i.e. I expect (that) they will not get here early)
4 E: Has the post come yet?
   F: I'm afraid not. (i.e. I'm sorry but it hasn't come yet)

211 The police **warned us of the danger.**

Structure[1]:

	A subject	B verb phrase	C direct object	D prepositional phrase
1	My cousin	told	me	about her neighbours.
2	My wife	will explain	the problem	to your father.
3	Jack	reminded	his friends	about the party.

The *prepositional phrase* cannot go before the *object* (so *Not* x We will explain (to) your father the problem x; « » 2)

Many *verbs* go in this structure; some common expressions are (**s/b =** **somebody** or **someone, s/t = something**): **accuse s/b of s/t, add s/t to s/t, blame s/b for s/t, blame s/t on s/b, compare s/b with s/b, compare s/t with s/t, congratulate s/b on s/t, convict s/b of s/t, explain s/t to s/b, introduce s/b to s/b, prevent s/b from s/t, provide s/b with s/t, provide s/t for s/b, put s/t to s/b, remind s/b of s/t, say s/t to s/b, spend s/t on s/t, supply s/b with s/t, supply s/t to s/b, tell s/b about s/t, thank s/b for s/t, warn s/b of s/t, waste s/t on s/t.** For the meanings of these and other expressions in this structure, students should consult a good dictionary.

Notice that the following *verbs* often have an **-ing** form as the *noun* in the *prepositional phrase*: **accuse s/b of doing, blame s/b for doing, convict s/b of doing, dissuade s/b from doing, excuse s/b for doing, forgive s/b for doing, keep s/b from doing, prevent s/b from doing** (« 203), **punish s/b for doing, save s/b from doing,**

scold s/b for doing, stop s/b from doing (« 203), **suspect s/b of doing, trick s/b into doing, warn s/b against doing,** e.g.

4   They accused him of stealing a fur coat.
5   I hope you'll excuse me for being late.
6   Nobody can prevent him from running away. (« » **203**.5)

---

[1] This is the *active* structure; examples of the *passive* structure are:

7   The problem will be explained to your father (by my wife). (« » 2)
8   His friends were reminded about the party. (« » 3)
9   He was accused of stealing a fur coat. (« » 4)

For a similar structure with *preposition* **as** « **105**.

212 Find out who did it.

Structure:

A *subject*	B *verb phrase*	C *direct object: noun clause* (« **181**)
1 Jill	was wondering	whether the baby would cry.
2 I	can't remember	if they came or not.
3 She	is learning	which things to concentrate on.
4 Mr Booth	will decide	how many catalogues to order.

Verbs that go in Column B include: **ask, care, consider, decide, discover, discuss, doubt** (with **if** or **whether** only), **enquire, examine, explain, find out, finish, forget, guess, imagine, know, learn, mind, notice, observe, perceive, remember, repeat, see, show, suggest, take, tell, think** (**about**)**, understand, wonder.**

5   I'd like to know where they're hiding.
6   Can you understand why she is so angry?
7   Jenny explained how to get to the station. (i.e. how he[1] should get to the station)
8   Have you thought about when to start? (i.e. when we[1] should start)

---

[1] or somebody else; in a *noun clause* without a *subject*, we understand the unmentioned *subject* from the context.

Also » **218**.

213 James **sent a letter to his cousin**.

Structure[1]:

	A *subject*	B *verb phrase*	C *direct object*	D to	E *indirect object*
1 2 3	Tom Simon She	gave offered lends	the flowers his collection her records	to to to	Mary. (« » **215**.1) the school. (« » **215**.2) anybody.

Verbs that go in Column B include: **award, bring, give, grant, hand, leave** (by legacy), **lend, offer, owe, pass, pay, promise, read, return, sell, send, show, teach, tell, throw, write.** *Pronouns* for both *objects* are in the *object* form, e.g.

    4   Tom gave them to Mary. (« » 1)
    5   Tom gave the flowers to her. (« » 1)
    6   Tom gave them to her. (« » 1)

This structure means that there is a direct transfer of the *direct object* to the *indirect object*, e.g.

    7   They brought the apples to my mother. (i.e. they gave the apples to my mother at the time; « » **214**.7)
    8   My grandfather left his furniture to me. (i.e. in his will; « » **214**.8)

_____

[1] This is an *active* structure. For the alternative *active* structure » **215**; for the *passive* structure « **174**.

214 We **bought a cassette for my mother**.

Structure[1]:

	A *subject*	B *verb phrase*	C *direct object*	D for	E *indirect object*
1 2 3	Helen Mrs Black The boys	will book made have chosen	the seats some cakes the records	for for for	her parents (« » **215**.3) the children (« » **215**.4) our club.

Verbs that go in Column B include: **book, bring, build, buy, call, choose, cook, do, fetch, find, gather, get, knit, leave** (not by legacy), **make, order, prepare, save, spare.** *Pronouns* for both *objects* are in the *object* form, e.g.

4 Helen will book them for her parents. (« » 1)
5 Helen will book the seats for them. (« » 1)
6 Helen will book them for them. (« » 1)

We use this structure when the *direct object* is intended for the *indirect object*, but the transfer is later, e.g.

7 They brought the apples for my mother. (i.e. intended for her, but not given to her at the time; « » **213**.7)
8 A messenger came and left this letter for Mr Brooks. (« » **213**.8)

---

[1] For the alternative *active* structure » **215**.

215 James **handed his wife the paintbrush**.

Structure[1]:

A subject ·	B verb phrase	C indirect object	D direct object
1 Tom	gave	Mary	the flowers. (« » **213**.1)
2 Simon	offered	the school	his collection. (« » **213**.2)
3 Helen	will book	her parents	the seats. (« » **214**.1)
4 Mrs Black	made	the children	some cakes. (« » **214**.2)

Verbs that go in Column B include: **award, book, bring, build, buy, call, choose, cook, cost, do, envy, fetch, find, forgive, gather, get, give, grant, hand, knit, leave, lend, make, offer, order, owe, pass, pay, prepare, promise, read, save, sell, send, show, spare, teach, tell, throw, write.** *Pronouns* for both *objects* are in the *object* form, e.g.

5 Tom gave her the flowers. (« » 1)
6 Tom gave Mary them. (« » 1)
7 Tom gave her them. (« » 1)

For the meaning of this structure « the alternative structures in **213** and **214**.

---

[1] This is an *active* structure; for the alternative *active* structure « **213**; for the *passive* structure « **174**.

216 Mother **asked David to telephone**.

Structure[1]:

A *subject*	B *verb phrase*	C *indirect object*	D (not)	E *direct object:* **to** *clause*
1	Tell	Jill		to come here.
2 They	advised	Mr Buck	not	to move it.
3 The bank	will force	you		to agree.
4 I	would like	him		to go to the post office.

This structure is sometimes called *accusative* + *infinitive*.

Verbs that go in Column B include: **advise, allow, ask, beg, bribe, cause, challenge, command, compel, dare, direct, drive, encourage, expect, forbid, force, get, hate, help, instruct, intend, invite, leave, like, love, mean, oblige, order, permit, persuade, prefer, remind, request, require, set, teach, tell, tempt, trust, urge, want, warn, wish.** A *pronoun* in Column C must be in the *object* form (4, 6, 7). There is no alternative structure with a *that clause,* so *Not* x Tell Jill that she comes here x (« » 1); *Not* x The bank will force you that you agree x (« » 3).

We use many of these words to report commands, requests, etc. (« 179). We also use this structure to express obligation (4), permission (5) and instruction (6) e.g.

> 5 The teacher got everybody to write it again. (« » **206**.1)
> 6 They will allow us all to bring a friend. (« » **206**.2)
> 7 The course taught us to work more effectively.

To can go alone if we can understand the rest of the *clause* from the context, e.g.

> 8 Mr Buck wanted to move the tree, but they advised him not to. (*Not* x they advised him not x; « » 2)

---

[1] This is the *active* structure. The *passive* structure is possible with all the *verbs* except **like, love, prefer, want** and **wish,** e.g.

> 9 Mr Buck was advised not to move it. (« » 2)
> 10 We were all allowed to bring a friend. (« » 6)

217 The guide **informed us (that) it was closed**.

Structure[1]:

	A *subject*	B *verb phrase*	C *indirect object*	D *direct object:* **that** *clause*
1	They	told	me	(that) she was ill.
2	Jack	will remind	the others	(that) Friday is a holiday.
3	Mrs Boot	has shown	her son	(that) it is quite easy.

Verbs that go in Column B include: **advise, assure, convince, inform, persuade, promise, remind, satisfy, show, teach, tell, warn. That** is optional. We use several of these *verbs* to report *statements* (« **177**.)

---

[1] This is the *active* structure; the *passive* structure is possible with the *indirect object* becoming the *subject* of the *passive* sentence, e.g.

    4   I was told (that) she was ill. (« » 1)
    5   The others will be reminded (that) Friday is a holiday. (« » 2)

218 They **showed my brother how to make omelettes**.

Structure[1]:

	A *subject*	B *verb phrase*	C *indirect object*	D *direct object:* *noun clause* (« **181**)
1	Mary	asked	me	where my wife was.
2	The note	reminded	my son	who he should ask for.
3	We	were teaching	Lucy	how to swim.
4	Our lawyer	will advise	us	whether to write again.

Verbs that go in Column B include: **advise, ask, inform, remind, show, teach, tell.**

In a *noun clause* without a *subject* (3–6), we understand the unmentioned *subject* from the context, e.g.

    5   The clerk told us where to go. (i.e. where we should go)
    6   The clerk asked us where to go. (i.e. where he should go)

¹ This is the *active* structure. The *passive* structure is possible with the *indirect object* becoming the *subject*, e.g.

    7   I was asked where my wife was. (« » 1)
    8   Lucy was being taught how to swim. (« » 3)

Also « **212**.

219 My sister often **sleeps** until 11 or 12 o'clock.

This sentence is *intransitive*, i.e. there is no *object* of the *verb* **sleeps**. Structure:

A *subject*	B *verb phrase*	C *(adverbials)*
1 Her friends 2 The girls 3 Some old men	came danced were listening	(by bus). (while the men clapped). (carefully).

Some *verbs*, e.g. **come** (1), are normally used only in *intransitive* sentences. Some *verbs*, e.g. **dance** (2) are used in *intransitive* or *transitive* sentences with little or no difference in meaning, e.g.

    4   The girls danced a flamenco while the men clapped their hands. (« » 2)

The girls danced a flamenco while the men clapped their hands.

Some *verbs*, e.g. **listen** (3), are used only in *intransitive* sentences but they have a corresponding *prepositional verb* (« **191**) for use in *transitive* sentences, e.g.

    5   Some old men were listening to the radio. (« » 3)

There are also certain common pairs of *verbs*, one for *intransitive* and the other for *transitive* sentences:

	intransitive		*transitive*
6	The bus arrived late.	7	The bus reached the hotel late.
8	The pens lay on the floor.	9	We laid the pens on the floor.
10	The sun rises in the east.	11	The cranes slowly raised the sunken ship.
12	We won.[1]	13	We beat our most important rivals.

---

[1] **win** can have a thing as *object*, but not a person, e.g. **win two matches, win the cup, win a battle,** etc. (*Not* ~~x we won our rivals x~~)

220 The paint **ran out** while we were asleep.

The paint ran out while we were asleep.

This sentence is *intransitive* (« **219**); **ran** is the *verb* and **out** is an *adverb* of place. All *adverbs* of place, e.g. **down, off, over,** can go in this structure; the *adverb* describes the position of the *subject* after the action of the *verb*, i.e. the paint ran and then the paint was out (of the paint tin).

1 Fred went out at 10 o'clock. (i.e. out of the building)
2 My son came up with a cup of tea. (i.e. up the stairs)
3 The baby seemed safe in the pram, but later he fell out. (i.e. out of the pram)

Adverbs of manner go in *mid-position* (4a) or last (4b):

4a The paint slowly ran out.
4b The paint ran out slowly. (*Not* x ~~ran slowly out~~ x)

221 The time **ran out** before I had finished.

This sentence is *intransitive* (« **219**); **run out** is a *phrasal verb*. *Phrasal verbs* are combinations of certain short *verbs* and certain *adverbs*, which are called *particles*[1]. *Phrasal verbs* often have several meanings, but the meaning is never a simple combination of the meanings of the *verb* and the particle. There is no absolutely clear line between the *verb* plus *adverb* of **220** and *phrasal verbs*. The same two words, e.g. **go out, come up**, etc., can have several meanings, ranging from a simple combination of their separate meanings (« **220**.1–3) to a totally different meaning, e.g.

1 The fire went out at 10 o'clock. (i.e. the fire died; « » **220**.1)
2 Your name came up at the meeting. (i.e. your name was mentioned; « » **220**.2)
3 At first they were friends, but later they fell out. (i.e. they argued and separated; « » **220**.3)

Adverbs of manner go in *mid-position* (4a) or last (4b), e.g.

4a Your name suddenly came up.
4b Your name came up suddenly. (*Not* x ~~came suddenly up~~ x)

---

[1] The most common *particles* are: **away, back, down, in, off, on, out, over**, and **up**.

All the common *intransitive phrasal verbs* are in the list of two- and three- part *verbs* in **260**.

For a comparison with *prepositional verbs*, « **191**; for *phrasal verbs* in *transitive* sentences, « **194**.

222 We all had to **stand clear**.

We use certain *verbs*, e.g. **stand**, with appropriate *adjectives*, e.g. **clear**, but without an *object*. Typical combinations are: **arrive late, come close, fly low, hold tight, jump high, lie flat, sit still, stand clear, stop short, wear thin**.

The *adjective* describes the state of the *subject* after the action of the *verb*, e.g.

1   Connie moved closer and then stood still.
2   These socks have worn thin very quickly.
3   Did you have to lie flat on the ground?

Also « **192**.

223 Do you often **go fishing**?

Structure:

A *subject*	B **go**	C **-ing** *clause*
1 I	have been¹	sailing only once.
2 Some people	go	shopping every day.
3 We	aren't going	skiing this weekend.

Verbs that go in Column C include: **camping, cycling, dancing, diving, flying, gliding, hiking, hunting, jogging, potholing, rambling, riding, running, sailing, shooting, shopping, skating, skiing, surfing, swimming, walking, waterskiing.**

We use this structure to talk about these activities considered as sports or hobbies or pastimes; in this meaning this structure is more common than the *verb* alone, e.g. **have sailed** in 1.

On the other hand, we cannot use this structure to talk about a means of transport (4) or to talk about how well or badly someone does the activity (5, 6):

4   A: How did you get to the village?
      B: We walked. (*Not* x we went walking x here)
5   Mary dances beautifully. (*Not* x goes dancing x here)
6   I don't swim as well as you do. (*Not* x go swimming x here)

---

¹ For **been** as the *past participle* of go « **146** *Note*.

224 I'm **waiting to play**.
I'm **waiting for my turn**.

I'm waiting to play is an *intransitive* sentence (« **219**); **I'm waiting for my turn** is a *transitive* sentence (« **191**). The *preposition*, e.g. **for**, is necessary if there is an *object* (1, 3), but it cannot be used with a **to** *clause* (2, 4). *Verbs* that have both these possibilities include: **agree**

(**to/with**), **aim** (**at**), **bother** (**about**), **care** (**for**), **consent** (**to**), **hesitate** (**about**), **hope** (**for**), **long** (**for**), **reckon** (**on**), **trouble** (**about**), **volunteer** (**for**), **wait** (**for**), **wish** (**for**), e.g.

1 Don't bother about the mess.
2 Don't bother to clean up the mess.
3 A: What did he volunteer for?
   B: (He volunteered for) the special mission.
4 C: What did she volunteer to do?
   D: (She volunteered) to send us all the magazines we need.

Note: Other *verbs* that can go in an *intransitive* sentence with a *to clause*, but which have no corresponding *prepositional verb*, include: **endeavour, pretend, proceed** and **tend**, e.g.

5 They were pretending not to see us.

225 Later Ken **became quite famous**.

We use certain *verbs*, e.g. **become**, to relate an *adjective*, e.g. **famous**, to the *subject*, e.g. **Ken**. There are different groups of these *verbs*.

Become and **get** are used to describe a change of state (1, 2). You will sometimes meet **come, fall, go, grow** and **turn** (3, 4) with this meaning, but you can always use **become** or **get**, e.g.

1 The weather will become warmer. (i.e. change so that it is warmer)
2 Did your shoes get dirty? (i.e. change so that they were dirty)
3 Milk turns sour quickly in hot weather. (or becomes)
4 In a big city snow soon goes grey. (or becomes)

Become can also relate a *noun phrase* to the *subject*; this expresses a change of state or role, e.g.

5 I think she will become a good actress.
6 After the children were born, he became a better husband.

Remain, stay and **keep** are used to describe a continuation in the same state, e.g.

7 Vegetables stay fresh in a fridge. (or remain, or keep; i.e. continue to be fresh)

Seem and **appear** are used for general appearance; for appearance to a specific sense we use **look, sound, smell, taste** and **feel**. All these verbs can be followed by an *adjective* (8–10) and also by a *clause* with **as if** (» 244). **Seem** and **appear** can also be followed by a **to** *clause* (8, 11), but not usually by a *noun phrase* alone; **seem, look, sound,**

smell, taste and **feel** can also be followed by a *prepositional phrase* with *preposition* like (12, 13):

8   The idea seemed (to be) quite sensible. (i.e. it was apparently sensible)

9   The meat smells delicious. (i.e. appears delicious to the nose)

10 Does this surface feel too rough? (i.e. appear too rough to the touch)

11 They appear to be doctors. (or seem to be doctors; *Not* x appear doctors x, *Not* x seem doctors x)

12 She looked rather like a tourist.

13 This tastes like real home-made soup.

For **seem** and **appear** also « **188.**

PART 6

Co-ordination and subordination

Introduction

Main clause and *subordinate clause*

A *main clause* is one that alone can make a sentence, e.g.

    1   Paul came early.
    2   The manager brought all the papers into the office.

On the other hand, a *subordinate clause* is one that cannot alone make a sentence, e.g.

    3   if it rains
    4   to give them the news
    5   because he's crazy

Subordinate clauses must be joined to a suitable *main clause* to make a sentence, e.g.

    6   If it rains, we'll stay at home. (« » 3)
    7   We rang them up to give them the news. (« » 4)
    8   He behaves like that because he's crazy. (« » 5)

However, in informal style, *subordinate clauses* are used as answers to *questions*, when the *main clause* can be understood from the context, e.g.

    9   A: Will you stay at home?
         B: If it rains. (« » 3)
   10   C: Why did you ring them up?
         D: To give them the news. (« » 4)
   11   E: Why does he behave like that?
         F: Because he's crazy. (« » 5)

Consider the two sentences:

   12   It was raining but we went for a walk.
   13   Although it was raining, we went for a walk.

In 12 there are two *clauses* joined by the *co-ordinator* **but**; both *clauses* give new information and both are equally important. These are called *co-ordinated main clauses* (» **226–228**).

In 13 there are two *clauses* joined by the *subordinator* **although**; the content of the **although** *clause* is given as background information to the new information in the other *clause*. The **although** *clause* is called the *subordinate clause*; the other is the *main clause* (» **229–252**).

Certain *main clauses* and *subordinate clauses* express similar meaning, e.g. 12 and 13 above, but there are differences; for learners the most important points are:

a) The meaning of the different *co-ordinators* and *subordinators*, which are together called *conjunctions*;

b) the order of the two *clauses* and the *conjunction*. The order in *co-ordinated main clauses* is always:

main clause + co-ordinator + main clause.

c) However, *subordinate clauses* are more complicated because different *subordinators* have different possibilities; the two most common ones are:

main clause + subordinator + subordinate clause, e.g.

14   I went for a walk although it was snowing.

subordinator + subordinate clause + main clause, e.g.

15   Although it was snowing, I went for a walk.

When the *subordinate clause* goes first (15), it is usually followed by a comma (,). For the possible order with the different *subordinators* » the different sections.

A **to** *clause* is a *subordinate clause* that begins with a **to** *verb*, e.g. **to come early; to be painted white; to have saved some money;** for its uses » Index.

A **that** *clause* is a *clause* that begins with optional **that** and has a *subject*, e.g. (**that**) **she writes to me;** (**that**) **they've bought a new car,** etc; for its uses » Index.

An **-ing** *clause* is a *clause* that begins with an **-ing** *form*, e.g. **drinking tea; being painted by me; having taken the money,** etc; for its uses » Index.

226 My father's out **and** my mother's in the bathroom.

This sentence consists of two *co-ordinated main clauses*; the *co-ordinator* is **and**. The order is always *main clause + co-ordinator + main clause*, and the *co-ordinator* can be **and** (1–3), **but** (4, 5) or **or** (6, 7). In some cases the two *clauses* are reversible, with the same meaning (1), but in others there is a relation of sequence in time (2) or cause and effect (3, 7), which will decide which *clause* goes first, e.g.

1a I clean the inside and John cleans the outside.
1b John cleans the outside and I clean the inside.
2 Everybody sat down and the meeting began.
3 You speak and I'll hit you. (i.e. If you speak, I'll hit you)
4 The plants are big but they're not very strong. (« » **237**.1)
5 Their representative came but we didn't buy anything.

Co-ordinated statements with **or** have optional **either**, e.g.

6 (Either) you can pay now or we'll send you the bill.
7 (Either) you keep quiet or I'm going out. (i.e. If you don't keep quiet, I'm going out)

And, but and **or** can also *co-ordinate imperatives*, e.g.

8 Sit down and watch this!
9 Listen carefully or go outside!
10 Come in but don't make a noise!

And, but and **or** can also join words and phrases when it is not necessary to repeat the whole *clause*, e.g.

11 The director and his staff sent their best wishes.
12 They worked quickly and efficiently.
13 The Wheelers came to the party but left early.
14 Lucy speaks French but Alan doesn't.
15 (Either) Gordon or Sheila must have told them the news.
16 The scissors are (either) in the drawer or on my desk.

227 Both Sue and her sister have had flu.

Co-ordinators **both. . . and** only rarely join two *main clauses*; normally they *co-ordinate noun phrases* (1, 2), *adjectives* (3), *adverbs* (4), etc., e.g.

1 Both you and I have made mistakes.
2 Robin did both the shopping and the cooking.
3 Tom is both impolite and boring. (« » **92**.1)
4 They worked both quietly and efficiently. (« » **226**.12)

For another use of **both** « **35**.

228 Neither the staff nor the students liked the exam system.

Co-ordinators **neither. . . nor** do not join *main clauses*; they are used in formal style to *co-ordinate noun phrases* (1–4), *adjectives* (5), *adverbials*, etc. When **neither . . . nor** is part of the *subject*, then the *verb* is *singular* (1, 3a) or *plural* (2, 3b) depending on the second of the two *noun phrases*.

Neither . . . nor is used to negate both of the phrases that it joins, e.g.

  1 Neither the president nor his secretary is interested. (i.e. both the president and his secretary are not interested)
  2 Neither the members nor the visitors are interested.
  3 Neither the members nor the president is interested.
  4 Neither the president nor the members are interested.
  5 I have been to neither Italy nor Greece. (« » **93**.2)
  6 Tom is neither polite nor interesting. (« » **93**.1)

Co-ordinators **neither . . . nor** are relatively rare; we more frequently use **not** with **either . . . or** (7) or the structures in **93**:

  7 I haven't been to either Italy or Greece. (« » 5)

For another use of **neither** « **38**.

229 When Mary comes to see us, we usually play cards.

Here, **when** is a *subordinator* in a sentence that refers to all time, i.e. past, present and future time all together. The *verb* in both *clauses* is a *present* form; in the **when** *clause* the *verb* is *present simple*[1], but in the *main clause* it can be *present simple* (1), *present perfect* (2), a *modal* (3) or an *imperative* (4). The **when** *clause* can be first or second (1a, b).

We use this structure to talk about two events that happen together regularly. **When** suggests that the thing happens more often than **if** (» **239**).

  1a When it snows, we stay at home. (i.e. every time that it snows; « » **239**.1)
  1b We stay at home when it snows.
  2   When I get up, my wife has usually had her breakfast. (« » **239**.2)
  3   We can have noisy parties when the neighbours are away. (« » **239**.3)
  4   Ask Mrs Thomas when you need to know anything. (« » **239**.4)

-----

[1] The **when** *clause* can also have a *present perfect*, but then **when** means 'after', e.g.

  5   When you've worked hard, you feel tired. (« » **239**.5)
  6   Mrs Aston goes to work when her children have gone to school.

230 **When** she **arrives,** everything **will be** ready.

Here, **when** is a *subordinator* in a sentence that refers to future time. Other *subordinators* that can join *clauses* that refer to future time are **as soon as** (2), **before** (3), **after** (4), **by the time** (5), **till, until** (6), **while** (» 233.6) and **if** (» 240). In all these cases the *subordinate clause* has a *present verb* form, usually a *present simple* (1–3, 5, 6) or a *present perfect* (4); the *main clause* usually has **will** (2, 5, 6), **shall** (4) or an *imperative* (1, 3, 6). The *subordinate clause* can go first or second (1a, b):

> 1a When she comes back, ask her to telephone me. (i.e. it is assumed that she will come back; « » **240**.1)
> 1b Ask her to telephone me when she comes back.
> 2 I'll write the letter as soon as I have time.
> 3 Clean your shoes before you go out!
> 4 Shall we do the washing up after the guests have gone?
> 5 It'll be dark by the time we finish.
> 6 Wait here until they call you. (or till they)

231 **When** the train **stopped,** everybody **jumped** out.

Here, **when** is a *subordinator* in a sentence that refers to past time. The *verb* in both *clauses* is a past form. The **when** *clause* can be first or second (2a, b).

This structure usually refers to single events; the event in the *main clause* usually follows closely after the event in the **when** *clause*, e.g.

> 1 When Jack and Joan came, we played cards.
> 2a When Peter came home, I told him the news.
> 2b I told Peter the news when he came home.
> 3 Did the car stop when you signalled to it?

This structure can also refer to a repeated event in past time (e.g. 1), but for this meaning it is clearer to use one of these structures:

> 4 Whenever Jack and Joan came, we played cards. (« **182**)
> 5 When Jack and Joan came, we used to play cards. (« **121**)

232 **When I opened** the curtains, it **was snowing.**

Here, **when** is a *subordinator* in a sentence that refers to past time. The *verb* in the **when** *clause* is *past simple*; the *verb* in the *main clause* is *past progressive*. The **when** *clause* can be first or second (2a, b).

The **when** *clause* refers to an event (*past simple*) that took place when something else was in progress (*past progressive*), e.g.

1 What was the orchestra playing when you turned on the radio?
2a When we arrived, Harry was bathing the baby. (« » **233**.1)
2b Harry was bathing the baby when we arrived.
3 When the assistant mentioned the price, I wasn't really listening.

When we arrived, Harry was bathing the baby.

Also « **151**.5, 6.

233 The phone rang **while** I was doing my exercises.

Here, **while** is a *subordinator* in a sentence that refers to past time. **While** emphasises duration, so the *verb* in the **while** *clause* is usually a *progressive* form (1, 2) or the *past* of **be** (3), (but « also **151**.7–10). The **while** *clause* can go first or second (2a, b).

While means 'during the period that'; the *main clause* refers to an event at some time during the period):

1 We arrived while Harry was bathing the baby. (« » **232**.2)
2a While we were working in the garden, it started to rain.
2b It started to rain while we were working in the garden.
3 Did the burglars get in while they were asleep?

1–3 all refer to past time, but a similar contrast can be made for all time, i.e. past, present and future, (4), present time (5) and future time

(6) with appropriate *verb* forms, e.g.

    4   Mary always interrupts me while I'm trying to study.
    5   Sit still while I'm talking!
    6   While you're having a rest after lunch, I'll go to the shops.

For another use of **while** » **238**.

234 I ran **because** I was late.

Because is a *subordinator*; the **because** clause usually goes second (1–3), but also « » 4. The **because** *clause* gives a cause or reason for the event in the *main clause*, e.g.

    1   They sat inside because it was raining. (« » **235**.1)
    2   Bill's off work because he's got flu. (« » **236**.1)
    3   The letter was returned because it had the wrong address.

The **because** *clause* is sometimes first, especially if the *main clause* is the only new information, e.g.

    4   They work hard, and because they work hard, they have the right to demand more money.

In informal style, especially in answer to a **why** *question*, we often use the **because** *clause* alone, e.g.

    5   A: Why was the letter returned?
           B: Because it had the wrong address.

235 **Since** he isn't very well, he mostly stays at home.

Here, **since** is a *subordinator*; the **since** *clause* usually goes first (1–3). A *subordinate clause* with **for** must go last (4, 5) and is usually preceded by a comma (,). **As** can replace either **since** or **for**, and all three words mean 'because', e.g.

    1   Since it was raining, they sat inside. (or As it; « » **234**.1)
    2   Since he understood very little German, he could not follow the conversation. (or As he; « » 5)
    3   Since you have ignored our letters, we must now contact our lawyers. (or As you)
    4   The girls were worried, for they were still a long way from home. (or as they)
    5   He could not follow the conversation, for he understood very little German. (or as he; « » 2)

These words cannot always replace **because**; for example, they cannot be used to answer a *question*, so e.g. *Not* x For it had the wrong address x in **234**.5.

Notice also the use of *preposition* **for** plus an **-ing** *form* to give an explanation or reason in such sentences as:

6 They were punished for cheating.
7 She was sent to prison for shoplifting.

Preposition **because of** is not possible in these sentences.

For another use of **since** « **148**.

236 I was late, **so** I ran.

When **so** joins two *clauses*, they are usually separated by a comma (,). The **so** *clause* goes second and expresses the consequence of the *main clause*, e.g.

1 Bill's got flu, so he's off work. (« » **234**.2)
2a They didn't like the designs, so we lost the contract.
3 There'll be plenty of things to do, so come early.

For other uses of **so** « **75**, » **251**.

237 **(Al)though** he smiled, he wasn't really happy.

Although is a *subordinator*; it has the alternative form **though,** with the same meaning. The *subordinate clause* can be first or second (2a, b).

We use **(al)though** to contrast two facts (1, 2). If the contrast is surprising, we can emphasise this by using **even though** (3):

1 (Al)though the plants are big, they are not very strong. (« » **226**.4)
2a (Al)though many people have tried to solve the mystery, nobody has succeeded.
2b Nobody has succeeded in solving the mystery (al)though many people have tried.
3 Even though we left home early, we didn't arrive until after lunch.

We can also express contrast with **yet** between the two *clauses* (4a) or with two separate sentences (4b):

4a The plants are big, yet they're not strong. (« » 1)
4b The plants are big. Yet they're not strong.

238 **While** some parts were funny, others were rather boring.

While is a *subordinator*; here it is used to balance contrasting facts[1]. In this sense, the **while** *clause* usually goes first, e.g.

1 While one witness was certain, the others expressed doubts.
2 While we admit to some carelessness, we cannot accept sole responsibility.
3 While the summer is pleasant, the winter is unbearably cold.

Since the facts in the two *clauses* are in contrast, these sentences are often similar in meaning to sentences with (**al**)**though** (« **237**).

———

[1] For **while** related to time « **233**.

239 **If** we **open** the door, (then) the flies **come** in.

If is a *subordinator*; here it is in a *conditional* that refers to all time, i.e. past, present and future. The **if** *clause* expresses the condition; it can go first or second (1a, b). If the *main clause* is second, (then) it begins with optional **then** (1a, 2). The *verb* in both *clauses* is a *present* form; in the **if** *clause* the *verb* is usually *present simple*[1], but in the *main clause* it can be *present simple* (1), *present perfect* (2), a *modal* (3), or an *imperative* (4).

We use this structure to talk about two events that happen together, but **if** suggests that they do not happen very often (« **when 229**), e.g.

1a If it snows, (then) we stay at home. (i.e. Every time that it snows, which is not very often, we stay at home; « » **229**.1)
1b We stay at home if it snows.
2 If I get up late, (then) my wife has usually had breakfast. (« » **229**.2)
3 We can have noisy parties if the neighbours are away. (« » **229**.3)
4 Ask Mrs Thomas if you need to know anything. (« » **229**.4)

———

[1] The **if** *clause* can also have a *present perfect*, e.g.

5 If you've worked hard, (then) you feel tired. (« » **229**.5)

240 If Keith **phones**, (then) I **will explain** everything.

If is a *subordinator*. The whole sentence is a *conditional*, often called the *first conditional* (« **241, 242**). The **if** *clause* expresses the *condition*, and it can go first or second (1a, b). If the *main clause* is second, (then) it begins with optional **then** (1b, 2, 3). In this *conditional* the **if** *clause* has a *present verb*, often the *present simple* (1, 2), but it can also be the *present perfect* (3), or a *modal*[1] (4); the *main clause* has *modal* **will** (2–4) or an *imperative* (1, 5).

This *conditional* refers to a possible event in future time. The *main clause* expresses a definite consequence of the **if** *clause*, but the *condition* in the **if** *clause* is not certain (« **when 230**), e.g.

> 1a If she comes back, (then) ask her to telephone me. (i.e. It is not certain that she will come back; « » **230**.1)
> 1b Ask her to telephone me if she comes back.
> 2 If we don't send the order, (then) they'll complain.
> 3 If Mrs Davies has heard about your illness, (then) she'll probably come and see you.
> 4 You'll be very welcome if you can come tomorrow.
> 5a Close all the windows if it rains!

We sometimes use **should** in the **if** *clause*, with the same meaning, and this often goes with an *imperative* in the *main clause*. An **if** *clause* with **should** usually goes first, e.g.

> 5b If it should rain, (then) close all the windows!

---

[1] The **if** *clause* cannot have **will** with a future meaning, so e.g. *Not* ~~if it will rain~~ (« » 5a). However, you will occasionally meet **will** ('is willing') in the **if** *clause*, e.g.

> 6 If they'll pay half the cost, (then) we'll pay the rest. (i.e. If they are willing to pay)

241 If I **had** a thousand pounds, (then) I **would take** a long holiday.

If is a *subordinator*. The whole sentence is a *conditional*, often called the *second conditional* (« » **240, 242**). The **if** *clause* expresses the condition, and it can go first or second (1a, b). If the *main clause* is second, (then) it begins with optional **then** (2–5). In this *conditional* the **if** *clause* has a *past verb*, often the *past simple* (1–3, 5–7) or the *past progressive* (4), but sometimes a *past modal* (8, 9). The *main clause* usually has **would** (1, 3–7, 10) but in formal style **should** can replace **would** with *subject* **I** or **we** (8, 10). We can also use **might** to express possibility (2; « **116**) and **could** to express 'would be able to' (9).

Although the *verb* forms are *past*, this *conditional* is used of present and future time. When we use it for present time (1–4), it expresses something that we know is not true, e.g.

1a It's a pity that it's raining now. If it was[1] fine, (then) I would go for a walk. (i.e. I am not going for a walk because it is raining.)

1b I would go for a walk if it was[1] fine.

2 If it was[1] fine, (then) I might go for a walk. (i.e. I would possibly go)

3 If you had a million pounds, (then) what would you do?

4 They aren't doing anything, but if they were working, (then) they wouldn't be so bored.

We also use this *conditional* to refer to future time (5–10) either when we think that it is improbable (5, 6) or when we mention future possibilities without considering whether they will happen or not (7, 9), or when we want to be very formal and polite (8, 10):

5 If your hair went white tomorrow, (then) what would you do?

6 I'd live in the country if I ever won a lot of money.

In 7 a husband and wife discuss possibilities:

7 A: It would be simpler if my parents came to visit us at Easter, but of course if they came in the summer, the weather would be better for them and they'd see more of the children.
B: To be honest, I think it would be better if we went to visit them. They would avoid the long journey and we would enjoy the change.

8 We should be grateful if you could provide us with this information. (or We would; **could** means 'were able to')

9 If Peter's car was[1] repaired by Friday, (then) we could go to London at the weekend. (**could** means 'would be able to')

10 I should be pleased if you would give this matter your attention. (or I would; **if you would** means 'if you were willing')

_____

[1] In formal style we use **were** instead of **was** in the **if** *clause*, e.g. **if I were, if he were, if she were**, etc., without change of meaning:

1c If it were fine, (then) I would go for a walk.

Notice also the fixed expression **if I were you**, which we use to give advice, e.g.

11 A: What shall I do?
B: If I were you, I'd see the doctor.

242 If I **had studied**, (then) I **would have passed** the exam.

If is a *subordinator*. The whole sentence is a *conditional*, often called the *third conditional* (« » **240, 241**). The **if** *clause* expressed the condition, and it can go first or second (1a, b). If the *main clause* is second, (then) it begins with optional **then** (1a, 2, 4, 6). In this *conditional* the **if** *clause* normally has a *past perfect* (1–4, 6), but can also have **could have** (5). The *main clause* normally has **would have** plus a *past participle* (1–5), but in formal style **should** can replace **would** with *subject* **I** or **we**. We can also use **might have** to express possibility (2; « » **131**) and **could have** to express 'would have been able to' (6).

The *third conditional* refers to past time. The **if** *clause* mentions something that is not true; the *main clause* expresses a consequence that is not true because the *condition* was not fulfilled, e.g.

  1a (It rained last Saturday, but) if it had been fine, (then) I would have gone for a walk. (i.e. I did not go for a walk because it was not fine; « » **241**.1)
  1b I would have gone for a walk if it had been fine.
  2 I might have gone for a walk if it had been fine. (i.e. I would possibly have gone; « » **241**.2)
  3 A: I'm glad I was working when my wife came home.
    B: Yes, if you hadn't been working, she wouldn't have believed that the job was urgent.
  4 C: Did you see the horror film on TV yesterday?
    D: No, but I wouldn't have enjoyed it if I had watched it because I don't like horror films.
  5 If we could have borrowed my mother's car, we would have got there in time. (i.e. If we had been able to borrow)
  6 If they had sent the spare parts earlier, we could have mended the machine last weekend. (i.e. we would have been able to mend)

With a present consequence of a past condition we have, e.g.

  7 If you had been born in Britain, (then) you would be British.

Note: In formal style the condition can be expressed without **if** and with **had** before the *subject*, e.g.

  1c Had it been fine, I would have gone for a walk.

243 **Even if** we took a taxi, we wouldn't get there in time.

Even if is a *subordinator*. The whole sentence is a *conditional*; the **even if** *clause* expresses the condition, and it can go first (1, 3) or second (2).

The *main clause* expresses a consequence that is in contrast to the condition, and so it is somewhat unexpected. The *verb* forms in the two *clauses* can correspond to the *first* (1; « **240**), *second* (2; « **241**) or *third conditional* (3; « **242**):

1 Even if you give me five pounds, I still won't have enough.
2 I wouldn't go to their party even if they asked me on their bended knees.
3 Even if we had inspected the cables last week, we wouldn't have realised the danger.

244 It looks **as if** he's coming to our house.

As if is a *subordinator*; it has the alternative form **as though**. When **as if** refers to a present appearance which we assume to be true, then we use *present* (1) or *future verb* forms:

1 It smells as if it's got garlic in it. (or as though)
2 It looks as if it's going to rain. (or as though)

When we assume that the appearance is not true, we use *past* forms for present and future time, e.g.

3 Ron is talking as if he was the winner. (or as though; or he were; « **241**[1])
4 They will treat you as if you were one of the family. (or as though)

When we refer to past time, we use *past* forms both for when the appearance was true (5) and for when it was not (6):

5 They spoke as if they were in a hurry, and they were.
6 They spoke as if they were in a hurry, but they weren't.

245 I **wish** (that) they **were** cheaper.

Certain expressions require the same *verb* forms as the **if** *clause* of the *second* (« **241**) or *third conditional* (« **242**), i.e. for present and future time they use a *past* form (1, 2) and for past time they use a *past perfect* (3). The most common expressions are the *verb* **wish** (1, 3) and **it's time**, which is used only for present time, e.g.

1 We wish (that) you could stay until tomorrow. (i.e. We're sorry you can't stay)
2 It's time the children went to bed. (i.e. It's time for the children to go to bed)
3 My brother wishes (that) he had learnt French. (i.e. he is sorry that he did not learn French)

Also « **122**.14.

246 We will do the work **provided** (that) they pay in advance.

Provided is a *subordinator*. The whole sentence is a *conditional*; the **provided** *clause* expresses the condition, and normally it goes second. **Provided** means 'only if'; it has the alternative form **providing**, both with optional **that**. The *verb* forms in the two *clauses* can correspond to the *first* (1; « **240**), the *second* (2; « **241**) or the *third conditional* (3; « **242**):

1   I will lend you the tools provided (that) you promise to bring them back before the weekend. (i.e. only if you promise; « » **247**.1)
2   They would make all the arrangements providing (that) they had all the details by the end of this week.
3   Jack would have come provided (that) his wife had been in better health.

247 We can't write to her **unless** we have her address.

Unless is a *subordinator*. The whole sentence is a *conditional*; the **unless** *clause* expresses the condition, and it can go first or second (1a, b). **Unless** means 'if not'. The *verb* forms in the two *clauses* can correspond to the *first* (1; « **240**), the *second* (2; « **241**) or the *third conditional* (3; « **242**):

1   I won't lend you the tools unless you promise to bring them back before the weekend. (i.e. if you do not promise; « » **246**.1)
2   They wouldn't see you next week unless you had made a previous arrangement. (i.e. if you had not made)
3   We wouldn't have gone to the play unless they had invited us personally. (i.e. if they had not invited)

248 I'll definitely come tomorrow **in case** you need some help.

In case is a *subordinator*. *The main clause* mentions something that is certain, i.e. these sentences are not *conditionals*. The **in case** *clause* mentions something that is not certain; it anticipates something that might possibly happen later (1, 3, 5) or an unknown present possibility (4). Compare 1 with 2:

1   I'm taking my umbrella in case it rains. (i.e. I am definitely taking my umbrella, because it might perhaps rain)

2   I'll take my umbrella if it rains. (i.e. If it does not rain, I will not take my umbrella)
3   I telephoned in case they wanted to tell me something.
4   We'd better not call now in case they're having lunch.
5   I'll buy some extra cakes in case Ann brings her friends home.

Note: There is a *preposition* **in case of**, used in formal style, but its meaning does not correspond to **in case**; it has conditional meaning, e.g.

6   In case of rain the match will be postponed. (i.e. If it rains)

249 The more you read, the more you learn.

Here, **the** is an *adverb*. **The** goes with a *comparative* in both *clauses* to talk about something that changes in proportion to something else. We usually understand the second *clause* to express a consequence of the first, e.g.

1   The more money you spend, the less you can save.
2   The more you eat, the fatter you get.
3   The more clearly people write, the easier it is for other people to read.

For use of **the** as a *determiner* « **14, 15**.

250 We sat close together (in order) to keep warm.

In order is a *subordinator*; it has the alternative form **so as**, with the same meaning. The *subordinate clause* usually goes last, but occasionally goes first (5). With *positive clauses*, especially with *verbs* of movement, we can omit the *subordinator*, with the same meaning (1a, b), but with a *negative clause* the *subordinator* cannot be omitted (2a, b). We use these *clauses* to express purpose, e.g.

1a They left early (in order) to avoid the rush hour.
1b They left early (so as) to avoid the rush hour.
2a They left early in order not to arrive late.
2b They left early so as not to arrive late.
3   We spent very little money in order to have a holiday later. (i.e. so that we could have a holiday; « » **251**.1)
4   So as not to waste time, I have made a list of suggestions.

A **to** *clause* has no *subject*. When we use this structure, we understand the unmentioned *subject* of the **to** *infinitive* from the context. If the *subject* cannot be understood, we use a different structure (» **251**.)

251 She spoke slowly **so (that)** everyone would understand.

So that is a *subordinator*; it has the alternative form **in order that,** which is formal style. The *subordinate clause* usually goes second; for past time it usually has **would** (1), for all time or for present time it usually has the *present simple* (2), and for future time it usually has **will** (3), but we often avoid **will** in both *clauses* (4). The **so that** *clause* expresses the purpose of the action in the *main clause*:

1   We spent very little money so (that) our children would have enough for a holiday. (« » **250**.3)
2   They always start early so (that) they don't have to run.
3   I've sent the letter first class so (that) it'll get there tomorrow.
4   I'll send the letter first class so (that) it gets there tomorrow. (or it will get)

When it is not necessary to mention a *subject* in the **that** *clause*, i.e. because it is understandable from the context, then we can use a different structure (« **250**).

For other uses of **so** « **75, 236**.

252 I need some scissors **to cut this paper (with)**. Scissors are **for cutting paper (with)**.

We use the **to** *clause* to talk about the purpose of a human action (1, 3, 5); we use **for** plus an -**ing** *clause* to talk about the function of a thing (2, 4, 5). *Preposition* **with** is optional after a *noun phrase*.

1   I want a small brush to do some delicate work (with).
2   These big brushes are for painting the large surfaces (with).
3   I need a cloth to clean the windows (with).
4   These cloths are very good for cleaning the windows (with).
5   I went to the shop to get some glue. I needed it to mend a glass vase, but look what they gave me! Glue for sticking wood together!

Prepositions, e.g. **for,** cannot go with a **to** *verb*, so *Not* x~~for to do~~ x (« » 1).

Also « **55**.

Appendixes

253 *Positive* and *negative*; **some** *words* and **any** *words*

Negative clauses are those containing one of the *negative* words: **not** (or **n't**), **no, none, nobody, nothing, nowhere, never, neither, nor.** *Clauses* that do not contain one of these words are *positive.* However, there are other words that provide a sufficiently negative context to require **any** *words* (when a choice must be made between **some** words and **any** words.) These are:

a) *Adverbs* **hardly, barely, seldom,** e.g.

    1   They hardly ever buy anything. (*Not* x something x)

b) *Verbs* such as **deny, fail, forget, refuse,** etc., e.g.

    2   They refused to go anywhere on foot. (*Not* x somewhere x)

c) *Adjectives* with a *negative* prefix, e.g. **unlikely, unwilling, incapable, improbable,** etc., and also **difficult** and **reluctant,** e.g.

    3   It's unlikely that anyone will come tomorrow, either. (*Not* x someone x, *Not* x too x)

d) *Nouns* such as **denial, failure, difficulty, reluctance,** etc., e.g.

    4   Their failure to inform anyone was the main problem. (*Not* x someone x)

e) *Preposition* **without,** e.g.

    5   We did it without any outside help. (*Not* x some x)

When the words **never, neither, nor, hardly, barely, scarcely, rarely, seldom,** and also **not only** go first in a *clause,* they are followed by the *auxiliary* plus the *subject* plus the *main verb,* i.e. the same *verb* form and word order as in *questions* (« p 94), e.g.

    6a Never have we enjoyed a holiday so much.
    6b We have never enjoyed a holiday so much.
    7a Hardly had she begun when the audience became restless.
    7b She had hardly begun when the audience became restless.
    8a Not only did the directors ignore the protest, (but) they also lied to the press.
    8b The directors not only ignored the protest, (but) they also lied to the press.

Some *words* are words and phrases that appear in *positive* contexts. *Positive* contexts are *positive statements* that do not contain words in a)–e) above (9), *questions* that expect a *positive* answer (10, 11), and *conditional clauses* when the condition is probable (12).

Any *words* are words that appear in neutral or *negative* contexts. These are *negative statements*, i.e. *statements* with a *negative* word or a word from a)–e) above (13), *questions* that do not expect a *positive answer* (14, 15), and *conditional clauses* when the condition is improbable (16):

9   Some people have already arrived.
10   Would you like some biscuits, too?
11   He asked if I'd like some biscuits.
12   If there's something I can do, please tell me.
13   They never tell me anything at all.
14   Have you (got) any brothers or sisters?
15   He asked if I had any brothers or sisters.
16   If there's any trouble at the meeting, come home.

Any *words* alone are not *negative*, so e.g.

17   A: Who came?
      B: Nobody. (*Not* x Anybody x)
18   C: What happened?
      D: Nothing. (*Not* x Anything x)

Table 5: some *words*, any *words* and *negative words*

some *word*	**any** *word*	*negative word*	**some** *word*	**any** *word*	*negative word*
some[1]	any[1]	no none	already	yet	——
somebody	anybody	nobody	still[1]	any more,	no more,
someone	anyone	no one		any longer	no longer
something	anything	nothing	too	either	neither, nor
sometimes	ever	never	a long way	far	——
somewhere	anywhere	nowhere	a long time	long	——
			a lot (of)[1]	much, many[1]	——
			——	at all	——

[1] These words are in fact more complicated; « separate sections.

254 Numbers

The *cardinal* numbers are:

1 one	11 eleven	21 twenty-one	40 forty
2 two	12 twelve	22 twenty-two	50 fifty
3 three	13 thirteen	23 twenty-three	60 sixty
4 four	14 fourteen	24 twenty-four	70 seventy
5 five	15 fifteen	25 twenty-five	80 eighty
6 six	16 sixteen	26 twenty-six	90 ninety
7 seven	17 seventeen	27 twenty-seven	100 a[1] hundred
8 eight	18 eighteen	28 twenty-eight	1,000 a[1] thousand
9 nine	19 nineteen	29 twenty-nine	1,000,000 a[1] million
10 ten	20 twenty	30 thirty	

31–99 are formed in the same way as **21–29**, e.g. **41 forty-one, 73 seventy-three**, etc. Examples of other numbers are:

105: a[1] hundred and five
326: three hundred and twenty-six
4,536: four thousand five hundred and thirty-six
6,500,000: six million five hundred thousand

When **hundred, thousand, million,** and also **dozen,** are *premodified,* e.g. **two hundred books, ten million people, three dozen eggs,** etc., they do not have a *plural* form. However, alone they have a normal *plural* form, e.g. **hundreds of people, thousands of tiny creatures, dozens of problems,** etc.

There is no absolute rule for when to use figures and when to use words in writing, but it is quite common to use words for **one** to **ten** and then to use **11, 12,** etc.

The number **0** has different names in different circumstances. In mathematics we usually say **nought,** (but see decimals below); for temperatures we say e.g. **25 degrees below zero** (i.e. **−25°**; *Not* x nought x), **nought degrees** (i.e. o°; *Not* x zero degrees x); in telephone numbers we usually say /əʊ/, like the letter o; in football and hockey we say **nil,** e.g. **Leeds three, Arsenal nil** (3–0); in tennis we say **love,** e.g. **forty love** (40–0).

In decimals **0** is often pronounced /əʊ/, but sometimes **nought.** After a decimal point the figures are pronounced separately, e.g.

0.5: nought point five or /əʊ/ point five;
3.875: three point eight seven five;
2.025: two point /əʊ/ two five.

Decimals after **1** go with a *plural noun,* e.g. **1.3 miles.**

Years are pronounced as follows:

1535: fifteen thirty-five; 1790: seventeen ninety; 1805: eighteen /əʊ/ five; 1910: nineteen ten; 1985: nineteen eighty-five, etc. Notice also e.g. **the eighteen nineties (1890–1899), the nineteen twenties (1920–1929),** etc.

The *ordinal* numbers are:

1st first	11th eleventh	21st twenty-first
2nd second	12th twelfth	22nd twenty-second
3rd third	13th thirteenth	23rd twenty-third
4th fourth	14th fourteenth	24th twenty-fourth
5th fifth	15th fifteenth	25th twenty-fifth
6th sixth	16th sixteenth	26th twenty-sixth
7th seventh	17th seventeenth	27th twenty-seventh
8th eighth	18th eighteenth	28th twenty-eighth
9th ninth	19th nineteenth	29th twenty-ninth
10th tenth	20th twentieth	30th thirtieth

40th fortieth	100th hundredth
50th fiftieth	1,000th thousandth
60th sixtieth	1,000,000th millionth
70th seventieth	
80th eightieth	
90th ninetieth	

31st–99th are formed in the same way as **21st–29th**; they are like the corresponding *cardinal* number except that the last word has the *ordinal* form, e.g.

51st: fifty-first; 83rd: eighty-third; 112th: hundred and twelfth; 422nd: four hundred and twenty-second, etc.

Fractions ½ and ¼ are **a¹ half** and **a¹ quarter** (or **a¹ fourth**). All other fractions use *ordinal* numbers, e.g.

⅔ **: two thirds;**   ⅙ **: a¹ sixth;**   1⅘ **: one and four fifths;**
3¾ **: three and three quarters;** 15/16 **: fifteen sixteenths,** etc.

Fractions are *postmodified* by an of *phrase*, not a *noun* alone, e.g. **a quarter of an hour, two thirds of the meat, three eighths of a mile,** etc. However, with a *noun*, **half** can go with or without **of**, e.g. **half (of) the bread, half (of) the apples,** etc. (« » **69**). With a *pronoun* **of** is essential, e.g. **half of it, half of them,** etc.

Fractions after **one** go with a *plural noun*, although there is an alternative form, e.g.

1¼ **miles: one and a quarter miles** or **a mile and a quarter**
1½ **hours: one and a half hours** or **an hour and a half**

We usually use *ordinal* numbers for dates, e.g.

5 July 1979: the fifth of July 1979 or **July the fifth 1979**

¹ We can replace **a** with **one** for emphasis e.g.

    1   Not ten thousand. I said one thousand.
    2   Not three quarters. I said one quarter.

255 Times

Times of the clock have two spoken forms: one for everyday use (Column B) and one for timetables, etc. (Column C), e.g.

A	B	C
6.00	six o'clock	six o'clock
6.01	one minute¹ past six	six 0 /əʊ/ one
6.04	four minutes¹ past six	six 0 /əʊ/ four
6.05	five (minutes)¹ past six	six 0 /əʊ/ five
6.10	ten (minutes)¹ past six	six ten
6.15	a quarter past six	six fifteen
6.20	twenty (minutes)¹ past six	six twenty
6.25	twenty-five (minutes)¹ past six	six twenty-five
6.26	twenty-six minutes¹ past six	six twenty-six
6.30	half past six	six thirty
6.35	twenty-five (minutes)¹ to seven	six thirty-five
6.40	twenty (minutes)¹ to seven	six forty
6.45	a quarter to seven	six forty-five
6.50	ten (minutes)¹ to seven	six fifty
6.53	seven minutes¹ to seven	six fifty-three
6.55	five (minutes)¹ to seven	six fifty-five

We distinguish the hours of midnight to midday from those of midday to midnight as follows:

Column A: either **6.15 a.m.** and **6.15 p.m.** or **6.15 and 18.15;** Column B: **a quarter past six in the morning** and **a quarter past six in the evening,** (*Not* ~~a quarter past eighteen~~); Column C: either **six fifteen a.m.** and **six fifteen p.m.** or **six fifteen** and **eighteen fifteen.**

We usually pronounce **a.m.** and **p.m.** as initials, i.e. /ei em/ and /pi: em/; we very rarely use the complete words **ante meridian** and **post meridian.**

Note: The *question* about time has two forms, e.g.

    What time is it?   or   What is the time?
    What time was it?   or   What was the time?

---

¹ With **five, ten, twenty** and **twenty-five** the word **minutes** is optional; with all other numbers it is essential.

256 Spelling rules for regular endings

Vowels are **a, e, i, o** and **u**; all other letters are *consonants*.

1 For the *plural* of *count nouns* (« **1**) and for the (**e**)**s** ending of the *present simple* (« **141**):

   a) if the ending is a *consonant* + **y**, omit **y** and add **ies**, e.g. **spy, spies; party, parties; marry, marries; try, tries**, etc.

   b) if the ending is **ch, s, sh, x** or **z**, or a *verb* ending in single **o**, add **es**, e.g. **match, matches; pass, passes; brush, brushes; box, boxes; buzz, buzzes; go, goes**, etc.

   c) in all other cases, except *verbs* **have** and **be** and irregular *plurals* (» **257**), add **s**, e.g. **top, tops; day, days; gate, gates; bridge, bridges; call, calls; walk, walks**, etc.

2 For the *comparative* and *superlative* of short *adjectives* and *adverbs* (« **71**):

   a) if the ending is a *consonant* + **y**, omit **y** and add **ier** and **iest**, e.g. **pretty, prettier, prettiest; happy, happier, happiest**, etc.

   b) if the ending is **e**, add **r** and **st**, e.g. **large, larger, largest; wide, wider, widest; free, freer, freest**, etc.

   c) if the ending is one *vowel* + one *consonant*, then double the *consonant* and add **er** and **est**, e.g. **big, bigger, biggest; fat, fatter, fattest**, etc.

   d) in all other cases, except irregular forms (» **258**), add **er** and **est**, e.g. **long, longer, longest; thick, thicker, thickest; broad, broader, broadest**, etc.

Note: The rules for *comparative* ending **er** also apply to the ending **er** for people who do a certain activity, e.g. **carry, carrier** (« **a**); **bake, baker** (« **b**); **dig, digger** (« **c**); **teach, teacher** (« **d**), etc.

3 For the *past simple* and the *past participle*:

   a) if the ending is a *consonant* + **y**, omit **y** and add **ied**, e.g. **cry, cried; marry, married; certify, certified**, etc.

   b) if the ending is **e**, add **d**, e.g. **live, lived; tie, tied; chase, chased; free, freed; agree, agreed**, etc.

   c) if the ending is a stressed syllable, including *verbs* of one syllable, with one *vowel* and one *consonant*, then double the *consonant* and add **ed**, e.g. **stop, stopped; drag, dragged; permit, permitted; prefer, preferred**, etc.

   d) if the ending is **ic**, add **ked**, e.g. **picnic, picnicked; panic, panicked**, etc.

   e) in all other cases[1], except irregular *verbs* (» **259**), add **ed**, e.g. **walk, walked; leak, leaked; play, played; vomit, vomited; murder, murdered**, etc.

4 For the -ing *form*:

a) if the ending is a *consonant* + **e**, omit **e** and add **ing**, e.g. **live, living; hope, hoping; convince, convincing**, etc.

b) if the ending is **ie**, omit **ie** and add **ying**, e.g. **lie, lying; tie, tying**, etc.

c) if the ending is a stressed syllable, including words of one syllable, with one *vowel* and one *consonant*, then double the *consonant* and add **ing**, e.g. **stop, stopping; drag, dragging; permit, permitting; prefer, preferring**, etc.

d) if the ending is **ic**, add **king**, e.g. **picnic, picknicking; panic, panicking.**

e) in all other cases[1] add **ing**, e.g. **walk, walking; leak, leaking; play, playing; vomit, vomiting; murder, murdering**, etc.

---

[1] Britons, but not Americans, use the endings of **c**) for **worship**, i.e. **worshipped, worshipping**, and for *verbs* ending in **al, el, il** and **ol**, e.g. **signalled, travelling, devilled, carolling**, etc. For Americans these words do not double the consonant.

257 Irregular *nouns*

1 A few *nouns* end in **s** but go with *singular determiners* and *pronouns*, etc. (« Table 1, p 3) and a *singular verb*, including **barracks, headquarters, means, works**, e.g.

There is a barracks near here. It was built in 1941.

2 A few *nouns* end in **s** but go with *mass determiners* and *pronouns*, etc. (« Table 1, p 3) and a *singular verb*, including: **news; measles, mumps; linguistics, mathematics**, and other subjects ending in **ics; billiards, bowls, dominoes**, e.g.

The news is important. It must be announced at once.

3 Tools and clothes that have two equal parts often end in **s** and are *plural*, although their meaning is one article, including: **binoculars, pliers, scales, scissors, tongs, tweezers, braces, glasses, jeans, knickers, panties, pants, pyjamas, shorts, spectacles, tights, trousers, trunks**, e.g.

A: Can I wear these jeans?
B: No, they aren't dry yet.

If it is necessary, we can make it explicit that we are referring to one article with **a pair of**, which is *singular*, e.g.

A pair of damp jeans was hanging in the bathroom.

4 A few *nouns* do not end in **s**, but are *plural*, (» also **9** below), including: **cattle, clergy, people, police** (« also **8**), e.g.

Those people are waiting to see if they have won.

5 Some *nouns* ending in **o** form the *plural* with **s**, some with **es**, and some with either:

with **s**	with **es**
kangaroos, radios, studios, zoos, kilos, photos, pianos, concertos, dynamos, solos, sopranos	echoes, heroes, negroes, potatoes, tomatoes
Others can add either **s** or **es**.	

6 A few compound *nouns* form the *plural* with the first word, in particular **mothers-in-law, sons-in-law**, etc., and **passers-by**. But most compounds form the *plural* with the last word, e.g. **grown-ups, print-outs, male nurses, apprentice butchers**, etc.

7 Many *nouns* ending in **f** or **fe** are regular, e.g. **beliefs, chiefs, safes**, but a few omit **f** or **fe** and add **ves**, including: **calf, half, knife, leaf, life, loaf, shelf, thief, wife, wolf**, e.g. **calves, knives**, etc.

8 A few *nouns* form the *plural* with a change of vowel: **foot, feet; goose, geese; tooth, teeth; louse, lice; mouse, mice; man, men; woman, women**. Notice also the compounds of **man** and **woman**, e.g. **postmen, policewomen**, etc.

9 Most words for animals have regular *plurals*, e.g. **dogs, elephants**, etc., but there are a few that have the same form for *singular* and *plural*, including: **deer, fish, plaice, salmon** and **sheep**. **Fish** also occasionally has the regular *plural* **fishes**.

10 The *plural* of **child** is **children**; the *plural* of **ox** is **oxen**.

11 There are also many other words that have been borrowed from other languages and which still form the *plurals* as in the original language. Most of these words are rare or technical; some of the more common ones are: **analysis, analyses; basis, bases; crisis, crises; diagnosis, diagnoses; hypothesis, hypotheses; oasis, oases; thesis, theses; stimulus, stimuli; curriculum, curricula; criterion, criteria; phenomenon, phenomena.**

258 Irregular comparisons

For the endings of regular *comparatives* and *superlatives* « **256 2**. There are a few irregular forms for *comparatives* and *superlatives* (« **27–29, 71, 72**):

	comparative	superlative		comparative	superlative
many	more	most (« **27**)	well	better	best
much	more	most (« **27**)	bad	worse	worst
little	less	least (« **28, 29**)	ill	worse	worst
few	fewer	fewest (« **29**)	far	farther	farthest
			far	further	furthest
good	better	best			

Adjective **old** has the regular forms **older** and **oldest**, but **elder** and **eldest** are often used for family relationships, e.g. **Michael is my elder brother.**

259 Irregular *verbs*

For the endings of regular *verbs* « 256.
Archaic and very rare *verbs* have been omitted.

plain verb	past simple	past participle	plain verb	past simple	past participle
arise	arose	arisen	flee	fled	fled
awake[1]	awoke	awoken	fling	flung	flung
be	was, were	been	fly	flew	flown
bear	bore	borne	forbid	forbade	forbidden
beat	beat	beaten	forecast	forecast	forecast
become	became	become	forget	forgot	forgotten
begin	began	begun	forgive	forgave	forgiven
bend	bent	bent	forsake	forsook	forsaken
bet	bet	bet	freeze	froze	frozen
bid	bid	bid	get	got	got
bind	bound	bound	give	gave	given
bite	bit	bitten	go	went	gone[2]
bleed	bled	bled	grind	ground	ground
blow	blew	blown	grow	grew	grown
break	broke	broken	hang	hung	hung
breed	bred	bred	have	had	had
bring	brought	brought	hear	heard	heard
broadcast	broadcast	broadcast	hide	hid	hidden
build	built	built	hit	hit	hit
burn[1]	burnt	burnt	hold	held	held
burst	burst	burst	hurt	hurt	hurt
buy	bought	bought	keep	kept	kept
cast	cast	cast	kneel[1]	knelt	knelt
catch	caught	caught	know	knew	known
cling	clung	clung	lay	laid	laid
come	came	come	lead	led	led
cost	cost	cost	lean[1]	leant	leant
creep	crept	crept	leap[1]	leapt	leapt
cut	cut	cut	learn[1]	learnt	learnt
deal	dealt	dealt	leave	left	left
dig	dug	dug	lend	lent	lent
do	did	done	let	let	let
draw	drew	drawn	lie[3]	lay	lain
dream[1]	dreamt	dreamt	light[1]	lit	lit
drink	drank	drunk	lose	lost	lost
drive	drove	driven	make	made	made
dwell[1]	dwelt	dwelt	mean	meant	meant
eat	ate	eaten	meet	met	met
fall	fell	fallen	mistake	mistook	mistaken
feed	fed	fed	mow[1]	mowed	mown
feel	felt	felt	put	put	put
fight	fought	fought	quit[1]	quit	quit
find	found	found	read	read	read

plain verb	past simple	past participle	plain verb	past simple	past participle
rid	rid	rid	spring	sprang	sprung
ride	rode	ridden	stand	stood	stood
ring	rang	rung	steal	stole	stolen
rise	rose	risen	stick	stuck	stuck
run	run	run	sting	stung	stung
saw[1]	sawed	sawn	stink	stank	stunk
say	said	said	strew[1]	strewed	strewn
see	saw	seen	stride	strode	—
seek	sought	sought	strike	struck	struck
sell	sold	sold	string	strung	strung
send	sent	sent	strive	strove	striven
set	set	set	swear	swore	sworn
sew[1]	sewed	sewn	sweep	swept	swept
shake	shook	shaken	swell[1]	swelled	swollen
shine	shone	shone	swim	swam	swum
shoot	shot	shot	swing	swung	swung
show[1]	showed	shown	take	took	taken
shrink	shrank	shrunk	teach	taught	taught
shut	shut	shut	tear	tore	torn
sing	sang	sung	tell	told	told
sink	sank	sunk	think	thought	thought
sit	sat	sat	throw	threw	thrown
sleep	slept	slept	thrust	thrust	thrust
slide	slid	slid	tread	trod	trodden
sling	slung	slung	understand	understood	understood
smell[1]	smelt	smelt	upset	upset	upset
sow	sowed	sown	wake[1]	woke	woken
speak	spoke	spoken	wear	wore	worn
speed	sped	sped	weave	wove	woven
spell[1]	spelt	spelt	wed	wed	wed
spend	spent	spent	weep	wept	wept
spill[1]	spilt	spilt	wet	wet	wet
spin	spun	spun	win	won	won
spit	spat	spat	wind	wound	wound
split	split	split	wring	wrung	wrung
spoil[1]	spoilt	spoilt	write	wrote	written
spread	spread	spread			

[1] These *verbs* can also be regular, e.g. **dream, dreamed, dreamed**.

[2] For **been** as the *past participle* of **go** « **146** *Note*.

[3] **Lie** ('tell a lie') is regular, e.g. **He lied about the accident.**

This is a list of common two- and three-part *verbs*.

abide by [1] [8]
account for [1] [6] [8]
act up [4]
add to [1] [8]
add up [2] [4]
add up to [3]
admit to [1] [5] [8]
agree to [1] [6] [8] [9]
agree with [1] [8] [9]
aim at [1] [9]
alight on [1]
allow for [1] [6] [8]
allude to [1] [6] [8]
amount to [1] [5]
angle for [1]
answer back [2] [4]
answer for [1] [8]
apologise for [1] [5] [6] [8]
appeal to [1]
apply for [1] [9]
approve of [1] [5] [6] [8]
arrive at [1]
ask after [1] [9]
ask for [1] [9]
attend to [1] [8]
average out [4]

back away [4]
back down [4]
back onto [1]
back out [4]
back out of [3] [5]
back up [2]
bail out [2]
bale out [4]
bandy about [2] [8]
bank on [1] [5] [6]
bargain for [1] [8]
bear down [2]
bear down on [3]
bear off [2]
bear on [1] [8]
bear out [2] [8]
bear up [4]
bear up under [3]
bear with [1]
become of [1]
believe in [1] [5] [6] [8]
belong to [1]
beat about [4]
beat down [2]
beat in [2]

beat up [2]
bite back [2] [8]
black out [2] [4]
blot out [2] [8]
blow away [2] [4]
blow back [4]
blow down [2] [4]
blow in [4]
blow out [2] [4]
blow over [4]
blow up [2] [4]
blurt out [2] [7] [8]
boast about [1] [5] [8]
boast of [1] [5] [8]
bog down [2]
bone up on [3]
book in [2] [4]
book out [2] [4]
bother about [1] [5] [8] [9]
bow out [4]
break away [4]
break down [2] [4]
break in [2] [4]
break in on [3]
break into [1]
break off [2] [4] [5]
break out [4]
break out of [3]
break through [1]
break up [2] [4]
break with [1]
bring about [2]
bring around [2]
bring back [2]
bring down [2]
bring forward [2]
bring in [2]
bring into [1]
bring off [2]
bring on [2]
bring out [2]
bring through [2]
bring to [2]
bring up [2]
bristle with [1]
brown off [2]
brush away [2]
brush down [2]
brush off [2]
brush up [2]
buck up [2] [4]
build up [2]

build up to [3] [5] [6] [8]
bump into [1]
burn away [2] [4]
burn down [2] [4]
burn off [2]
burn out [2] [4]
burn up [2] [4]
burst in [2] [4]
burst in on [3]
burst into [1]
burst out [4]
butt in [4]
buy off [2]
buy out [2]
buy up [2]

call away [2]
call back [2] [4]
call by [4]
call down [2]
call for [1]
call in [2]
call off [2]
call on [1]
call out [2]
call up [2]
calm down [2] [4]
cancel out [2] [4]
care about [1] [8] [9]
care for [1] [9]
carry away [2]
carry forward [2]
carry off [2]
carry on [2] [4] [5]
carry on with [3]
carry out [2]
carry over [2] [4]
carry through [2] [4]
cash in on [3]
cast off [2] [4]
catch at [1]
catch on [4]
catch out [2]
catch up [2] [4]
catch up on [3]
catch up with [3]
cater for [1]
cave in [4]
chalk up [2]
change into [1]
check up [4]
check up on [3] [8]

cheer up [2] [4]
choke back [2]
clean down [2]
clean out [2]
clean up [2]
clear away [2]
clear off [2] [4]
clear out [2] [4]
clear up [2] [4]
close down [2] [4]
close in [4]
close up [2] [4]
close with [1]
come about [4]
come across [1] [4]
come across as [3]
come across with [3]
come again [4]
come along [4]
come apart [4]
come around [4]
come at [1]
come between [1]
come down [4]
come down on [3]
come down to [3] [5] [6]
come down with [3]
come for [1]
come forward [4]
come from [1]
come in [4]
come in for [3]
come into [1]
come of [1]
come off [4]
come on [4]
come out [4]
come out against [3]
come out for [3]
come out in [3]
come out with [3]
come over [4]
come round [4]
come through [1] [4]
come to [1] [4]
come under [1]
come up [4]
come up against [3]
come up with [3]
compete for [1]
compete with [1]
complain about [1] [5] [6] [8]

concentrate on [1] [5] [8]
confide in [1]
consent to [1] [9]
consist in [1] [5]
consist of [1]
cope with [1] [5]
count on [1] [6]
crack down [4]
crack down on [3]
crop up [4]
cry off [4]
cry out against [3] [5] [6] [8]
cry out for [3]
cut across [1]
cut away [2]
cut back [2]
cut down [2]
cut down on [3] [5]
cut out [2] [5] [8]
cut up [2]

deal in [1]
deal with [1]
delight in [1] [5] [8]
depend on [1] [8]
die away [4]
die down [4]
die off [4]
die out [4]
dig at [1]
dig in [4]
dig into [1]
dig out [2]
dig over [2]
dig up [2]
do away with [3]
do down [2]
do for [1]
do in [2]
do out [2]
do over [2]
do up [2]
do with [1] [5]
do without [1]
draw aside [2]
draw away [2] [4]
draw back [2]
draw down [2]
draw in [2] [4]
draw off [2]
draw on [1] [2]
draw out [2]
draw up [2] [4]
dress up [2] [4]
drink down [2]
drink up [2]
drink to [1]

drive at [1]
drive away [2]
drive back [2]
drive off [2]
drive out [2]
drop away [4]
drop back [4]
drop behind [4]
drop by [4]
drop in [4]
drop in on [3]
drop off [4]
drop out [4]
drop round [4]
dry out [2] [4]
dry up [4]
dwell on [1]

eat away [2]
eat into [1]
eat up [2]
egg on [2]
eke out [2]
end up [4] [5]
enter into [1]

face up to [3]
fall about [4]
fall away [4]
fall back [4]
fall back on [3] [8]
fall behind with [3]
fall down [4]
fall for [1]
fall in [4]
fall in with [3]
fall into [1]
fall off [4]
fall out [4]
fall through [4]
fall to [1] [4]
feed on [1]
feel for [1]
fight back [2] [4]
fight down [2]
fight off [2]
fight on [4]
fight out [2]
fill in [2]
fill in for [3]
fill out [2] [4]
fill up [2] [4]
find out [2] [4] [7] [8]
finish off [2] [8]
finish up [2] [4]
fire at [1]
fit in [2] [4]

fit in with [3]
fit into [1]
fit out [2]
fit up [2]
flirt with [1]
fly at [1]
fold back [2]
fold up [2] [4]

get about [4]
get across [2]
get ahead [4]
get along [4]
get around [4]
get at [1]
get away [2] [4]
get away with [3] [5] [6] [8]
get back [2] [4]
get behind [4]
get by [4]
get down [2] [4]
get down to [3] [5]
get in [2] [4]
get into [1]
get off [1] [4]
get on [1] [4]
get on with [3] [5] [8]
get out [2] [4]
get over [1] [2] [5] [6]
get round [1]
get round to [3] [5]
get through [2] [4]
get up [2] [4]
get up to [3]
give away [2]
give back [2]
give in [2] [4]
give off [2]
give onto [1]
give out [2] [4] [7]
give over [4]
give up [2] [4] [5]
go about [4]
go after [1]
go against [1]
go ahead [4]
go along [4]
go along with [3]
go around [4]
go at [1]
go away [4]
go back [4]
go back on [3]
go beyond [1] [8]
go by [1] [4] [8]
go down [4]
go down with [3]

go for [1]
go in [4]
go in for [3] [5]
go into [1]
go off [4]
go on [1] [4] [5] [8]
go on with [3]
go out [4]
go over [4]
go round [4]
go through [1] [4]
go through with [3]
go to [1]
go up [4]
go without [1] [5]
grab at [1]
grind down [2]
grow up [4]

hand around [2]
hand back [2]
hand down [2]
hand in [2]
hand on [2]
hand out [2]
hand over [2]
hand round [2]
hang about [4]
hang around [4]
hang back [4]
hang down [4]
hang on [1] [4]
hang onto [1]
hang out [2] [4]
hang over [4]
hang up [2] [4]
head for [1]
head off [2]
hear from [1]
help out [2] [4]
hesitate about [1] [5] [9]
hire out [2]
hit back [2]
hit back at [3]
hit out [4]
hit out at [3]
hold back [2] [4]
hold down [2]
hold forth [4]
hold in [2]
hold off [2]
hold on [4]
hold out [2] [4]
hold out for [3]
hold out on [3]
hold over [2]
hold to [1]

hold up [2][4]
hold with [1][5][6][8]
hope with [1][9]
hunt for [1]
hurry up [2][4]

insist on [1][5][6]
interfere in [1]
interfere with [1][6]
iron out [2]

join in [1][4]
join in with [3]
join up [4]
jump at [1]
jump for [1]
jump to [1]

keep at [1]
keep away [2][4]
keep away from [3]
keep back [2][4]
keep down [2][4]
keep in [2][4]
keep in with [3]
keep off [2][4]
keep on [2][4][5]
keep on at [3]
keep out [2][4]
keep out of [3]
keep to [1]
keep up [2][4]
keep up with [1][8]
knock about [2][4]
knock back [2]
knock down [2]
knock off [2][4]
knock out [2]
knock up [2]

laugh at [1][8]
lay aside [2]
lay down [2]
lay in [2]
lay into [1]
lay off [2][4][5]
lay on [2]
lay out [2]
lay to [4]
lay up [2]
lead up to [1][5]
leave for [1]
leave off [2][4][5]
leave out [2][8]
lend out [2]
let down [2]
let in [2]

let off [2]
let on [4]
let out [2]
let up [4]
light on [1]
light up [2][4]
listen to [1][6][8]
live down [2]
live off [1]
live on [1]
live up to [3]
lock up [2][4]
long for [1]
look about [1]
look after [1]
look ahead [4]
look around [4]
look at [1][6][8]
look back [4]
look back on [3][8]
look down on [3]
look for [1][8]
look forward to [3][5][8]
look in [4]
look into [1][8]
look on [4]
look onto [1]
look out [2][4]
look out for [3]
look out on [3]
look over [1][2]
look round [4]
look through [1][8]
look to [1]
look up [2][4][8]
look up to [3]

make for [1]
make off [4]
make off with [3]
make out [2][4][7][8]
make up [2][4]
make up for [3][8]
make up to [3]
manage with [1][8][9]
manage without [1][5][9]
mark down [2]
mark off [2]
mark out [2]
mark up [2]
matter to [1]
meet with [1]
melt down [2]
mess about [2][4]
mess around [2][4]
mess up [2]
mess with [1]

miss out [2]
muddle through [4]

nip in [4]
note down [2]

object to [1][5][6][8]
occur to [1]
open onto [1]
open out [4]
open up [2][4]
own up [4]

pack up [2]
part with [1][8]
pass away [4]
pass by [4]
pass for [1]
pass off [4]
pass on [2][4]
pass out [2][4]
pass over [1][2]
pass round [2]
pass up [2]
pay back [2][4]
pay for [1][5][8]
pay in [2]
pay off [2][4]
pay out [2]
pay up [4]
persist in [1][5]
pick on [1]
pick out [2]
pick up [2]
pin down [2]
play about [4]
play around [4]
play at [1]
play down [2]
play off [2]
play on [1]
play up [4]
play up to [3]
play with [1]
plug away at [3]
point at [1]
point out [2][7]
point to [1][8]
polish off [2]
pose for [1]
pour out [2][4]
prepare for [1][8][9]
press for [1]
press on [4]
profit from [1][5][8]
provide for [1]
pull ahead [4]

pull at [1]
pull away [4]
pull back [2][4]
pull down [2]
pull forward [4]
pull in [2][4]
pull off [2]
pull out [2][4]
pull over [4]
pull round [4]
pull through [1][2][4]
pull up [2][4]
push ahead [4]
push along [4]
push for [1]
push forward [4]
push in [4]
push off [4]
push on [4]
put about [2]
put across [2]
put around [2]
put aside [2]
put away [2]
put back [2]
put by [2]
put down [2]
put forward [2]
put in [2][4]
put in for [3]
put off [2][5]
put on [1][2]
put out [2][7]
put over [2]
put round [2]
put through [2]
put up [2]
put up with [3][5][6][8]

qualify for [1]
quarrel with [1][8]

reach for [1][8]
react to [1][8]
reason with [1]
reckon on [1][5][9]
reckon with [1][9]
refer to [1][8]
reflect on [1][8]
refrain from [1][5]
rely on [1][6][8]
report on [1][8]
report to [1]
respond to [1][8]
rest on [1]
rest with [1]
result in [1][6]

revel in [1][5]
ring for [1]
ring off [4]
ring out [4]
ring up [2][4]
rise up [4]
rope in [2]
rub out [2]
rule out [2]
run across [1]
run after [1]
run along [4]
run at [1]
run away [4]
run away with [3]
run down [2][4]
run for [1]
run in [2][4]
run into [1]
run off [2][4]
run on [4]
run out [4]
run out of [3]
run over [2]
run through [1]
run up [2]
run up against [3]
rush at [1]

save up [2][4]
scrape through [1][4]
scrape up [2]
search for [1][8]
see about [1][5]
see off [2]
see out [2]
see over [1]
see through [1][2]
see to [1]
seek for [1][8]
sell off [2]
sell out [2][4]
sell out of [3]
sell up [4]
send away [2]
send away for [3]
send down [2][8]
send for [1][8]
send in [2][8]
send off [2][8]
send on [2][8]
send out [2][8]
send up [2][8]
serve as [1]
set about [1]
set aside [2]
set back [2]

set by [2]
set down [2]
set in [4]
set off [2][4]
set on [1]
set out [2][4]
set up [2]
settle down [4]
settle down to [3]
settle for [1]
settle in [4]
settle into [1]
settle on [1]
settle up [4]
sew up [2]
shake off [2]
shake up [2]
share out [2]
shoot at [1]
shoot down [2][4]
shoot off [2][4]
shoot out [4]
shoot up [4]
shout at [1]
show around [2]
show off [2][4]
show out [2]
show round [2]
show up [2][4]
shut down [2][4]
shut off [2]
shut up [2][4]
sink into [1]
sit back [4]
sit down [4]
sit for [1]
sit in [4]
sit in for [3]
sit in on [3]
sit out [2]
sit up [4]
slip off [2]
slip on [2]
slip up [4]
smell at [1]
smell out [2]
smile at [1][8]
smoke out [2]
sort out [2][8]
speak for [1]
speak out [4]
speak up [4]
speak up for [3][8]
speed up [2]
split up [4]
stand between [1]
stand by [4]

stand down [4]
stand for [1]
stand in [4]
stand in for [3]
stand out [4]
stand to [4]
stand up [2][4]
stand up for [3]
stand up to [3]
start off [2]
start out [4]
start up [2][4]
stay on [4]
stem from [1]
step out [4]
step up [2][4]
stick at [1]
stick out [2][4]
stick out for [3]
stick to [1]
stick up [2]
stick up for [3][8]
stick with [1]
stir up [2]
strike off [2]
strike out [2]
strive for [1]
succeed in [1][5]
suffer from [1]
swear at [1][9]
swear by [1][8]
swear in [2]
sweep up [4]
sympathise with [1][8]

take after [1]
take apart [2]
take away [2]
take back [2][8]
take down [2][8]
take in [2]
take into [1]
take off [2][4]
take on [2]
take out [2]
take over [2][4]
take to [1][5]
take up [2][5]
take up with [3]
talk down to [3]
talk out [2]
talk over [2][8]
tear apart [2]
tear down [2]
tear into [1]
tear off [2]
tear up [2]

think about [1][5][8]
think of [1][5][6][8]
think out [2][8]
think over [2][8]
think through [2][8]
think up [2]
thrive on [1][5]
throw away [2]
throw in [2]
throw off [2]
throw out [2]
throw up [2][4]
tie down [2]
tie up [2]
tire out [2]
touch off [2]
touch on [1][8]
toy with [1]
track down [2]
trouble about [1][8][9]
trust in [1]
try for [1]
try on [2]
try out [2]
tumble to [1]
tune in to [1]
turn about [4]
turn against [1]
turn away [2]
turn back [2][4]
turn down [2]
turn in [2][4]
turn into [1]
turn off [2][4]
turn on [2][4]
turn out [2][4]
turn over [2][8]
turn to [1]
turn up [1][4]

use up [2][8]

volunteer for [1][9]
vote for [1]

wait for [1][9]
walk off with [3]
walk out [4]
walk out on [3]
walk over [1]
wash away [2]
wash down [2]
wash out [2]
wash up [2]
waste away [4]
watch out [4]
wear away [2][4]

wear down [2] [4]	win over [2]	work at [1]	wrap up [2]
wear off [4]	win round [2]	work away [4]	write down [2] [8]
wear on [4]	win through [4]	work for [1]	write off for [3]
wear out [2] [4]	wind up [2] [4]	work out [2] [4]	write out [2] [8]
weigh down [2]	wipe out [2]	work up [3]	write up [2] [8]
weigh out [2]	wish for [1] [9]	work up to [3]	
whip up [2]	wonder at [1]	worry about [1] [5]	yearn for [1] [9]

---

[1] These *verbs* (at least in some of their meanings) are *prepositional verbs*, (« **191**).

[2] These *verbs* (at least in some of their meanings) are *transitive phrasal verbs*, (« **194**).

[3] These *verbs* are *phrasal-prepositional verbs*, (« **195**).

[4] These *verbs* (at least in some of their meanings) are *intransitive phrasal verbs*, (« **221**).

[5] These *verbs* can be followed by an -**ing** *form* (« **199, 200**), but not by an *infinitive*, e.g.

    1   Do you believe in helping young criminals? (*Not* x to help x)
    2   Carry on working where you left off. (*Not* x to work x)
    3   They didn't object to paying last time. (*Not* x to pay x)
    4   We're looking forward to seeing you. (*Not* x to see x)

[6] These *verbs* can be followed by a *noun phrase* and an -**ing** *form*, (« **201, 202, 205**), e.g.

    5   Tim was banking on them getting here early.
    6   Has Susan complained about us making a noise?
    7   I don't hold with young people staying out late.
    8   They won't put up with the boss ignoring the safety rules.

[7] These *verbs* can be followed by a **that** *clause*, (« **209**), e.g.

    9   June made out (that) we'd never told her.
   10   Miss Payne pointed out (that) the figures weren't correct.

[8] These *verbs* can go with a *noun clause* (« **212**), most usually with **what**, e.g.

   11   Do you really think I approve of what they did?
   12   Ian objected strongly to what I proposed.

[9] These *verbs*, without the *preposition*, can go with a **to** *infinitive*, (for examples « **224**).

Index of grammatical terms functions, etc.

The most important references are <u>underlined</u>

Index of words

The most important references are <u>underlined</u>

disturbed **80**
do *p91*, *p92*, *p94*, **110, 136, 141, 214,**
215
does *p91*, *p92*, *p94*, **110, 141**
doubt **209, 212**
down **88, 193, 194, 220, 221**
dozen **254**
dread **198, 200**
dream **209**
dress(ed) **173**
drive **216**
due to **106**
during **101, 106, 148**

each *p3*, **36**
each other **48**
eager **81**
east **88**
easy **189**
either *p3*, **38, 93, 226, 228, 253**
elect **196**
else **52**
embarrassed **81**
encourage **216**
endeavour **224** *Note*
endure **198, 200**
enjoy **199**
enough *p3*, **31, <u>32</u>,** *p57*, **<u>78</u>**
enquire **178, 212**
entertaining **189**
envy **142, 215**
equal **142**
even **27–29, 84c**
even if **243**
even though **237**
eventually **89**
ever **84c, 98, 153, 253**
every *p3*, **37**
everybody **33, 44¹, <u>54</u>**
everyone **33, 44¹, <u>54</u>**
everything **33, <u>53</u>**
evidence **3**
examine **212**
except **99²**
excuse **211**
excited **81**
exist **142,** **173** *Note* b
expect **142, 176, 198, 209, 210, 216**
explain **209, 211, 212**

face **199**
fact **106**
fail **142, 173** *Note* b, **198, 253**
fairly **74**
fall **225**
family **8**
fancy **199, 201**

far **27–29, 31, 71, 77, 167, 253**
fascinated **81**
fascinating **189**
fashion **85**
fast **83**
favour **201**
fear **142, 176, 209**
feel **112, 142, 176, 197, 204, 205,**
209, 225
fetch **208, 214, 215**
(a) few *p3*, **20, <u>25</u>, <u>26</u>, 27, 29, 31, 70, 75**
fewer, fewest **29**
finally **89**
find (out) **57, 176, 197, 202, 209, 212,**
214, 215
finish **199, 212**
first **67, 89, 150** *Note*, **254**
fit **142, 173** *Note* b
fly **222**
following **177**
foot **30**
for **97, 101, 148, 167, 191, 235, 252**
forbid **216**
force **206, 216**
forget **142, 207, 209, 212, 253**
forgive **211, 215**
fortunate **80**
forward **193**
free **81**
frequently **84c**
friendly **83**
frightened **80**
fun, funny **189**
furious **81**
furniture **3**

gallon **30**
gang **8**
gather **209, 214, 215**
generally **84c**
get **79, 173, 175, 203, 206, 214–216,**
225
give **208, 213, 215**
glad **80, 81**
go **145, 150, 177, 225**
gone **146**
go on **207**
going to **145, 152**
good **189**
good deal **24, 27–29**
government **8**
gram **30**
grant **213, 215**
grass **3**
grateful **80**
great **189**
great deal **24, 27–29**

very **23, 26, 74, 109**
volunteer (for) **224**

wait (for) **224**
want **57, 122, 142, 197, 198, 199** *Note*, **208, 216**
want to know **178**
warn **211, 216, 217**
was **84c**, *pp91–94*, <u>**108**</u>, **151, 152, 158**
wash(ed) **173**
waste **211**
watch **204, 205**
way **85**
we **35, 42, 45, 107, 110, 241, 242**
wear **222**
weather **3**
weigh **142, 173** *Note* **b**
well **68**
went **150**
were **84c**, *pp91–94*, <u>**108**</u>, **151, 152, 158, 241**
west **88**
what *p3*, <u>**41**</u>, **158,** <u>**159**</u>**, 166, 169, 172, 181, 183, 190, 191**
what . . . for **172**
what . . . like **164**
what time **170**
whatever **182**
when **62, 101, 106,** <u>**170**</u>**, 181, 229–232**
whenever **182**
where **62, 88, 169,** <u>**171**</u>**, 181**
wherever **182**
whether **178, 181**
which *p3*, **59, 60, 61, 63, 64, 161, 169**
whichever **182**
while **106, 230, 233, 238**
whisper **209**

who **59, 60, 63, 158,** <u>**160**</u>**, 169, 181, 190, 191**
whoever **182**
whole *p3*, **33, 34**
whom **59, 60, 63, 160, 169, 181**
whose *p3*, **61, 162, 169**
why **62, 172, 181, 234**
will *pp91–94*, *p96*, **117, 125, 128** *Note*, **145, 155–157, 173, 230, 240**
willing **81**
win **219**
wish (for) **142, 209, 216, 224, 245**
with **47, 55, 65, 87, 191, 252**
without **253**
wonder **178, 212**
won't *p94*, **117**
work **3, 104**
worried **80, 81**
worth **79**
would *pp91–94*, *p96*, **122, 173, 200, 241**
would have *pp92–93*, **242**
would like **122**
would rather **122**
would sooner **122**
write (about) **202, 213, 215**

yard **30**
yes **178**
yesterday **89, 177**
yet **94, 153, 237, 253**
you **35, 42, 43, 45, 107, 110, 136**
your **44, 45**
yours **46**
yourself **47**
yourselves **47**

zero **254**